MISUNDERSTOOD MARX

Chen Xianda

8th House Publishing

Canada

Cataloging in Publication (CIP) Data

MISUNDERSTOOD MARX / By Chen Xianda
Chinese Version: China Renmin University Press, 2016.1
English Version: 8th House Publishing 2018.12

ISBN 978-1-7751040-1-8

MISUNDERSTOOD MARX

By Chen Xianda

Publication: 8th House Publishing

Region: Montreal, QC, Canada

Website: http://www.8thhousepublishing.com

Edition: 1st issue, January 2016 (Chinese)
       1st issue, December 2018 (English)

Impression: 1st print, December 2018

TABLE OF CONTENTS

INTRODUCTION   TO UNDERSTAND MAX ACCORDING TO THE TRUE FEATURES OF MARXISM

Lenin (Vladimir Ilyich Ulyanov) once said: "Marxism is a very profound and comprehensive knowledge. And therefore, in the 'reasons' put forward by those who turned away from Marxism, we often see just a few words and phrases quoted from Marx, which is not surprising, especially for the wrong quotations."[1] The history of theoretical struggle for more than 100 years proves that it is an extremely important aspect of the ideological struggle to distort Max with Marx's words, to create all kinds of myths, to misunderstand Marx with all kinds of tricks and tactics, and to prevent Marx from becoming Marx as the founder of Marxism.

It is not rare for the image change of the founder of a certain theory in cultural history, but the extensive, lasting, worldwide debate and great controversy with differences like ice charcoal caused by Max is few and far between. As for Marxism in the time after Marx, the farther away from Marx's own time it is, the greater the differences in the understanding of Marx. Just as the pedestrians going away, where the farther away it is, the harder it is to discern. Accordingly, when we say that we should take Marxist theory as our guiding ideology, we must have a correct premise, that is, we must understand and restore the true nature of Marx and Marxism. This is the great mission given by the times to the theorists of Marxist.

1

In world today, almost all schools that promote Marxism call themselves Marxism and are true Marxism. However, their views are different, and even opposite to each other by accusing each other and arguing endlessly, which raises the question that what is exactly Marxism?

---

[1]*The Collected Works of Lenin*, Chinese Edition 1, Vol. 26, Page 192, Beijing, People's Publishing House, 1959.

If true Marxism means to only adhering to all the views of Marx and Engels, and upholding the "all" principle, Marxism should inevitably end in 1883 or 1895. According to this criterion, Leninism does not belong to Marxism because Lenin has indeed broken through some of Marx's and Engels' views in some respects and replaced some old principles with some new ones. Seeing Marxism in this way is to treat Marxism as a historical category, just like Aristotelianism and Hegelianism, which exists only at a certain time in history. In fact, Marxism is a system of thought that still plays a guiding role in reality. Marxism, by its nature, is always contemporary. It is a rigid dogmatism that "what Marx and Engels have not said is not Marxism".

However, we cannot adhere to the principle of "nothing" and put any schools that deviate from and oppose the fundamental views of Marx and Engels into Marxism. If a school has its own unique philosophical views and political opinions, it can show its own brand, with no need to squeeze in the ranks of Marxism. Freudianism is Freudianism, while Existentialism is Existentialism. Freud Marxism or Existentialism Marxism, just like the round square and iron wood, is hard to blend. If we admit that they are also Marxism and belong to a school of Marxism, there is no difference from admitting that any school of thought can call itself Marxism, as long as they are willing to do so. This is not the development of Marxism, but the dismemberment of Marxism.

For more than half a century, from the West to the Orient, there is a long and fierce debate about what is Marxism.

For example, Lukács (György Lukács) thought, in the book of *What is Orthodox Marxism,* that the standard to measure whether it was Marxism was the method. Even if all the conclusions and principles of Marxism had been changed, as long as we persisted in dialectics, we were adhering to Marxism, and it was orthodox Marxism. Lukács admitted the variability of the principle, which was not bound to a principle, with its own rationality, but if we abandoned all the principles of Marxism, where did the Marxist method come from? Moreover, dialectics itself had different forms. Just sticking to dialectics may be a Hegel.

Professor Binkley (Luther J. Binkley) in the United States set another standard. He regarded Marxism as a theory of value, and thought that the standard to adhere to Marxism or not lied in whether to stick to the moral ideals of Marx. He said: "The attraction of Marxism to us today is a moral prophecy. If one examines the facts of the present society in the light of human values, and then acts upon one's own discoveries, so that our world may become a place where all human beings can become more creative and freer, we are loyal to Marx."[2]

It has been seen that since 1930s, after the full texts of Marx's *Economic and Philosophic Manuscripts of 1844* was published, there had been a wave of reinterpretation of Marxism. Some theorists regarded Marxism as a faction of humanitarianism and advocated humanitarianism Marxism; some regarded the alienation theory as the core of Marxism and advocated the alienation theory of Marxism; and some emphasized the ethical nature of Marxism and propagated the ethics of Marxism. Other schools were numerous and innumerable, such as Freud Marxism, existential Marxism, structural Marxism, phenomenological Marxism, and ecological Marxism. What people see through the prism of theorists is misunderstood or deformed Marxism rather than true Marxism.

The question is whether there is objective and original Marxism or not, or each school at each time can have its own Marxism. Some scholars flatly deny the former for the latter. For example, Wright Mills (Charles Wright Mills), the American sociologist, clearly said in *The Marxist* that:" Marx has not gained unified understanding. It depends on our own interests for us to make what kinds of explanations on his writings according to the books, pamphlets, papers, and letters written by him in different stages of development, hence any of these explanations

---

[2]Luther J. Binkley: *Conflict of Ideals: Changing Values in Western Society*, Page 106, Beijing, Commercial Press, 1983.

cannot represent the 'real Marx'."[3] He also stressed: "People do not have a unified understanding of Marx. Every researcher must know Marx through their own efforts."[4] As many researchers as there are, there are as many Marx, which is the complacency theory of some Western scholars. What is Marxism seems to be a metaphysical problem under the proposition full of epistemology. The search for this problem is purely a meaningless move, and is completely wrong.

We do not deny the diversity and difference of the understanding of Marxism. However, as for Marxism as a scientific system, its content does not depend on the subjective understanding of the people, but depends on its scientific nature. On this issue, the view of Heilbroner (Robert L. Heilbroner), the American scholar, is more objective in his book *Marxism: For and Against*.

Heilbroner did not deny that there were many interpretations of Marxism at the present time, but he emphasized the existence of an objective Marxism. He said:" I firmly believe that there is something in common that can be recognized in Marxism, or more precisely the thoughts inspired by the writings of Marx (what we call 'Marxism' collectively)." Heilbroner summarized the common grounds into four parts, namely, (I) dialectical attitude to cognition; (II) materialism; (III) the general view of capitalism based on the social analysis of Marx; and (IV) the belief in socialism.[5] Although specific criteria can be discussed, he believed that attention should be paid to the view that Marxism should have a common and objective standard.

We should distinguish what the Marxism is from what "I" think the Marxism is. Otherwise, it will become the hot air with everyone acts as he pleases to adhere to

---

[3]Charles Wright Mills: *The Marxist*, Page 39, Beijing, Commercial Press, 1964.

[4]Charles Wright Mills: *The Marxist*, Page 39, Beijing, Commercial Press, 1964.

[5]See Robert L. Heilbroner: *Marxism: For and Against*, Page 4, Beijing, Institute of Information, Chinese Academy of Social Sciences, 1982.

the Marxism.

As for the question of what is the Marxism, we can look into it from two angles: one is its founder, and the other is its contents.

There is no doubt that Marxism is inseparable from its founder. Lenin once said: "**Marxism** is the system of Marx's thoughts and doctrines."[6] This is defined from the point of view of its founder. What Lenin stressed is that Marxism is the thoughts and doctrines of Marx (including Engels), that is, one cannot impose his or her own fiction, additional ideas and interpretations on Marx and Engels. He also emphasized that Marxism was the system of Marx's thoughts and doctrines, rather than the sum of all the works or statements. But Marxism cannot be defined solely from the point of view of its founder. After the death of Marx and Engels, Marxism continued to be enriched and developed in the practice of the proletarian revolution and socialist construction. Marx and Marxism cannot be completely equated. Marxism was founded by Marx, but was not exclusive to Marx. Thus, Marxism, as a scientific system, studies the changes of the whole objective world and social formation and the law of proletarian revolution and construction. Its most fundamental mission is to guide the proletariat and the masses in socialist revolution and communist construction.

According to the above analysis, we can say that Marxism is a scientific and theoretical system founded by Marx and Engels, developed by their successors with the ultimate goal to oppose capitalism and construct communism. In this sense, Marxism is the theory of scientific communism. It should be the greatest mockery of Marxism if its scientific criticism on capitalism is removed from Marxist theory; the goal of socialist revolution is abandoned; but he is still called as a Marxist by himself.

2

---

[6]*Selected Works of Lenin*, Edition 2, Vol. 2, Page 580, Beijing, People's Publishing House, 1972.

What exactly is the nature of the ideological system that Marxism belongs to? Is it the simply scientific system or critical system? Is it a closed system with continuous improvement only on its own basis or an open system with continuous contact with the outside world, collision and communication with other ideological system? How shall we regard Marxism? These are questions of great significance.

First of all, Marxism is a theory of unity of revolutionary and scientificity.

Compared with any school in history and reality, Marxism has the most powerful and unstoppable attraction. It has developed from a small school of thought in the labor movement of Western Europe in the 1840s, swept the world, and became the ideological system with the most followers, the strongest power and the greatest influence. The fundamental reason is that it combines scientificity and revolutionary inwardly and inseparably in the theory itself.

The thoroughly critical spirit is a concentrated expression of the revolutionary nature of Marxism, which is permeated by all the works of Marxism. The subtitle of Marx's *Das Kapital* and its manuscripts is "Critique of Political Economy", that is to critically review the capitalist economic system and its economic theory. As early as his youth, he once declared: "The advantages of the new trend of thoughts are that we do not want to dogmatically anticipate the future, but just hope to find a new world in criticizing the old world." and declared publicly **"to be ruthless in criticizing everything that exists."**[7] The criticism spirit of Marxism is manifested in its opposition to the theory that the old system and old things are regarded as fixed and unchanged and opposition to all doctrines that defend for the old system. It observes the capitalist system from the viewpoint of thorough dialectics, exposes the contradictions and confrontations of the capitalist system at various levels in economic, political and ideological aspects, investigates its emergence and

---

[7]*Marx/Engels Collected Works*, Chinese Edition 1, Vol. 1, Page 416, Beijing, People's Publishing House, 1960.

evolution, and explains the inevitability of its transitory and transformation into a higher social form.

Some people say that the criticism spirit of Marxism only applies to capitalism, but to socialism and Marxism itself, it is non-critical, and is a kind of conservative self-defense theory, which is absolutely a misunderstanding.

Criticalness is the essential characteristic of Marxism, and it is also applicable to socialist society. Marxism has never regarded the socialist society as a solidified society that does not require adjustment and reform, nor has it ever confused everything that exists in the socialist society with socialism. In the socialist society, there is obviously a social phenomenon which is incompatible with the nature of socialism. "Everything that exists is reasonable". This is not the way of thinking of Marxism. Marxism considers the problem of socialism in a critical manner, that is to say, it constantly sums up and reflects, rejects erroneous and outdated policies and measures, and truly explores the socialist model and road suitable for the characteristics of the country.

Marxism treats all kinds of theories that safeguard the interests of the exploiting class in a critical attitude. It always adheres to the principle of party spirit, defends the purity of the Marxist Theory, and opposes various doctrines that misinterpret and attack Marxism. At the same time, it also takes a critical attitude towards itself. Both Engels and Lenin have proposed to treat the problems of Marx in the attitude of Marx. This attitude is a kind of non-dogmatic and critical attitude, namely, to against the theory as "the peak", and dare to replace the old outdated principles with new principles. It is through this critical spirit that Marxism maintains its own purity and vitality.

The critical spirit has a bearing on what kind of Marxism we really need: The revolutionary Marxism that dares to uphold the truth and insist on the critical spirit or the peaceful Marxism with no distinction between right and wrong with consonance and compromising? This is not simply a question of the image of

Marxists, but concerns the essence of Marxism. Mao Tse-tung pointed out shortly after the beginning of the War of Resistance against Japan in 1938: "Had our Party has a hundred to two hundred comrades who have learnt Marxism-Leninism systematically rather than piecemeal, actually and hollowly, out Party's fighting power will be greatly enhanced, and our work in defeating the Japanese imperialism will be speeded up."[8] So far, the conclusion is still of urgent practical significance. Our Party needs a large number of theoretical soldiers who always creatively adhere to Marxism and carry forward the critical spirit of Marxism on the theoretical front.

The essence of Marxism is critical, but its criticism is combined with science. Meanwhile, Marxism is also a kind of scientific theory. As far as its theoretical source is concerned, it critically inherits the outstanding achievements in the cultural heritage of mankind; as far as its content is concerned, based on the facts and taking the laws as the object, it deeply reveals the regularity of its research objects; and as far as its verification is concerned, it regards practice as the only criterion for testing truth. Practice has a dual function that: It can be verified as well as falsified. It proves its correctness through the achievements of its expectations and its errors through repeated failures of its anticipations. Marxism bases its theory on practice, which is the most reliable guarantee of Marxism as a scientific truth.

Some scholars in the West try their best to oppose the conclusion that Marxism is a scientific theory. They have created a variety of misinterpreted theories of Marxism, the most popular of which is the religious Marxism, to belittle Marxism. For example, Kolakowski (Leszek Kolakowski) once said: "Marxism plays a religious role, and its efficacy has a religious character. But it is a comic and false form of religion,

---

[8]*Selected Works of Mao Tse-tung*, Edition 1, Vol. 2, Page 499, Beijing, People's Publishing House, 1952.

because it has taken its secular eschatology as a scientific system of religious mythology that does not want to be self-righteous."[9] The existentialist Camus (Albert Camus) believed that Marxism "is a mixture of the most valuable methods of criticism and the most problematic theory of idealistic salvation".[10] Tucker (Benjamin Ricketson Tucker) claimed that Economic and Philosophic Manuscripts of *1844* showed that Marx was not the kind of social analyst he wanted to be, but was firstly a moralist or a religious thinker. Russell (Bertrand Arthur William Russell, 3rd Earl Russell) listed communism as a world religion, along with Buddhism, Hinduism, Christianity and Islam, and believed that they were "all false and harmful."[11]

It is a demagogic and preposterous analogy to call Marxism as a religious doctrine. The beautiful dream of Marxism on communism is fundamentally different from the "Millennialism" proclaimed by the theologians. Marxism is an absolute atheism that opposes any religious doctrines. Religion, though a sigh of oppressed beings, is a protest against the suffering of reality and the feeling of the merciless world. However, it makes people indulge in the illusion about their own situation, rather than teaching people to abandon the situation that needs illusion. To compare Marxism to religion is to completely deny its scientific and revolutionary nature.

Moreover, we should also see that the Marxism system has an open nature. In the history, all thinkers who attempt to establish a complete system are trying to solidify their views and theories and describing them as the final and last absolute truth. Even the great dialectics, like Hegel, is of no exception.

Some Western scholars also try to describe Marxism, especially Engels as the

---

[9]Quoted from Bell (Daniel Bell): *The Social Sciences Since the Second World War*, Page 132~133, Beijing, Social Sciences Literature Press, 1988.

[10]Quoted from *The Philosophy of Existentialism*, Page 412~413, Beijing, China Social Sciences Press, 1986.

[11] Russell: *Why I Am Not a Christian*, Page 8, Beijing, Commercial Press, 1982.

constructor of a closed system. For example, McLellan (David McLellan) regarded Engels as the imitator of Hagel closed system in his book *Marxism after Marx*. He said: "There are indeed some similarities between the system established by old Hegel and Engels' tendency to systematize Marxism on the basis of natural science."[12] He also said that Engels "portrays Marxism as a dogmatic metaphysical system like the dialectical materialism textbooks of Soviet (and other countries)".[13]

The closed system is incompatible with the nature of Marxism. As early as 1843, in a letter to Ruge (Arnold Ruge), Marx publicly declared his opposition to any dogmatism, and laughed at the idea that believed all the answers to riddles were in the philosopher's desk, and that the fatuous and mundane world only needed to open its mouth to accept the absolutely scientific roasted grouse. Later, Engels fiercely criticized German college students who tried to create the ultimate truth system, especially Dühring (Eugen Karl Dühring) in his book *Anti-Dühring*. In Engels' view, it is absurd that if human beings reach the point where only eternal truth needs to be applied and no new truth has to be discovered, which means that history and cognition have stopped at one point. He said: "The system of all-embracing and ultimately complete recognition of nature and history is in contradiction with the basic laws of dialectical thinking."[14]

As for the relationship between Marxism and the objective world, it is not self-reflection, but facing reality, facing the world, that is, contacting and interacting with the real world of its own time. It has been in this way not only when Marxism was born, but also in the whole development history of Marxism, which is a history of the unity of theory and practice. Marxism will always focus on reality and pay

---

[12]McLellan: *Marxism after Marx*, Page 12, Beijing, China Social Science Press, 1986.

[13]McLellan: *Marxism after Marx*, Page 9.

[14]*Karl Marx and Frederick Engels: Selected Works*, Edition 1, Vol. 3, Page 64, Beijing, People's Publishing House, 1972.

close attention to and study the most urgent problems raised in its own time. We can say that the basic principles and important propositions in the Marxism scientific system are like open pockets, which are ready to develop and enrich by generalizing new experiences at any time.

In terms of the relationship between Marxism and other non-Marxism schools, it is not a sectarian system isolated from the world civilization development. Marx and Engels critically assimilated the precious legacy of their pioneers in the creation of Marxism. It should continuously absorb the new achievements of contemporary natural science and social science after Marxism was founded. Even in modern times, we should not take the attitude of simple rejection to the Western philosophy, but should seriously study their important problems and some enlightening thoughts to broaden one's horizons while criticizing their mistakes. For each generation of Marxists, if we neglect the critical examination of the contemporary theoretical achievements, we will isolate ourselves from the cultural background and social thoughts of the whole era, and will be withered from isolation.

The open nature of the Marxism system is also manifested in that it is never self-styled and poses itself as the ultimate truth. The relay of Marxism has been handed down from generation to generation, and no generation has reached the end, but in the process. In this sense, the ideological system of Marxism is never completed, and its development will not end.

Finally, Marxism is a creative science with its vitality lying in its creativity.

Historical experience has proved that any thought system which boasts the ultimate truth will be on their way out, just like the feudal dynasty hoping to live forever. The reason why Marxism is always full of vitality and become the essence of each era lies in that Marxism is consciously rooted in practice and developed with the development of practice.

Marx and Engels, as the founders of Marxism, spent their whole life summing up new experiences and never stopping creative researches. For example, in the preface to the German edition of *The Communist Manifesto 1872*, according to the experience of the revolution in 1848, especially the Paris Commune in 1871, Engels pointed out: "Because of the great development of great industry in the last 25 years, and the working-class political parties have also developed along with it, because of the practical experience of the revolution in February, especially the practical experience of the Paris Commune where the proletariat took power for the first time for two months, this guiding principle is out of date in some places now. Especially the commune has proved that: 'The working class cannot simply master the ready-made state apparatus and use it to achieve their own purposes.'"[15] On the basis of practical experience, Marx and Engels' scientific attitude towards their own theory has been shown by publicly declare that one of their arguments is out of date.

Just because Marxism is rooted in practice and is creative, every era has its outstanding representatives. There are many schools in history gradually declined with the death of the founder, but Marxism will not. As it has the practical basis of the largest number of people, even after the death of Marx and Engels, there are a great many of Marxists emerged generation after generation. They have made contributions of different degrees to the development and promotion of Marxism.

Creativity is the fundamental characteristic of Marxism. But some Western scholars described dogmatism as the inevitable fate of the development of Marxism. Just as McLellan said: "Marx asked his followers not only to explain the world, but also to change the world. But the more they succeeded in this aspect, the more Marxism tended to become a dogma of mass movement."[16] He also declared arbitrarily: "Marxism had become a pure faith to its hundreds of millions of followers, and for

---

[15]*Karl Marx and Frederick Engels: Selected Works*, Edition 1, Vol. 1, Page 229.

[16]McLellan: *Marxism after Marx*, Page 2.

them it can provide a guarantee of final victory. For this reason, it became increasingly different from Marx's original ideas, and evolved into a dogmatic system opposed to heresy as was often called revisionism."[17]

We do not deny that there is a danger and tendency of dogmatism in the process of the development of Marxism. However, this is not inevitable and insurmountable. Socialist practice is the most creative, but also most in need of creativity. It is of great difficulty to build the socialist system with characteristics of its own country by only copy the general principles of Marxism or the patterns of other countries. The socialist construction practice of hundreds of millions of people can once again break the dogmatic deadlock, and push forward Marxism.

Marxism must be combined with the actual conditions of each country, which is the most effective way and method to prevent dogmatism. Will it cause the so-called "transformation" of Marxism, that is, its successors are further and further away from the original ideas of the founders to emphasize creativity and combination with the actual conditions of each country? Many Western scholars preach this point. For example, they believe: "As the focus of Marxism moves eastward, the success of the Chinese revolution, which is based on the peasants rather than proletarian, clearly shows that the connection with Marx's own thoughts is becoming more and more distant."[18]

This is a very complex problem. From the longitudinal perspective, there will be differences in the theory between a successor school and its founder. For instance, the Confucianism, through the revolution in the Han Dynasty, Tang Dynasty, Song Dynasty and Ming Dynasty, is apparently not exactly the same as the one in the Pre-Qin Period; from the horizontal perspective, the spread of the same system of thought in other countries will also change. Take Buddhism for example, it is not

---

[17]McLellan: *Marxism after Marx*, Page 2.

[18]David McLellan: *Marxism after Marx*, Page 4.

exactly the same with that in India after being introduced to China

The development and dissemination of the Marxism definitely cannot be achieved without the characteristics of each era, and the economic and political situation and cultural traditions of each country. But there is no simple analogy between this and the ideological deformation. If the deformation in the field of former thought is often manifested as a thinker of a particular class, to adapt to the new political needs, the original system of thought needs to be transformed and reconstructed. However, the development of the Marxism is brought into the scope of human understanding of the truth, which manifests itself as a new accumulation of scientific knowledge. Marx's successors move forward along with the truth path opened by its founder, which is more close to the objective truth, rather than far from it.

3

As to the composition of Marxist scientific system, Lenin clearly listed Marxist philosophy, political economy and socialism theory as the "three compositions" of Marxism in his famous paper titled *The Three Sources and Three Component Parts of Marxism*, and briefly discussed their contents by combining with their sources. The prominent points of Lenin's exposition lies in its connection with the historical mission of the proletariat and discussion any of its components as an overall component.

Some scholars or researchers always have questions, such as why does Marxism have three components, instead of four or five components? Why can't literature and art, ethics, aesthetics and thought be part of it? Why can't the components of Marxism be divided into parts about general laws and parts about special laws according to other criteria, such as the scope of the law? We should be clear that when we say that Marxism consists of three components, our foothold is the fait accompli of the development history of Marxism, not its abstract possibilities, and what it should or may include. Marxism can be used to guide various sciences, and one can find several reasons to re-include them in the scientific system structure of Marxism, but this is only a personal view of a scholar, not a historical fact. The scientific system structure of Marxism is determined by the great historical mission of the proletariat and the inherent logic of Marxist theory. Without this basis point, we can only get stuck in trivial arguments.

It is necessary to establish a scientific theoretical form commensurate with its class status and mission for the proletariat to change from a free class to a self-made one. Although Britain, France and Germany have made great achievements in the field of theory before the birth of Marxism, none of the theories accord with the interests and aspirations of the proletariat and the need for the proletariat to fulfill its great historical mission. The British classical political economy is a great achievement in economic theory, but the attempt to introduce the conclusions favorable to the working class from the theory of labor value is only utopian socialism, just as Bray (John Francis Bray), the British utopian socialist, showed; the believers of critical utopian socialism and communism transformed into reactionary sects, and into a social quack selling a cure for all diseases, which showed that, in the 19th century, the role of the three utopian socialism was inversely proportional to the development of the history; and those conceived from the philosophy of Feuerbach (Ludwig Andreas von Feuerbach) were "real socialists" just like Huss (Walter Rudolf Hess). The proletariat needs a new theory which not only overcomes the national unilateralism of Britain, France and Germany (the separation of political economy, socialism theory and philosophy), but also obtains the form of science. But to change the theory of socialism from utopia to science is a comprehensive task involving many subjects, which cannot be fulfilled by only limited to the theory of socialism itself. Only under the guidance of dialectical materialism and historical materialism, and based on the analysis of the inherent contradictions in the production mode of capitalist, can it be possible to scientifically clarify the position, mission and way to complete liberation of the proletariat in the capitalist society. Consequently, Marxism, the theoretical form to be adapted to the struggle of the proletariat, is bound to be a unified whole including philosophy, political economy and scientific socialism theory.

The scientific system structure of Marxism also depends on its own internal logic. Engels profoundly revealed the inner logic of the scientific system structure of Marxism by summarizing the history of human thought in the 'Introduction' to *Anti-Dühring*. After describing Marx's epoch-making achievements in the field of philosophy and political economy, he said: "These two great discoveries, namely, the materialist conception of history and the uncovering of the secrets of capitalist production through surplus value, should be attributed to **Marx**. As a result of these discoveries, socialism has become science."[19]

Marxist scientific theory itself needs philosophy, especially a new theory that can not only explain the world but also change the world. Marx attached great importance to philosophy. He regarded philosophy as the "mind" and "spiritual weapon" of the emancipation of the proletariat, and the "Gallic Rooster" of the proclamation of human liberation in *The Introduction to The Critique of Hegel's Philosophy of Right*.

Political economy is the theoretical basis of Marxism. Marxism is a scientific system, not a speculative system. The theoretical content of Marxism theory comes from economic analysis rather than the deduction or derivation of philosophy. The reason why Marxism is scientific lies in that it reveals the inherent contradiction, operation mechanism and law of capitalist society truthfully based on the facts. Without economic analysis on capitalist society, there would be no Marxism.

In Marxist scientific system, the theory of scientific socialism is at the core. In a broad sense, Marxism is the scientific socialism, because the complete liberation and historical mission of the proletariat have manifested the aim, task and mission of Marxism in a concentrated manner. After all, the Marxist philosophy and political

---

[19]*Karl Marx and Frederick Engels: Selected Works*, Edition 1, Vol. 3, Page 67.

economy serve this fundamental purpose.

It is proved that in Marxist scientific system, philosophy is the guiding principle of the world view and methodology, and political economy is the intermediary from the philosophy to the real life (the analysis on capitalist society). The scientific socialism theory about the nature, condition and mission of the proletarian liberation movement is the scientific conclusion about the social development after the analysis on the economic relations in the capitalist society by philosophy. The world view and methodology, the theoretical analysis on the capitalist economy and the conclusion drawn from this is strict, complete and consistent in theory and logic. They permeate and complement each other, constituting the unified Marxist theory. Once the scientific socialism theory leaves Marxist philosophy and Marxist political economy, it is no different from average communism or utopian socialism; on the contrary, without the guidance of Marxist philosophy, without the socialist revolution and socialist construction, the so-called Marxist political economy will inevitably fall into the embrace of bourgeois political economy. Similarly, if we ignore the great historical mission of the proletariat and the social and economic phenomena, especially the analysis on the emerging economic phenomena, Marxist philosophy will return to the trivial scholasticism divorced from life. To separate any part of Marxism from the whole will make it lose its original nature and lead to the misinterpretation of the whole scientific system of Marxism.

Not only is the structure of Marxist scientific system determined by the need of the proletarian practice, but it is also formed and matured in the course of practice. Unlike Hegel, Marx and Engels did not predetermine the structure of their own ideological system. *The Phenomenology of Spirit* is the secret and birthplace of Hegel's system. In this book written in 1806, Hegel outlined the structure of his entire system. Marx and Engels are not just scholars buried in the London Library, just as some politicians described. They did not create the system according to the pre-conceived system, but according to the need of practice, especially in order to answer the practical problems in the proletarian revolutionary process, and made their theory perfect and mature.

The reason why Marx and Engels began their theoretical activities from accepting German classical philosophy is also determined by the historical and cultural background of Germany. Marx's doctoral dissertation *The Difference Between the Democritean and Epicurean Philosophy of Nature*, and Engels's *Schelling On Hegel*, *Schelling and Revelation*, and *Schelling-Christian Philosopher*, are typical philosophical papers. The starting point of theoretical thinking process of Marx and Engels is philosophy. But unlike their own German philosophical pioneers, they did not stop in philosophy .Marx and Engels, who were forging weapons for the liberation of the proletariat, realized that the ultimate cause of social change should not be found in people's minds, but in the economy, that the communist movement can only find the basis of experience and theory for itself in the private property movement, that is, in the economy, and gradually turn to the study of political economy.

This kind of change is of decisive significance to the establishment of Marxist scientific system, and is promoted by practice. Taking Marx as an example, Marx turned to the study of political economy for the first time mainly after the suspension of *The Deutsch–Französische Jahrbücher (German–French Annals)* in March 1844. Marx studied the works of some economists of Britain and France in Paris, and made excerpts of notes, which were well known as *The Paris Manuscripts*. Among them, *Economic and Philosophic Manuscripts of 1844* was particularly important. *Economic and Philosophic Manuscripts of 1844* attempted to combine philosophy, political economy, and socialist theory, and could be regarded as the embryonic form of Marxist scientific system. Although *Economic and Philosophic Manuscripts of 1844* was not mature, it tried to prove communism from the angle of economics by analyzing the movement of private property, and took a decisive step in socialism from space to science. The second time for him to focus on political economics was after moving to Brussels in the spring of 1845. Marx continued his research started in Paris in Brussels. He read a lot of political economics books, went to Britain with Engels for field investigations, and studied some economic works at the Chettem Library in Manchester. Marx's economic research achievements were condensed in *The German Ideology* co-authored by him and Engels. This important work not only completely cleared Feuerbach, established historical materialism in an all-round way, but also investigated the inevitability and necessity of socialist revolution based on the contradiction movement laws of productivity and relations of production, so as to build the theoretical argumentation of socialism on the basis of historical materialism and economic analysis and further deepened the Marxist scientific system initially established in *Economic and Philosophic Manuscripts of 1844*. The European Revolution of 1848 interrupted Marx's economic research. After the failure of the revolution, Marx arrived in London in August 1849 and began the research of economics again. Henceforth, it can be said that Marx devoted his life to the preparation and writing of *Das Kapital*. Marx not only left a large number of drafts of *Das Kapital*, but also published the first volume of *Das Kapital*. *Das Kapital* is a great work on economics and the most important philosophical work, or, as Lenin called "capital logic." What is of particular importance is that *Das Kapital* logically reproduced the historical process of the emergence, development and extinction of capitalist, and convincingly proved the historical inevitability of the deprivation of capitalist private ownership. Taking the economic analysis on capitalist production relations as the center, and combining philosophy, political economics and scientific socialism, *Das Kapital* is the most profound and comprehensive demonstration of Marxism scientific system.

We should grasp the scientific system of Marxism as a whole and see the inherent and inseparable connection between the various components of Marxism. Historical experience has proved that antagonizing each component of Marxism is an important aspect of dismemberment of Marxism.

The theorists in the later period of the Second International tried to expel philosophy from Marxism, denied that Marxism had its own philosophical foundation, and advocated to replenish Marxism with Kantianism and Maherism. For example, Kautsky (Karl Johann Kautsky) once claimed: "I do not understand Marxism as any philosophy, but as an experimental science, namely, a special view of society." He also said: "Marxism does not declare any philosophy, but declares the end of all philosophy." He also declared that historical materialism "is linked not only to Maher and Avenarius (Richard Ludwig Heinrich Avenarius), but also linked to many other philosophies."[20] Bernstein (Eduard Bernstein) tried to cut off the inherent relationship between Marxist scientific socialism and its economic and philosophical theories, denied that socialist society was the inevitable results of economic development, and thought that it was an ethical requirement derived from human impulses. He declared that "it is both impossible and unnecessary to provide a purely materialistic argument to socialism."[21]

If the theorists in the later period of the Second International tried to negate the Marxist scientific system by negating Marxist philosophy, the contemporary Western Marxism and Western scholars were completely opposite with an attempt to attribute Marxism only to philosophy and to the greatly reduced theory of humanism and alienation. D. Bell, an American socialist and political philosopher, discussed this trend in *The Debate on Alienation*. He said today in Britain and France, peoples' interests in Marx went around the theme of alienation. People did not regard Marx as an economist or political theorist, but regarded him as the first philosopher to reveal the alienation.[22] Marx was only a philosopher, a humanitarian and alienation theory philosopher. All the core areas of Marxism were

---

[20]Quoted from Vranicki (Predrag Vranicki): *History of Marxism*, Vol. 1, Page 352, Beijing, People's Publishing House, 1986.

[21]Bernstein: *The Preconditions of Socialism and the Task of the Social Democratic Party*, Page 255, Beijing, Sanlian Bookstore, 1973.

[22]See *Alienation* II, Page 1, Beijing, Culture and Art Publishing House, 1986.

human nature, humanity and alienation. This is the Marxism in the eyes of the Western Marxists.

Some Western scholars have similar views. For example, Binkley, a professor of philosophy at the Franklin Marshall College in the United States, also publicized this view in the book *Conflict of Ideals*. He believed that Marx's economic theory had been surpassed by that of Keynes (John Maynard Keynes, 1st Baron Keynes); Marx's prediction about the elimination of the middle class, the struggle between the bourgeoisie and the proletariat, and the capitalism bound to be replaced by socialism had been proved to be incorrect. The only thing left was a theory of moral value. So he declared publicly: "Regarding Marx as a philosopher, a prophet, or a founder of a new world religion, or even as a 'value legislator', we can understand the significance of Marx more clearly."[23] "Marx, as an influential prophet in our choice of world view, will live forever," he added. "However, Marx, as an economist and a prophet of the inevitable path of history, has fallen to a forgotten point that can only arouse historical interests."[24] Marx was completely misunderstood. Marxism, as a complete scientific system, including philosophy, political economy and scientific socialism theory, had only philosophy left. Marxism was cut off from the revolutionary movement of the proletariat and turned into a harmless holy idol of prophecy.

The British scholar Perry Anderson (Francis Rory Peregrine "Perry" Anderson) said: "Marx, the founder of historical materialism, is constantly shifting from philosophy to politics and economics, and taking it as a central part of his thinking; but the traditional successor, who emerged after 1920, has been constantly shifting from economics and politics to philosophy, giving up issues that are of great concern to

---

[23]Luther J. Binkley: *Conflict of Ideals: Changing Values in Western Society*, Page 96.

[24]Luther J. Binkley: *Conflict of Ideals: Changing Values in Western Society*, Page 106.

mature Marx."[25] It should be said that this is an objective comment on the formation of the Marxism scientific system and its contemporary encounter from one side.

4

How to treat the function of Marxism, that is, to insist on or deny the guiding role of Marxism, is a question related to whether the proletariat can realize its great historical mission, and related to the fate of Marxism in the present age. We should not only correctly understand the function of Marxism, but also study the mechanism and conditions for Marxism to play its function to fully realize the guiding role of Marxism.

Generally speaking, any philosophical and social ideological system has dual functions: cognitive function and value function. Cognitive function refers to its ability to provide some objective knowledge for human beings, while the value function means that it reflects the interests and wishes of a particular subject. The relationship between the two functions is complex. It can be partially consistent with each other, or it can be contradictory or even antagonistic. For example, when the bourgeoisie is on the rise, there is some consistency between the cognitive function and the value function of its ideological system, so the British classical political economy, which reflects its interests, is scientific to a certain extent. However, when the bourgeoisie is in the dominant position, especially after the contradiction between it and the oppressed proletariat is intensified, the sociological theory which meets the needs of the bourgeoisie is less scientific.

Marxism also has dual functions. The difference is that the cognitive function and value function of Marxism are consistent. Engels once said: "The more unscrupulous and selfless science is, the more it meets the interests and aspirations

---

[25]Anderson: *Considerations on Western Marxism*, Page 68~69, Beijing, People's Publishing House, 1981.

of workers."[26] The fundamental interests of the proletariat require it to understand the world scientifically in order to find a way to complete liberation. We must correctly handle the relationship between these two functions. Once any of them is ignored, the guiding role of Marxism will be hindered.

Marxism is a scientific system with great cognitive function. It reveals the emergence, development and extinction of capitalism, the general laws of the proletarian revolution, the objective and truthful cognition in the field of philosophy, political economy and scientific socialism by revealing the most common laws of nature, society and human thinking to provide great cognitive tools for mankind, and open up a great possibility for man to know the truth.

More importantly, the cognitive function of Marxism is not limited to itself, but is prominently manifested as a practical function. If the former philosophy and social theory seeks to explain the world, Marxist focuses on changing the world. In the Marxism, the purpose to correctly understand the world is to change the world. Excluding practice from cognitive function is a misinterpretation of the cognitive function of Marxism.

There are two wrong views on the cognitive function of Marxism.

One is dogmatism, which regards Marxism as a "Morrison pill" to cure all diseases. In fact, Marxism is not a dogma. It does not provide a ready-made answer to all questions. There are no ready-made answers to contemporary problems from the classic works of Marxism, which cannot be blamed on Marx, but on its own ignorance of the scientific nature of Marxism. Long before the October Revolution, Lenin had mocked some Marxists in Russia for finding answers to the Russian revolutionary leadership in Marx's works, which was "vulgar Marxism" and "the laughing at dialectical materialism". He said: "The elements of this or that type of development of capitalism are likely to be intertwined infinitely and intricately. Only

---

[26]*Karl Marx and Frederick Engels: Selected Works*, Edition 1, Vol. 4, Page 254.

the irredeemable nerd will simply cite Marx's discussion of another historical era to solve the unique and complex problems that are currently occurring."[27] It is to turn Marxism from science to apocalypse with the attempt to find a ready-made answer to contemporary problems from the classics of Marxist.

However, it is absolutely wrong to contempt and even to deny the cognitive function of Marxism just because of this. Failure to provide ready-made answers is not its weakness, but its strength and invincibility. The doctrine that claims to contain all the answers is not science, but theology. We can only expect what it can do in accordance to the scientific nature of the Marxism system, but cannot ask it to do what it cannot do. The scientific function of Marxism lies in the fact that it does not provide a permanent conclusion, but scientifically reveals the true features of the objective world and the objective laws of its movement, thus providing a correct method to know and change the world. Just as what Engels said: "The whole world view of Marx is not a doctrine, but a method. It provides not the existing dogma, but the starting point for further research and the way to **use** this research."[28]

Marxism is both a scientific system and an ideology of the proletariat. The value function of Marxism is embodied in its nature as ideology. Marxism has a distinct class inclination, consciously defends and reflects the interests of the proletariat and all workers, repudiates and opposes various hostile doctrines and ideologies in the ideological field.

The research on the function of Marxism cannot be separated from its practical utility. It is not difficult to see that in the century and a half since the birth of Marxism, it not only plays a role of scientific world view and methodology in

---

[27]*Selected Works of Lenin*, Edition 2, Vol. 1, Page 159.

[28]*Marx/Engels Collected Works*, Chinese Edition 1, Vol. 39, Page 406, Beijing, People's Publishing House, 1974.

guiding people to understand and change the world correctly, but also plays the role of constantly excluding and eliminating all kinds of wrong theories and doctrines from the workers' movement in the process of mobilizing, propagating and organizing the masses of workers, establishing political parties for workers in various countries, and leading the proletarian revolution and socialist construction. A history of Marxism is not only the practice history of the proletariat and its political party, but also the history of ideological struggle. Marxism has been developed and disseminated in the struggle against various external and internal bourgeoisie and petty bourgeoisie ideology.

In contemporary times, the dual function of Marxism has been challenged and misinterpreted.

Some Western scholars strongly denied the scientific function of Marxism, vigorously advocating the theory of "outdated Marxism". They regarded Marxism as the product of the second wave. Today, the use of Marxism is just like using magnifying glass in the age of electron microscope. This argument is wrong. The most vital of Marxism is not its individual argument or prophecy, but its revelation of the objective law. Its validity lies in its truth. Absolutely, it does not end the truth, but provides a support for the human beings to know the new truth. More importantly, the world is developing, so is the Marxism. The contradiction between fixed Marxism and immutable objective reality is a fictional contradiction in the minds of Western scholars. This fiction is a violation of the dialectical nature of Marxism.

Some Western scholars also opposed the value function of Marxism and strongly advocated the "end" or "downplay" of ideology. They opposed the science and ideology, and accused Marxism of "institutionalized ideology".

In fact, science and ideology are not absolutely opposite. There are various ideologies. The criticism of Marx and Engels on the German ideology in *The German Ideology* is a criticism of German philosophy and "real socialism" represented by

Feuerbach, Bauer (Bruno Bauer) and Schmidt (Johann Kaspar Schmidt), rather than the negation of all ideologies. As a kind of ideology of the summation of various thoughts and viewpoints produced on the basis of specific relations of production, it is an objective social phenomenon, and the problem is its nature. Marxism is also an ideology, but it is a scientific ideology.

In our time, there is no "end" or "non-ideology" of ideology. The opposition of various ideologies is still fierce. Despite the ecological problem and nuclear testing have aroused the concern of all mankind, this does not mean that it is a supra-state, supra-nation and supra-class problem. It is not difficult for people to see the antagonism of different ideologies from the politicians' understanding of these problems and their solutions.

The political situation in the world today has eased somewhat, and the links and exchanges between different social systems are closer than ever before. But the struggle of ideology has not stopped. Imperialism has not given up the purpose and policy of fundamentally changing the socialist system. It attempts to continuously penetrate through ideology so as to "win without war." Marxism must exert its ideological function and carry on necessary and persuasive criticism and struggle against various hostile ideologies.

Especially in socialist countries that have already acquired political power, we must adhere to the guidance of Marxism and give full play to its regulation and guidance in the whole social life. This is a major issue related to the future and destiny of the socialist countries. Abandoning the guidance of Marxism and letting the bourgeois liberalization trend of thought overflow, we will definitely ruin the socialist society.

The functions of Marxism and its enforcement are different. Some countries in the East have won the revolution, but the West is still in the silent period of revolution. Some socialist countries have successfully applied Marxism to the struggle to seize political power, but they are still groping for it in the course of socialist construction. Does this mean that Marxism has lost its function? No, the key is that we don't have a correct understanding of the mechanism for functioning.

As a scientific system, the universal principle of Marxism is universally applicable to both the East and the West, and can guide both the socialist revolution and the socialist construction. However, the utility of Marxism does not depend solely on its universal principles, but on the practical application of these principles. Accordingly, whether the function of Marxism can be brought into play or not, except for other objective conditions, as for Marxism itself, the following problems must be addressed:

First of all, there must be a group of Marxists with high theoretical accomplishment and practical experience. The exertion of Marxism, to a great extent, depends on the type and level of Marxists. Since the birth of Marxism, there have been several generations of Marxists with different situations. Historical experience has proved that the Russian Marxists represented by Lenin and the Chinese Marxists represented by Mao Tse-tung played a key role in the successful application of Marxism to the Russian and Chinese revolutions.

Secondly, it is necessary to understand the national conditions. The exertion of Marxism depends on the degree to which Marxism is combined with the actual conditions of each country. There are a series of intermediate links (such as the understanding of national conditions, the formulation of actual policies, the implementation of policies, etc.) between Marxism and its actual effects. If any one of these links fails, the intended purpose may not be achieved.

Moreover, creative scientific research must be carried out. Marxism is science and requires us to treat it in a scientific manner. The application of Marxism to the East, the West, the socialist revolution and socialist construction will inevitably meet many new problems, which requires us to carry out arduous scientific research and exploration.

Finally, we must be good at summing up the experience. It is a process of repeated practice and failure to give full play to the function of Marxism. History has a large scale. It is wrong to deny the guiding function of Marxism only based on one or short-term error. Marxism cannot guarantee that people do not make mistakes, but it points out a path from error to success.

***

Marxism was developed in struggle. A highly scientific summary of the law of the development of Marxism has been made by both Lenin in his *The Historical Destiny of the Doctrine of Karl Marx* and Mao Tse-tung in his *On the Correct Handling of Contradictions among the People*.

"A thunder shook the earth, a goblin born from a pile of bones." Truth and falsehood always exist in comparison and struggle for development. Every step forward in the development of Marxism must be fought. The misinterpretation of Marxism by various theories, ideological trends and schools of thoughts can be said to have started from the day Marx and Engels founded Marxism. Heinrich Cunow, a German social democratic theorist, described the situation in German in the Preface to his *Die Marxsche Geschichts, Gesellschafts- und Staatstheorie; Grundzüge der Marxschen Soziologie, 1920/21 – Marxist Theory of History, Society and the State* in 1920s. He said: "Today, the Social Democratic Party of Germany based on Marxism splits into a series of rival parties." In quoting Marxist theories, they all set out from the basic point of view of various social philosophies. Moreover, within their own ranks, even many widely different theories have been branded as Marxism. Marx's theory, and the political struggle that arises from it, has completely no unanimous conclusion can be drawn."[29] In the contemporary world, this situation has become more serious than that in 1920s.

Historical experience has proved that the fate of Marxism is closely linked to the

---

[29] Heinrich Cunow: *Die Marxsche Geschichts, Gesellschafts- und Staatstheorie; Grundzüge der Marxschen Soziologie, 1920/21 – Marxist Theory of History, Society and the State*, Vol. 1, Page 1, Beijing, Commercial Press, 1988.

proletarian revolution and socialist construction. When the storm of the proletarian revolution comes and the socialist construction flourishes, the position of Marxism is constantly consolidated and expanded with high prestige and widespread dissemination; while when capitalism is relatively stable, the revolutionary situation is "silent", the socialist countries suffer setbacks, the critics of Marxism, like poisonous mushrooms after the rain, spring out of the ground. But we firmly believe that Marxism, as a kind of scientific truth, is invincible regardless of what kind of struggle it encounters in the course of its life.

CHAPTER 1   PROLETARIAN PROMETHEUS

On March 18th 1843, young Marx published a political cartoon—Chained Prometheus on the newspaper to protest against the close down of *Rheinische Zeitung* by the Prussian government. It was a self-portrayal of Marx's image. Indeed, Marx was Prometheus, not God, and all his works were science, not revelation.

Mehring (Franz Erdmann Mehring) said: "Marx is neither a god nor a demigod, and he is not a pope who has no faults. He is a thinker who has fundamentally expanded the limits of human understanding."[30] This assessment should be said to be pertinent.

1. Marx As A Great Scientist

Marx was the "fire thief" who forged the truth for the proletariat and mankind. He brought science and light to the human beings who were wandering and groping blindly in the dark. For Marx's lofty position in the history of science, Engels made a full affirmation. On March 17th 1883, standing in front of his dead friend's grave, he praised Marx as "the greatest thinker of the contemporary era"[31], and "the great master of science"[32].

---

[30]Mehring: *In Defense of Marxism*, Page 301, Beijing, People's Publishing House, 1982.

[31]*Karl Marx and Frederick Engels: Selected Works*, Edition 1, Vol. 3, Page 574.

[32]*Karl Marx and Frederick Engels: Selected Works*, Edition 1, Vol. 3, Page 575.

It was not Engels' personal feelings and simple personal evaluation of his dead friends. At the time of Marx's death, telegrams of condolences and newspaper editorials from workers' organizations in many countries all over the world expressed the same view. There were many editorials such as *A Vibrant and Productive Thinker* in *The Sun* of New York, *The Greatest Thinker of This Century* in *Liberty*, *Scholar and Thinker* in *Chicago Tribune*, *He Laid the Scientific Foundation of Socialism* in Zurich's *Worker's Voice, His Works Set Up An Everlasting Monument* in Zurich's *Social Democrats, An Erudite Thinker* in Rome's *League for Democracy, The Discoverer of the Laws of Economic Development* in *The People* of Milan, *An Excellent Economist* in *The Weltbild* of St. Petersburg, *One of the Greatest Representatives of Modern Economics* in *Judicial Bulletin* of Moscow, *An Unparalleled Scholar* in *Moscow Telegraph*, and *The Most Talented Son of the Jews* in *Dawn Chronicle Weekly* of St. Petersburg. Although they have different political colors, they all show great respect for Marx. They all praise Marx as "the greatest thinker of this century", "the founder of modern socialism" and "the pioneer of new science".[33]

All the reactionary forces in old Europe, such as the Pope and the Tsar, the reactionary officials and the police, regarded Marx as a "demagogue", an "agitator", and a "schemer". In fact, Marx was a great scientist, but his organization skills and revolutionary achievements concealed his image as a great scientist.

Marx has been respected by his friends for his profound thoughts since his youth. In the autumn of 1841, when Marx was a young student who had just stepped out of college, in his letter to his friend, Hess highly praised Marx for "not only surpassing Strauss but also transcending Feuerbach in the development of thought or in philosophical spirit", and said to his friend: "Imagine that the combination of

---

[33]See Philip Sheldon Foner: *When Karl Marx Died: Comments in 1883*, Beijing, Beijing Press, 1983.

Rousseau (Jean-Jacques Rousseau), Voltaire (François-Marie Arouet), Holbach (Paul Henri Thiry d'Holbach), Lessing (Gotthold Ephraim Lessing), Heine (Christian Johann Heinrich Heine) and Hegel (Georg Wilhelm Friedrich Hegel) into one person (I mean combination, not mixing), which will give you a concept of Dr. Marx."[34] That is to say, when Marx was young, he had France's most radical democratic ideas, Germany's profound philosophical ideas, and the temperament of poets. Then, in May 1842, when Marx's first article on the debate on freedom of the press of the Rhine Provincial Assembly was published in *Rheinische Zeitung*, Ruge praised that: "He is so erudite, so knowledgeable, and so good at mastering problems that have been confused by ordinary people."[35]

At the age of 25, Marx wrote Critique of Hegel's Philosophy of Right, which challenged the view of state of Hegel, who was the most authoritative in the philosophical field of Germany. When Marx completed *The Communist Manifesto*, which proclaimed the inevitable demise of the old world, he was only 29 years old. This groundbreaking and enlightening proclamation that combined the most profound scientific analysis and beautiful literary style fully demonstrated Marx's scientific genius.

In particular, Marx devoted nearly 40 years to the creation of *Das Kapital*. He had read more than 2000 books on economics and 4000 kinds of newspapers and periodicals, as well as a large number of official documents and blue books, and carried out careful analysis and hard researches. The sheer number of manuscripts in *Das Kapital* alone is staggering. In human history, there has been no such work on social sciences as *Das Kapital*, which can achieve to such a scientific height on the analysis on the activity laws and development mechanism of a social form.

---

[34]*Marx/Engels Collected Works*, International Edition, Part I Vol. 1-II, Page 261.

[35]Nalski: *Marxist Philosophy in the 19th Century* I, Page 47, Beijing, China Social Sciences Press, 1984.

Referring to scientists, people always think about Copernicus (Nicolaus Copernicus), Galilei (Galileo Galilei), Newton (Isaac Newton), Darwin (Charles Robert Darwin), and Einstein (Albert Einstein). As for social theory, it is not science but ideology, which is a bias. In fact, the social field is an extremely complex field of the whole physical world. There are also differences in truth and falsehood as well as science and fantasy in the understanding of society, and it is more difficult to know society than to know nature. *Das Capital* fully demonstrates the scientific nature of social theory. Just as Darwin overthrew the view that animal and plant species were regarded as unrelated to each other, incidental, God-made and unchanged things, and put biology on the basis of complete science for the first time, Marx also overturned the view that society can be randomly changed, accidentally produced and changed, and mechanically combined with individuals according to the will of the superior by analyzing the capitalist social formation in *Das Capital*, regarded the development of capitalist social formation as a natural historical process and set up a model for scientific analysis of society. *Das Capital* is the treasure and pride of social science.

Marx spent his whole life in scientific exploration. In his old, sick and extremely difficult final years, Marx also devoted himself to the study of eastern and primitive societies. In order to study the question of land rent, Marx paid great attention to the study of Russian land relations and extensively read the relevant works of Russian scholars and the compilation of documents and statistics published in Russia after 1861. He also made summaries and commentaries on *The System of Commune Land Ownership and the Cause, Process and Result of Its Disintegration (Общинное землевладение etc. Mosk.1879)* by Kovalevsky, *Ancient Society* by Morgan (Lewis Henry Morgan), *Lectures Delivered by Maine for the Inns of Court were the Groundwork of Ancient Law* by Maine (Sir Henry James Sumner Maine), *The Origin of Civilization and the Primitive State of Man* by Lubbock (John Lubbock, 1st Baron Avebury, 4th Baronet), and *The Aryan Village in India and Ceylon* by Phear (Phear John B.). This is Marx's *Anthropology Notes*, which aroused the increasingly attention and growing interests of the theoretical circles, and was the witness of Marx's scientific exploration in his later years.

From the whole history of human science, Marx is a worthy great scientist. His field of study is very broad. His major is law, but he has studied philosophy, political economy, socialist theory, history, literature in depth with outstanding achievements even in the field of natural science. The various natural science achievements he used in *Das Capital*, especially his *The Mathematical Manuscripts of Karl Marx*, are proof. Engels said: "Marx has made unique discoveries in every field he studies (even in mathematics). There are many such fields, and neither of them is a superficial study."[36] In particular, his historical materialism and the surplus value theory are two great discoveries in the history of human thought. Marx has a lot of works, and the international edition of *Marx/Engels Collected Works* has 100 volumes. In the world, it should be Mark's works that at the top list of the world works with the largest number of publications and the highest number of translated works. If we put the published Marx's works and their translations together, we can imagine that no library in the world can accommodate them.

"The style is the man", which applies not only to writers, but also to scientists. Marx, as a great scientist, has an extremely bright personality, which can be called as "Marx's style", and Marx has noble scientific morality and scientific conscience. He respected science and facts with no fear in power and no consideration in personal gains or losses. In his letter to Ruge in September 1843, he called for a merciless critique of everything that existed, and "such criticism is not afraid of his own conclusions, nor does he shrink from offending those in power."[37] In 1859, Marx called this spirit the spirit of "going to hell" in his *A Contribution to the Critique of Political Economy*. When he spoke of his *Critique of Political Economy*, he said: "my

---

[36] *Karl Marx and Frederick Engels: Selected Works*, Edition 1, Vol. 3, Page 574~575.

[37] *Marx/Engels Collected Works*, Chinese Edition 1, Vol. 1, Page 416.

opinion, no matter how people comment on it, and no matter how unsuited to the selfish prejudice of the ruling class, it is the result of many years of honest discussion. But in the scientific entrance, as in the hell entrance, such demands must be made: All hesitation here must be eradicated; and all cowardice here is of no avail."[38]

Marx fulfilled his promise. Although Marx was persecuted and expelled many times throughout his life, especially in his later years, when he was poor and ill with great hardship in life, he never bowed down, never "sold theory for officials", nor wavered in his faith and pursuit of truth. It is Marx's scientific conscience to seek truth silently, declare truth loudly, and defend truth bravely.

Marx always faced the reality and looked at the pressing problems of society. He was born in Germany with a tradition of speculative philosophy. When he began to enter the University of Berlin, he was still obsessed with creating a speculative system. For example, he wrote about 300 prints of the theory of law, "trying to make some kind of philosophy of law run through the whole realm of law."[39] But his association with the doctor's club and his participation in the youth Hegel movement changed Marx's direction of life. He abandoned the pure academic path of making up the philosophical system, took part in the actual struggle, and thought about urgent social problems theoretically. It can be said that none of Marx's works is a pure academic problem which has nothing to do with reality. The subject of his doctoral thesis *The Difference Between the Democritean and Epicurean Philosophy of Nature* seems to be purely philosophical, but in fact is the struggle against Prussian autocracy and religion in the form of philosophy. One of the prominent manifestations of the reality of Marx's works is timeliness, which is almost always

---

[38]*Karl Marx and Frederick Engels: Selected Works*, Edition 1, Vol. 2, Page 85.

[39]*Marx/Engels Collected Works*, Chinese Edition 1, Vol. 40, Page 10, Beijing, People's Publishing House, 1982.

an analytical study of important events that have just occurred or are taking place. *The Review of Prussia's Latest Order for Checking Books and Newspapers* he wrote in January 1842 was a review of the order for checking books and newspapers issued by King William IV, The Conqueror of Germany on December 24th 1841. Several famous comments published in *Rheinische Zeitung* in 1842 was an attack on the debate in the Rhine Provincial Assembly held in 1841. The famous articles *On the Jewish Question* and *The Introduction to The Critique of Hegel's Philosophy of Right* published in *Deutsch–Französische Jahrbücher (German–French Annals)* in early 1844 answered the Jewish questions that Germany was discussing at that time, especially the question of political liberation and human liberation. His famous book *The Poverty of Philosophy* was written in 1847 as an answer to the economic and philosophical arguments of French anarchist Pierre-Joseph Proudhon set forth in his 1846 book *The System of Economic Contradictions, or The Philosophy of Poverty*. *The Eighteenth Brumaire of Louis Napoleon*, Marx's genius work, is an analysis of the political events that are taking place and is not over. Marx's account of China was all what was happening at that time, for example, the Opium War, the Taiping Heavenly Revolution, and the military and economic aggression of the powers against China. Even *Das Capital*, the most scientifically advanced masterpiece, is Marx's analysis of the social forms in which he lives to solve the problem of where the capitalist society was headed at that time mainly through the exploration of the emergence and laws of development of capitalist social forms. As for Marx, it was incompatible with his style to turn his back to the present and face the past. As early as in the 1842, in the debate with the *Collen Daily*, Marx attacked the purely philosophical study of escapism, criticizing that "philosophy, especially German philosophy, likes to be quiet and lonely, closed to the outside world and obsessed with the indifference of self-intuition",[40] pointing out that "any true philosophy is the essence of the spirit of its times", and "philosophy should not only

---

[40]*Marx/Engels Collected Works*, Chinese Edition 1, Vol. 1, Page 120.

contact and interact with the real world of its times from the inside in terms of its content, but also from the outside."[41] Marx adheres to this principle all his life until death. *Anthropology Notes* in his later years is formally facing the past, but in fact, still based on reality. He studied the ancient society and the oriental society in order to deeply analyze the capitalist social form and explore the need of human social development laws.

Marx is a scientist and a great social scientist. But unlike previous philosophers and social scientists, Marx not only has outstanding and multifaceted academic achievements, but also is in the lofty position of "fire thief" in the history of mankind. Or as Lenin put it, Marx taught the working class self-knowledge and self-consciousness, replaced fantasy with science, and gave mankind great tools of understanding, especially to the working class. Marx forged a great tool of understanding for mankind, especially for the working class, so that the human being who had been wandering in the dark for a long time had a torch to illuminate the way forward. Marx is the proletarian Prometheus.

In the history of human thought, there are quite a number of successful thinkers who have contributed to human culture to varying degrees and in different fields, but not every thinker is in the position of "fire thief." It not only purely depends on the intelligence of the individual, but the time is more important. The first half of the 19th century that Marx was living was the era of "century transformation". This is the era of rapid development of productive forces, which broke free from feudal restraints, and of the intensification of contradictions in the capitalist mode of production. The first economic crisis in 1825 and the June revolution in France in 1830 shook people's minds. What kind of person is needed in such an era? Is Jesus Christ, Sakyamuni, the founder of Buddhism or a scientist who explains their historical status and mission and their way out needed? In 1840s, the furious storm

---

[41]*Marx/Engels Collected Works*, Chinese Edition 1, Vol. 1, Page 121.

made all kinds of utopian socialists boasted themselves as the savior and prophet, disappeared from the political stage one by one, and the new proletariat, which began to grow, needed science, not fantasy; it is the trumpet of battle, not tears and warmth; and it is the understanding of reality, not the prophecy of the afterlife. Anyone who can scientifically analyze the contradictions that have begun to emerge and point out the ways and means to solve them can be in the position of "fire thief" and forever engraved on the monument of history. Just at the right time, Marx sent the scientific torch for the liberation of mankind with his intelligence and revolutionary enthusiasm.

2. Marx as a Great Revolutionary

Marx is a scientist and a revolutionary, and according to Engels, "first of all, a revolutionary. It is, in fact, his lifelong mission to participate in the cause of overthrowing the capitalist society and the state system it built in some way and to participate in the cause of liberation of the modern proletariat who realized their positions, demands and their own liberation conditions for the first time by depending on Marx".

This, in fact, was also an international commentary at the time of Marx's death. An editorial in *Collen Daily* called Marx "the unselfish and fearless liberator of the working class", and Budapest's *Chronicle of Workers* praised Marx as "one of the most remarkable people to push the movement of the earth".[42]

In the eyes of some contemporary West scholars, Marx's image as a revolutionary has been forgotten; Marxism is no longer a theory of proletarian revolution, but a cultural phenomenon; it is not born out of the needs of the labor movement and the proletariat, but the products of the cultural development. Marx himself is not a revolutionary, but a philosophical anthropologist, even a kind-hearted evangelist who preaches the gospel to all living beings. Hook (Sidney Hook) preached this kind

---

[42]See Philip Foner: *When Karl Marx Died: Comments in 1883.*

of view in *The Second Coming of Karl Marx*. He said: "For the second coming, Marx was not an economist in a dusty dress and the author of *Das Capital*, nor a revolutionary and the author of the inspiring *The Communist Manifesto*, but is Marx who dressed in the clothes of philosophers and moral prophets and brought the delightful message of human freedom. The power of this message transcends the narrow view of the class, the political parties and the sects."[43]

Marx as a scientist and Marx as a revolutionary are two in one. Marx is a scientist, a revolutionary scientist; Marx is a revolutionary, a scientific revolutionary. The fusion of revolutionary and scientific nature is the characteristic of Marx as a new thinker.

Marx's revolutionary road went through the process from fighting for spiritual freedom to striving for material interests, from defending intellectuals and peasants to exploring the essence of private ownership and wage labor, and from striving for political liberation to human liberation. At the beginning, Marx was a revolutionary democrat. His doctoral thesis, especially *The Review of Prussia's Latest Order for Checking Books and Newspapers*, and a series of brilliant and sharp comments published in *Rheinische Zeitung*, shown Marx's political stand against Prussian autocracy. Since October 1843, after left Germany and arrived in Paris, the capital of France, the new world, through the study of the history of the French revolution and the social reality of France, through the study of the political economy, Marx gradually took the struggle for the proletariat and human liberation as his lifelong mission. *On the Jewish Question* and *The Introduction to The Critique of Hegel's Philosophy of Right* are the key points of this turning point.

Marx as a revolutionary concentrated in founding revolutionary theory, establishing revolutionary organization and participating in actual revolutionary struggle.

Marx attached great importance to the founding of revolutionary theory. As early

---

[43]Hook: *The Second Coming of Karl Marx*, Published on *New York Times*, May 22, 1966.

as October 1842, in the article *Communism and the Augsburg Allgemeine Zeitung*, Marx commented on the practice of some utopian socialists who were still obsessed with all kinds of experiments in immigration areas. Marx considered it extremely urgent to conduct scientific theoretical arguments on communism, not experiments, and to put the theory of communism above all kinds of experiments. He said: "We firmly believe that the real **danger** is not the **actual experiment** of communist thought, but its **theoretical argumentation**."[44] Because in Marx's view, only truly scientific theory is the rational power that "controls our consciousness and dominates our faith".[45]

In *The Introduction to The Critique of Hegel's Philosophy of Right*, Marx vividly compared revolutionary theory to "the lightning" to greet the revolutionary storm, saying: "once the lightning of thought really shoots at the untouched people's garden, **the Germans** will be liberated as **human beings**."[46]

Engels made the same point. He said very humorously and profoundly that: "If we have philosophers thinking with us, and workers working with us for our cause, what else in the world can stop us from moving forward?"[47] The proletarian revolution is not a rational revolution based on the head, nor a brain-less revolution. Its head is Marxism. The focus of Marx's revolutionary work is to lay the head for the proletarian heart of human liberation.

For Marx, the problem is not only to create a scientific theory, moreover, it is

---

[44]*Marx/Engels Collected Works*, Chinese Edition 1, Vol. 1, Page 134.

[45]*Marx/Engels Collected Works*, Chinese Edition 1, Vol. 1, Page 134.

[46]*Marx/Engels Collected Works*, Chinese Edition 1, Vol. 1, Page 467.

[47]*Marx/Engels Collected Works*, Chinese Edition 1, Vol. 2, Page 595, Beijing, People's Publishing House, 1957.

necessary to propagate this theory to the workers[48], in order to fundamentally change the situation in which the former socialist theory was divorced from the labor movement. For this reason, Marx and Engels set up a Communist Communications Commission in Brussels in 1846 to actively establish contacts with socialists and workers' groups in various countries, to communicate with each other about the socialist movements in various countries, and to disseminate their views to them. Marx also carried out propaganda and education through the German Workers Association in Brussels. His important work *Wage Labour and Capital* was the report given at the German Workers Association in December 1847. Marx expounded the complicated economic problems in a very popular way, which made the ordinary workers have a correct understanding of the nature of wage and wage labor. It can be said that Marx devoted his whole life to educating workers in various ways. All his works are not simply for "the academia", but first of all for the workers.

A very notable feature of Marx's revolutionary work of creating and propagating his scientific views was that Marx attached great importance to newspaper. In *No. 179 Editorial of Collen Daily* dated June 1842, he criticized German speculative philosophy, and proposed "changing the priesthood of asceticism into the light fashion of newspaper."[49] Newspapers are an important position for Marx to state his views, for example, *Rheinische Zeitung* in 1842, *Vorwärts* of Paris in 1844, *Deutsche-Brüsseler-Zeitung* in 1847, *Neue Rheinische Zeitung* in 1847, *The People* in 1859, *New York Daily Tribune* in 1852-1861, and so on. Marx published a great deal

---

[48]"We have an obligation to demonstrate our point of view scientifically, but it is equally important for us to convince the European proletariat, above all the German proletariat, that our convictions are correct." (*Marx/Engels Collected Works*, Chinese Edition 1, Vol. 21, Page 248, Beijing, People's Publishing House, 1965.

[49]*Marx/Engels Collected Works*, Chinese Edition 1, Vol. 1, Page 120.

of war-fighting, realistic and scientific comments and articles in the newspaper, and expounded and propagated his own scientific views.

Marx also attached great importance to the organizational work of the revolution. Before Marx, workers' organizations of all kinds had already appeared, for example, "Equality League" of Babeyf (Francois Noël Babeyf), "Four Seasons Commune" of Blanqui (Louis Auguste Blanqui), "Egalitarian Workers' Society" of Dézamy (Théoddre Dézamy), and "League of the Just" of Weitling (Wilhelm Christian Weitling), and groups with mutual nature organized by workers to defend wages were even more common. But the workers' group at the time was either a purely economic organization or a small number of conspiratorial organizations lacking scientific theory, which could not take on the task of leading and organizing workers to engage in mass struggle. In October 1843, after his arrival in Paris, Marx began to come into contact with workers' organizations and their leaders, gradually discovered their political and theoretical weaknesses and realized that the proletariat had to build a revolutionary organization different from the organizations dominated by all kinds of utopian socialism and the equalitarianism of the petty bourgeoisie. Marx joined The Communist League, attended the Second Congress of The Communist League in London, and together with Engels drawn up *The Communist Manifesto*, which is the programmatic document for the league. Although The Communist League was finally dissolved with the defeat of the revolution in 1848, Marx reformed The Communist League, especially the protocols of *The Communist Manifesto*, which is a useful attempt to establish a proletarian political party.

In July 1863, representatives of workers from Britain and France agreed to set up an international political organization of the proletariat. Marx was invited to participate in the preparatory work. On September 28, 1864, the workers' delegations of Britain and France as well as representatives of democratic and exiled organizations from other countries, met in London and formally established the first proletarian mass international organization, namely the International

Workers' Association (IWA), commonly known as the First International. Marx was elected as a member of the leading committee and was chosen as a member of the small committee responsible for drafting the programmatic documents of the International Workers' Association. The first batches of programmatic documents of the International Workers' Association were written by Marx. Marx is the soul of the First International as well as the founder and leader of the First International. Marx's activities in the First International are Marx's most important organizational activities. Marx also paid close attention to the movement of establishing mass socialist political parties in European and American countries, and gave guidance and help theoretically and ideologically.

In the age of Marx's life, capitalism was in the process of its industrialization. Production developed rapidly, but various social contradictions were gradually becoming sharp and increasingly intensifying. Marx focused on these contradictions in theory, but as long as the revolution took place, Marx would devote himself bravely into the battle. Marx personally participated in the 1848 revolution in Europe. He took an active part in the armed revolt of the republic faction in Brussels and gave a large sum of money to arm the local workers. When the German revolution took place in March, Marx organized the German workers, members of the Communists League and members of the Workers' Club returned to Germany to take part in the struggle and drafted *Demands of the Communist Party in Germany*, which were printed and distributed in Germany with *The Communist Manifesto*. Marx also returned to Collen, Germany, founded *Neue Rheinische Zeitung*, and actively participated in the German revolution.

Marx's attitude towards the Paris Commune was that of a true revolutionary. Although Marx began to oppose the hasty rise of Parisian workers in adverse circumstances, when the Parisian workers rose up to the revolution, Marx tried his best to support. Marx had direct contact with the leaders of the commune, put forward constructive opinions, and launched the struggle of solidarity and support for the commune. After the commune failed, he also enthusiastically organized assistance to the exiles of the commune.

Marx also enthusiastically supported the struggles of China, India and other oppressed nations.

Engels had enthusiastically praised the giants of the Renaissance: "Some people use tongues and pens, some people use swords, and some people combine the two. So there is the integrity and strength of the character that makes them perfect. The scholars in the study are the exception: they are not second-rate or third-rate figures, namely, the cautious mediocrity that fears to burn his fingers."[50] The perfect man who truly fought with his pen and sword and who was complete and strong in character was Marx, and as a perfect combination of a scientist and a revolutionary, he became a giant in the era of proletarian revolution. Although he was persecuted and vilified during his life time, after his death, he received great honor, and was always the revolutionary leader at the peak of proletarian practice and theory.

3. To Conquer the World with Truth

The truth was always in the hands of a few at the very beginning. When Marx and Engels declared war on the old world hand in hand, they were only two young men of nobody in Europe.

The period of Marx's life is the period of the establishment and spread of Marxism, and the period of striving for their own right to exist and trying hard to deepen the rising labor movement.

In the first half century of Marxism, Marxism is not dominant in the labor movement, and it is only one of numerous socialist factions and ideological trends. In his life, Marx was constantly struggling with various hostile theories. In the first half of 1840s, he criticized the Young Hegel School, "The Real Socialists" and the

---

[50]*Karl Marx and Frederick Engels: Selected Works*, Edition 1, Vol. 3, Page 446.

Weitling Doctrine; in the late 1840s, he carried out the struggle against Prudonism in the aspect of economic theory; in the 1850s, he criticized the parties and doctrines that had shown their predominance in the European revolution in 1848; in the 1860s, he opposed the Lassalism; and in the 1870s, he opposed the Bakuninism and the Durlinism. No representative of any school of thought or ideological trend called himself a Marxist, but opposed Marx's point of view with their own. This kind of struggle is not a struggle between Marxism and various ideological trends under the banner of Marxism, but a struggle between Marxism and various hostile theories.

The advantage of this struggle is that the both parties in the dispute have definite views and clear differences, unlike the false Marxist views under the banner of Marxism, which are often ambiguous and elusive.

The mission given to Marx by history is not only to create a scientific theory, but also to inculcate it into the labor movement. If the contemporary struggle is characterized by trying to drive Marxism out of the labor movement, the characteristic of Marx's era is to squeeze in and make Marxism a dominant ideology in the labor movement.

Prior to the emergence of Marxism, workers in the more developed countries of capitalism in Western Europe had already carried out struggles such as the Luddite Movement that destroying the machines and all kinds of economic struggles. Workers' groups of all kinds and even political organizations have also appeared. In the first half of the 19th century, the Lyon Workers' Uprising, the British Charter Movement, and the Sirisian Textile Worker Uprising in Germany culminated, but at that time the entire labor movement lacked a scientific and complete guiding ideology. The top priority of Marxism after its emergence was to fight against all kinds of erroneous theories in the labor movement. Whether it is to oppose "True Socialism", to criticize Kriege (Hermann Kriege), to oppose Weitling or to oppose Proudhon (Pierre-Joseph Proudhon) in the early days, or to oppose Lassalle

(Ferdinand Lassalle) and Bakunin (Mikhail Alexandrovich Bakunin), it is to concentrate on trying to drive out all kinds of sectarianism, utopism, petty-bourgeois equalitarianism, anarchism and syndicalism from the labor movement.

Engels clearly clarified the essence of this struggle. Why did he and Marx attach so much importance to the insignificant Dühring? The reason was that Dühring revived what Marx had expelled from the labor movement. In his letter to Sorge (Friedrich Adolph Sorge), Engels said: "We have spent a lot of time and energy removing **utopian** socialism and the whole set of illusions about the future social structure from the minds of German workers, so as to make them theoretically (and therefore, in practice) superior to the French and the British, but now these things are in vogue, and their form is empty, not only more than the great French and English visionaries, and even more than Weitling."[51]

In the 19th century, in England, France and Germany where Marx had lived and fought, the proletariat was the ruled class. By what force could Marx gradually defeat his theoretical opponents and become the guiding ideology of the labor movement? He could not rely on his power and position, as he was a poor and sick exile persecuted by the rulers. Marx did not infiltrate any non-theoretical factors in the theoretical struggle, but relied entirely on the power of truth.

"As long as theory is thorough, it can convince ad hominem [human beings]. The so-called thoroughness is to grasp the root of things."[52] This is Marx's dictum. Marx defeated the adversary precisely because he founded the historical materialism and the theories of surplus value, and on this basis gave the scientific explanation to the proletarian emancipation road and the condition, and gave a scientific explanation of the road and conditions for the liberation of the proletariat on this basis. Due to

[51]*Karl Marx and Frederick Engels: Selected Works*, Edition 1, Vol. 4, Page 418.

[52]*Marx/Engels Collected Works*, Chinese Edition 1, Vol. 1, Page 460.

its scientific and revolutionary nature, it is the most easily accepted and understood by the working class.

This is a real theoretical struggle, not a power struggle. Losers are not exiled, expelled and sentenced, but lost their influence in the labor movement. The result of the struggle was a series of important works: *The German Ideology*, *The Holy Family*, *The Poverty of Philosophy*, *The Critique of the Gotha Program*, *Anti-Dühring*, and a great number of reviews and papers. This is the triumph of truth over falsehood. This victory does not stifle truth, but develops truth. In the second half of the19th Century, Marxism was moving forward in this kind of struggle.

The 19th century was a period of theoretical victory for Marxism. It was in this process that Marxism gradually integrated and formed into a complete scientific system; and it was in this process that Marxism had become the dominant theoretical form in the labor movement.

Of course, in the era of Marx's life, all sorts of misinterpretations of Marxism began. Heinrich Cunow said: "As long as Karl Marx and Friedrich Engels were alive, the odd tampering and interpretation of Marxist theory has been repeated for many times, especially in France."[53] For example, in his later years, Marx was so dissatisfied with the narrow and dogmatic interpretation of Marxism by French Marxists that he denied that he was a Marxist.[54]

However, it was after the death of Marx and Engels that truly carrying out a "revision" of Marxism under the banner of Marxism and standing on the basis of Marxism. Bernstein, the chief figure in the late Second International period, should be the initiator.

---

[53] Heinrich Cunow: *Die Marxsche Geschichts, Gesellschafts- und Staatstheorie; Grundzüge der Marxschen Soziologie, 1920/21 – Marxist Theory of History, Society and the State*, Vol. 1, Page 1.

[54] See *Marx/Engels Collected Works*, Chinese Edition 1, Vol. 35, Page 385, Beijing, People's Publishing House, 1971.

CHAPTER 2   "CRISIS" IN THE GOLDEN AGE

Marx attracted many admirers with scientific logic and strong sense of the times for his doctrines. Under his name, a large number of talented thinkers formed a large lineup of Marxist theory. These theorists studied and propagated Marx's theory with great enthusiasm, making use of all kinds of pulpits, assemblies, newspapers and periodicals and so on, so that Marxism had been widely disseminated worldwide. This unprecedented grand occasion first appeared in the Second International Era (from 1889 to 1914). Even Kołakowski called this period as the golden age of Marxism.[55]

The fate of theory is often closely linked to the course of history. The historic turn at the turn of the 19th century and the 20th century led to such a dramatic change: The original form of the unified Marxist theory camp had been divided. In theory, this divergence is mainly manifested in the different views on the interpretation of Marxist theory, some of which tend to the opposite side of Marxism. This situation seems to indicate that Marxism has encountered a crisis in the face of reality, and the emergence of this kind of "crisis" under the prosperity urges people to reflect on the essence of Marxism and to inquire into the fate of Marxism.

1. At the Turning Point of History

People do not care about the fate of a theoretical doctrine that is hatched purely from the study, for it is far from history and out of touch with reality, with no problems such as "challenges" or "crises". However, people have always been concerned about the historical fate of the Marxist theory, which reflects the spirit of the times and is related to the fate of mankind.

---

[55]See Kołakowski: *Main Currents of Marxism*, Vol. 2, Page 1, Oxford, 1981.

At the end of the 19th century and the beginning of the 20th century, the economic situation and the labor movement of the major capitalist countries in Europe showed a turning point. The waves of the reality stirred up the wild whirlwind of the theory. Within the ranks of Marxist theory, there was a great controversy that attracted the attention of the whole world. Since the death of Marx and Engels, the doctrines found by the two thought masters were, for the first time, judged by their students on the scales of history. The core issue affecting the nerves of Marxist theorists within the Second International was: Is Marx's assessment of the fate of the capitalist system and the revolutionary strategy of the proletariat out of date? Along with this issue, they also debated some important theoretical issues on such fields as Marxist philosophy, political economy and scientific socialism.

At the end of the 19th century and the beginning of the 20th century, compared with the founding period of Marxism, there had been some new characteristics in Europe, which was firstly manifested in the development of capitalism from a period of free competition to the stage of monopoly. In the age of Marx, the capitalism presented in front of the people was the cruel competitions of capital, the increasing intensification of social contradictions, the miserable conditions of workers, the growing crises of economy and politics, and the destruction of capitalism seemed to be just round the corner. However, in the course of its development, capitalism adopted some new measures and regulatory adjustment, expanded the capacity of the capitalist relations of production, and promoted the development of productive forces and science and technology. When capitalism entered the stage of imperialism, some of the major capitalist countries in Europe saw a temporary picture of peace and prosperity, and therefore, the question of whether capitalism must collapse or not was poignantly raised.

In connection with the new characteristics of the development of capitalism mentioned above, the situation of the proletarian political movement also changed greatly. Germany was the center of the spreading of Marxism and the proletarian political movement at that time, and also the center of the debate between

Marxism and revisionism. The German Social Democratic Party was not weakened, but grew stronger and gained more and more supporters during the implementation of the extraordinary law of anti-socialists of Bismarck (Otto Eduard Leopold, Prince of Bismarck, Duke of Lauenburg). The party won more than 10% votes in the elections at the end of 1870s and more than half a million votes in the late 1980s. In January 1890, the German government abolished the anti-socialist law and began to adopt a liberal "new policy" and a "moderate" policy against the proletariat. In February, the party won nearly 1.5 million votes in the election, a huge victory. The rise of the Social Democratic Party in parliament created the illusion that socialism can be peacefully introduced. Not only in Germany, but also in Britain, France, Austria, Italy and other countries, the contrast of political power between the proletariat and the bourgeoisie also changed in favor of the former. Proletarian parties had been able to make greater use of bourgeois laws for legitimate struggles. In addition, the pre-emergence of socialism in each country, such as the British trade unionism and Fabianism, France's possibility doctrine, Germany's Lassalle doctrine and Falmarism, also overflowed, playing a role in fuelling the idea of a violent revolution in the ranks of the proletariat. As a result, the question of whether Marx's argument on violent revolution was out of date was acutely raised.

With the urges of the economic and political situation of European countries, people not only think seriously about the fate of capitalism and the tactics of the political struggle of the proletariat, which are the two most sensitive issues, but also involve a series of important theoretical problems of Marxism, such as the nature of Marxist philosophical basis, the scientific nature of labor value theory and surplus value theory, the poverty of the proletariat, the basis of scientific socialism, the inevitability and contingency of social historical process, and the contradiction between science and value.

For the above problems, theorists in the later stage of the Second International launched a fierce debate. When Engels was alive, although there had been some divergences of principle within the "International", a clear pattern of two armies had not been formed as to the above major issues. Because of Engels' death, the inner party of the Second International lost its great revolutionary leader and theoretical authority. Thus, the former unified Marxist theory team split rapidly. On one side were revisionists represented by Bernstein. Under the slogan of "opposing dogmatism", they "revised" Marx's theory on the pretext that new situations in reality needed to be generalized. They founded the magazine *Socialist Monthly* as an equal to *New Age*, the official publication of the German Social Democratic Party. There were Ludwig Waltmann, Stauttinger, David, Heine, Compufmeier, Eisner and most Austrian Marxists going hand in hand with Bernstein. On the other side were the "Orthodox", with the leaders of the German Social Democratic Party and a group of leading theorists, including Bebel (Ferdinand August Bebel), Liebknecht (Karl Liebknecht), Luxembourg (Rosa Luxemburg), Zetkin (Clara Josephine Zetkin) and Russian Plekhanov (Georgi Valentinovich Plekhanov) and others. The "Orthodox" insisted on the basic position of Marxism and launched an offensive and fierce counterattack against the revisionists. As the two sides of the controversy were at the intersection of theory and reality, the views presented by each side were very complex.

Does this theoretical phenomenon appear in the later period of the Second International show that Marxism is really in crisis?

At that time, faced with the criticism on Engels' philosophy and socialism by Bernstein and others, Plekhanov wrote sadly in a letter to Kautsky: "We are now experiencing a crisis, and I feel deeply sorry for it."[56] This statement shown the mentality of many left-wing theorists in the Second International at that time. This mentality should be very natural, because the criticism on the thoughts of Marx and Engels arisen in the internal Marxists was far more shocking than the attack

---

[56] *Bernstein and the German Party*, Page 6, Beijing, Sanlian Bookstore, 1981.

from the outside of Marxists. Besides, the perpetrators were once close friends or students of Engels, and some once quite influential Marxist theorists. It should be definitely affirmed that most of the problems put forward by Bernstein and others are existing in reality. However, because of their failure to fully grasp the characteristics of the times and the essence of Marxism, the conclusion that it is not only against reality but also contradicts the scientific essence of Marxism is drawn.

The individual conclusions drawn by Marx and Engels under certain historical conditions may be corrected by historical development, but the essence of Marxism is not outdated because of the change of times. There are indeed some vulgar tendencies of Marxism in the Second International, which appear to be feeble and rigid in the face of the dynamic reality. But, anything belongs to the essence of Marxism should be distinguished from what is called "Marxism", which is added by others and which is incompatible with the nature of Marxism. The distortion of Marxism and revolt against Marxism by Bernstein and others cannot be regarded as the crisis of Marxism. They only put vulgar Marxism in a very embarrassing situation, but Marxism itself does not have a crisis. Thus, what can really be called a crisis are the vulgar things and dogmatic tendencies attached to Marxism by some theorists in the Second International.

The development history of Marxism shows that Marxism doctrine is subject to severe test in every turn of history. In the course of developing Marxism according to reality, there will inevitably be deviations and even fallacies, even for those who have good theoretical literacy, and those who hold firm Marxist positions. It was of the same nature and an extremely arduous work to develop Marxism, to fight against revisionism and to defend Marxism at that time. Marxism did not and cannot predict every change in the course of history. It is not the correct attitude towards Marxism to keep the concrete conclusions of Marx only. The left-wing theorists of the Second International had made outstanding contributions in defending Marxism, but also exposed many deficiencies and had a great influence on the descendants.

Throughout the history of the development of Marxism, Marx's theory has been interpreted and even "revised" comprehensively by later generations, which was started in the late period of the Second International. The theory is developed in the controversy. It is also of great benefit to the development of theory to investigate the debates appeared in history. There is no doubt that we will be enlightened for the development of Marxism by some perspectives on the various viewpoints appeared in the internal debates of Marxism at the turn of the 19th century and the 20th century.

2. Rebelled "Believers"

In the Second International period, there was no more dramatic figure than Bernstein.

Eduard Bernstein (1850—1932) was a famous authority of Marxist theory at the early stage of the Second International. He was editor in chief of *Social Democrats*, the official paper of German Social Democratic Party. After he published a series of articles in the *New Age* magazine in 1896-1898 under the headline of "*The Problem of Socialism*", he put the cat among the pigeons internally in the Second International. Later, he organized his views on "revision" to the Marxism into a book, and published *The Premise of Socialism and the Tasks of the Social Democratic Party* in February 1899. Lenin scolded the book as "the declaration of a genre completely separated from Marxism within Marxism"[57], and argued in this book that "Bernstein, who was once an orthodox Marxist, proposed a revision of the Marxist doctrine in the most arrogant manner and in the most complete form. The revision of the Marxist doctrine is exactly revisionism"[58]

---

[57] *The Collected Works of Lenin*, Chinese Edition 1, Vol. 17, Page 43, Beijing, People's Publishing House, 1959.

[58] *The Collected Works of Lenin*, Chinese Edition 1, Vol. 15, Page 14, Beijing,

Bernstein's "revision" of Marxism is the theoretical refraction of the realistic socialist movement. The "revision" is not the results of "insanity" as some people simply accuse, nor is anything that is made up purely in the study. When the fate of capitalism and proletarian political struggle strategy and other issues are put forward more acutely in the new situation, every Marxist should answer this question. The most deceptive about Bernstein's view is that he is holding the banner of anti-dogmatism. In his view, a new era had come, and the "spiritual weapon" used by the Social Democrats to welcome the new era must be examined. He thought the primary task of the Social Democratic Party in theory was to overcome utopian socialism and its theoretical premise-dogmatism. From his point of view, the utopian socialism, once criticized by Marx and Engels as "the menu for the future restaurant", that was the utopian socialism with a detailed description and design of the social organization of the future, had disappeared, but another kind of utopian socialism still existed. This utopian socialism assumed that "there is a leap from the capitalist society to the socialist society". Bernstein said: "They draw a line with this side as the capitalist society, and that side as the socialist society. There is no systematic work in the capitalist society."[59] The utopian socialism was "decorated" with the slogan of Marx and Engels.

"Even for the most scientific theory, if it is dogmatically interpreted, it will lead to utopianism."[60] Under the slogan of "anti-dogmatism", Bernstein gave a "new" interpretation of Marxist philosophy, economics and political theory, and demonstrated his views on the opposition to "collapse theory" and "violence theory".

Bernstein not only started a debate with the "Orthodox School" in the Second International, but also criticized Marx and Engels. He said that the theoretical basis

---

People's Publishing House, 1959.

[59]*Speech of Bernstein*, Page 28, Beijing, Sanlian Book Store, 1973.

[60] *Speech of Bernstein*, Page 28

of Marx and Engels to establish socialist theory was their view of history, whereas the core of their view of history was to emphasize the inevitability of history only, and to attribute all the processes and factors of history to the inevitability of mechanical material movement. Bernstein specially analyzed the classical expression of historical materialism in *A Contribution to the Critique of Political Economy* of Marx, and thought it had a serious mechanism tendency. "'Consciousness' and 'existence' are so opposite that it is almost possible to draw the conclusion that man is merely a living agent of historical power. He carried out the task of historical power almost against his own will... As a whole, man's consciousness and will are very subordinate to the material movement."[61] He also believed that in *Das Kapital*, Marx also had a "sentences of fatalism tone". Accordingly, Bernstein proposed to make a "revision" of the Marxist view of history. That is, the proposition should not be limited to Marx's exposition on the view of history, but shall take full consideration that the individual and the whole nation in the contemporary society have freed themselves from the influence of necessity of realization without their will or against their will. With this view, the historical materialism is "expanded", and this "revised" Marxist historical view does not think that the economic basis of each nationality's life has an unconditional and decisive impact on the life form of each nationality.

The second question that Bernstein is concerned with in Marxist philosophy is the question of dialectics, which, in his view, is "the deadliest heel of Achilles of Marx and Engels' theory."[62] In the study of economics, Marx was "deceived" by Hegel's contradiction dialectics remains. Marx and Engels seemed to have never completely got rid of the remains. Hagel's logic contradiction will make people imperceptibly into the trap of "self-development of concept". "Once the development is predicted

---

[61]*Speech of Bernstein*, Page 83.

[62]*Speech of Bernstein*, Page 99.

according to the principles, the risks of arbitrary conception must have emerged. The more complex the object referred to by the development is, the greater the risk."[63] As a consequence, Hegel's dialectics is an element of betrayal in Marxist theory and a trap that hinders any rational and correct investigation of things.[64] And therefore, we can draw a conclusion that the monographs of Marx and Engels on investigations on the political struggles according to dialectics and their theories taking the decisive influences of experience on violence as the starting point shall be examined from different angles from them.

The above viewpoints of Bernstein show that in his understanding of the philosophical basis of socialist theory, he is trying to weaken historical inevitability of Marxist philosophy, especially the view of the regularity of social and economic movement, and highlight the subjective factors in the historical process. Bernstein echoed the slogan "go back to Kant" because it "directly inspired" him from an epistemological point of view. In his view, Kant (Immanuel Kant) was a transcendental idealist. But in fact it was a much stricter realist than many materialists. Kant did not want to experience anything outside the world. In the world of experience, what is of great importance is to pay attention to the "motive force" of the socialist movement. This "motive force" is the power of interest, understanding and moral consciousness. Special attention should be paid to moral consciousness in the three "view power".

The moral force such as justice is a force that can play a creative role, and it is a powerful power in the socialist movement. Bernstein's philosophical interpretation of Marxist socialist theory aims at opposing the establishment of socialist theory and practice on the basis of the inevitability of social and economic movements, but advocates taking the ethics requests or the ethics impulse as the root of the

---

[63]*Speech of Bernstein*, Page 97.

[64]*Speech of Bernstein*, Page 103.

socialist movement. This is obviously a far cry from the original intent of Marxism.

Bernstein not only disagreed with Marxist philosophy, but also denied the scientific nature of Marxist political economy, especially Marx's theory of value. He believed that Marx's concept of "value" was "the conception of pure thinking", and "surplus value" was only "simple formula", which was "a formula based on hypothesis". This theory of value "is no different from the marginal utility value of the Gothen-Jervons-Berm School. Both of them are based on the actual relationship, but both are built on the abstract."[65] The value of labor is absolutely nothing more than a key...But from a certain point, this key fails. And therefore, it is fatal to almost every student of Marx. "Thus, the theory of labor value and the theory of surplus value" cannot make scientific demonstrations for socialism or communism.[66]

Bernstein was also against with Engels's judgment made in the preface to *The Poverty of Philosophy* that Marx proved his communist requirements according to the collapse of the capitalist production mode, which had been increasingly implemented. He thought that Marxist theory about capitalism social class relations and class structure did not conform to reality. He said: "If the society is constructed or developed as envisaged by the socialist doctrine, the economic collapse can certainly be only a problem happed in a very short period of time. But as we can see, the situation is not the same. The social structure is far from simple than before, but is highly polarized and differentiated regardless of income level or occupation activities."[67] He explained from two aspects that the income of the various classes of society would not lead to the intensification of class contradictions. On the one hand, the vast majority of the surplus products

---

[65]*Speech of Bernstein*, Page 119.

[66]*Speech of Bernstein*, Page 121~122.

[67]*Speech of Bernstein*, Page 126.

produced by the workers were not occupied by the bourgeoisie. Even if the stomachs of the capitalists were ten times larger than that of the workmen, and they had ten times more servants than they actually have, their consumption was nothing but "a feather on the scale" of the surplus products. If the surplus products were not in the hands of the proletariat in any way, they must have been taken away by other classes. On the other hand, the dispersion of social wealth had led to the emergence of a large number of middle classes, leading to an absolute and relative increase in the number of the wealthy. In a word, the polarization between the rich and the poor in capitalist society was gradually disappearing.

In Bernstein's view, the development of capitalist economy also eliminated its sharp opposition. "As the economic development moves forward, generally speaking, we will no longer encounter the usual business crisis. So we must abandon the meditation that takes it as the leader of great social changes."[68] The emergence of capital monopolies resulted in the elimination of competition between large and small enterprises. With the expansion of world markets, the improvements in communications and transport, the flexibility of modern credit systems and the rise of cartels, there will be no economic crisis like the previous type at least for a longer period of time. Bernstein asserted that if a general crisis was supposed to be the inherent law of capitalist production, it must prove its authenticity now or in the near future. Otherwise, the evidence of its inevitability would float in the air of abstract speculation.

After the "revision" of Marxist philosophy and Marxist economics, Bernstein further "revised" Marxist political theory, that is, scientific socialism.

Bernstein said: "Marx and Engels reached a theory very similar to the Blanquism on the basis of the radical Hegel dialectics."[69] "The revolutionary programme of action

---

[68]*Speech of Bernstein*, Page 37.

[69]*Speech of Bernstein*, Page 105.

of *The Communist Manifesto* is completely Blanquism."[70] He thought that the theory of class struggle advocated by Marx and Engels was merely a reprint of Blanquism which advocated violent struggle because it overestimated the creativity of revolutionary violence in the socialist transformation of modern society. Marx's socialism theory is a theory that taking the economy, which is the basis of the social development, as the starting point to bring the worship of violence to the top. The critique of Blanquism is the self-criticism of Marxism, of which the first is its dialectical self-criticism. The term "dictatorship of the proletariat" is completely outdated today. Only be removed from its practical meaning and given any weakened meaning, can it be consistent with the reality. Class dictatorship belongs to a lower culture and is a phenomenon of political atavism. The proletariat and its political parties should not be keen on class struggle and violent revolution, but should lay emphasis on such democratic rights as universal suffrage.

Bernstein made a comparison of Marx's construction of scientific socialism to "building a huge building within a ready-made scaffold"[71] When dialectics, the scaffolding, restricted the building and prevented it from developing freely; Marx did not demolish the scaffolding, but changed it at the expense of proportion, thus making the buildings more subordinate to the scaffolding. This shows that Marx, the "great scientific genius was in fact a prisoner of doctrine."[72] As a result, the scientific socialism has become a product of cutting one's feet to fit the shoes in the eyes of Bernstein. What should be the theory of socialism he understands? He said: "I don't actually think that the victory of socialism depends on its 'inherent economic necessity'. It is neither possible nor necessary to justify the provision of

---

[70]*Speech of Bernstein*, Page 106.

[71]*Speech of Bernstein*, Page 218.

[72]*Speech of Bernstein*, Page 218.

pure materialism to socialism."[73] He also believed that what the socialists should be concerned about was not the more distant future, but what needed to be done now and in the near future. It is an indispensable prerequisite for the realization of socialism to strive for democracy and to create democratic institutions of politics and economy. The various liberal systems in capitalist society are different from those of feudalism in the past. They are flexible with the ability to change and develop. It is unnecessary to blown down them, but continue to develop them. For this purpose, it requires organizational and positive action, not revolutionary dictatorship. Consumer cooperative is a viable social organism and a means to overcome exploitation. By relying on it, the working class can seize a large part of wealth of the society without resorting to violence. It was based on these arguments that Bernstein put forward his most famous formula: "To be honest, I have very little tastes and interests in what people usually think of 'the ultimate aim of socialism'. Whatever it is, it is completely insignificant to me. Movement is everything. As for the movement, I am referring to both the general movement of the society, that is, social progress, as well as the political and economic propaganda and organization that have been carried out to make it possible."[74] This is indeed "frankness". "The ultimate aim of socialism is insignificant, and movement is everything", which can better express Bernstein's betrayal of the essence of the socialist revolution than a thousand words. It is not hard to see from Bernstein's argument that he advised people not to expect and it was unnecessary to expect the imminent collapse of the capitalist economic system; what the proletarian political parties should do now and for a long time is to organize the working class politically and train them to use democracy in order to fight for the reform of the state system in accordance with the spirit of democracy. People don't have to fight for the ultimate aim. The richer the society, the easier and more

---

[73]*Speech of Bernstein*, Page 219.

[74]*Speech of Bernstein*, Page 40.

secure the realization of socialism will be. In short, in Bernstein's view, it is quite possible for capitalism to enter socialism peacefully.

Bernstein's "revision" of Marxism from various aspects is an important event in the history of Marxist theory. If it is admitted that his "revision" is correct, it is to declare that Marxist theory is in a full-blown crisis. If it is simply declared that he is making a "frenzy of nonsense", it is undoubtedly evading the question again, which is helpless for the people to seriously solve the problems raised by the reality to Marxism. It is necessary for us to further analyze the mistakes of Bernstein and others in connection with the struggle of the orthodox against revisionists in the Second International.

3. Problems & Answers

Revisionism has resulted in very bad consequences both in theory and in practice. Revisionism is usually seen as a betrayal of Marxism, which is correct. However, as a product of specific social and historical conditions and a special theoretical phenomenon produced within Marxism, revisionism is worth pondering for its characteristics and significance.

Revisionism does not abandon Marxism in theoretical form, but fights against Marxism by standing on the base of Marxism. Kautsky, as the representative of the "Orthodox" in the Second International, and the main opponent of Bernstein, was bewildered by the superficial phenomenon of revisionism at first. There is no wonder that at the beginning of Bernstein's attack on the "orthodox" Marxism, Kautsky's attitude wavered.

In a letter to Victor Adler, an Austrian Marxist, Kautsky argued that people without theory, such as Vandervelde （Emile Vandervelde）, the leader of Belgian socialism, were not revisionists, "because they have nothing to revise, and because they have no theory at all."[75] This reflects from another perspective that Bernstein and other

[75]Quoted from McLellan: *Marxism after Marx*, Page 24.

revisionists are familiar with Marxist theory, and they have a complete theory of revisionism.

The definite meaning of the concept of "revision" in "revisionism" refers to the betrayal of the fundamental principles of Marxism, but the revisionists deliberately confuse the boundary between revisionism and ordinary revision, and believe that Marx himself is constantly revising his own doctrine. Bernstein listed two principles in the preface to *Das Kapital*: "Even if a society explores the natural laws of its own movement... it can neither skip nor abolish the natural stages of development by statute. But it can shorten and alleviate the pain of birth."[76] "Today's society is not a solid crystal, but an organism that can change and is often in the process of change."[77] Bernstein believed that these two principles contained "significant limitations" or "weakening" of socialist revolutionary thoughts. He went on to say: "Any revisionist now accepts these two principles of Marx. Indeed, I am happy to admit that revisionists may attach more importance to their meaning and effectiveness than Marx himself, and in any case, pay more attention than some who belong to the Marxist school but in the view of revisionists to form a narrow Marxist orthodoxy. These people believe that Marx's principles based on certain historical premises have the power of enduring dogma, rather than admitting that it has only relative significance."[78]

Formally, the difference between revisionism towards Marxism and dogmatism lies in the fact that revisionism emphasizes the relativity of Marxist principles, while dogmatism adheres to the absoluteness of Marxist principles. This kind of bipolar

---

[76] *Marx/Engels Collected Works*, Chinese Edition 1, Vol. 23, Page 11, Beijing, People's Publishing House, 1972.

[77] *Marx/Engels Collected Works*, Chinese Edition 1, Vol. 23, Page 12, Beijing, People's Publishing House, 1972.

[78] *Speech of Bernstein*, Page 354.

antagonism is intertwined and coexisted in the development history of Marxism, which is often seen even in the debates against revisionism. Otto Bauer believed that: "The theory of revisionism is nothing but the antithesis of vulgar Marxism, and is only the inevitable shortage of Marx's doctrine when it rushed into an ever-larger field not belong to its fields for the first time."[79] This view unilaterally emphasizes that revisionism appears as a reaction to vulgar Marxism (including the tendency to mechanize and dogmatize Marxism). It seems that revisionism is filling in the void that Marx's doctrine has not dabbled in. If so, revisionism's "revision" of Marxism should be an unquestionable truth. But the problem is not.

Seen from the controversy with revisionism at that time, many social democrats defended Marx's basic theory, and recognized the "revision" of the basic spirit of Marxism by Bernstein and others on a series of issues. Bebel, Kautsky, Plekhanov, Luxembourg, Zetkin and others, refuted Bernstein from all angles, and criticized his formula that "The ultimate aim of socialism is insignificant and movement is everything." From their criticism and analysis, it is not difficult to see that one of the most basic features of Bernstein's revisionism is that: From the point of view of reality, one can get an incorrect answer that is not practical; while from the perspective of opposing dogmatism, one is going to the extreme of deviating from the basic spirit of Marxism.

When Marx and Engels created their own doctrine, there is no doubt that they would be limited by certain historical conditions. They cannot and did not hope to make accurate prediction and detailed description of the future of historical development. In the face of some new features arisen in the development of capitalist and the strengthening of democratic forces in the socialist movement, it is absolutely necessary and irreproachable to examine and test Marxism under the new historical conditions. Bernstein captured some of the major fateful problems in

---

[79]Quoted from McLellan: *Marxism after Marx*, Page 28.

the theory and practice of socialism, and also found that there were some conclusions in Marx's and Engels' works that need to be developed according to the new social reality. However, when trying to solve the problems he raised, or for the purpose of demonstration, he not only imposed those not belong to Marx on Marx, but also created the opposition in the Marx's theory, thus misinterpreted the "origin " of Marxism; or taking the historical condition change as an excuse, he not only simply opposed the "means" and "ultimate aim" of the socialist movement, but also exaggerated the relativity of the Marxist theory and negated its scientific contents.

In the remarks of Bernstein's revisionism, the most naive must be his understanding of Marxist philosophy. He confused vulgar materialism with Marx's historical materialism, muddled up the theory of fatalism and the science on the objective law of social development, criticized Marx's view of history by opposing vulgar materialism and fatalism, and tried to find the theoretical basis for seeking the realistic foundation of socialist movement beyond the inevitability of social economic process. He believed in Darwin's concept of evolution, hated Hegel's dialectics, and tried to remove the dialectical factors that had been scientifically modified from Marxism. In fact, Marx always treated Hegel's dialectics with a critical attitude, and used its reasonable form to scientifically investigate social reality. The precious essence of revolutionary and negative features in dialectics is completely compatible with the theory of scientific socialism. The former constitutes the core part of the methodology of the latter. The denial of dialectics undoubtedly removes the foundation stone of revolutionary theory. This is recognized not only by the vast majority of Marxists in the Second International. Moreover, Lukács, the founder of Western Marxism, put forward historical subject-object dialectics in response to Bernstein's contempt for dialectics.

Bernstein had an inherent tie with Neo-Kantianism. Cohen (Gerald Allan "Jerry" Cohen), the founder of Marburg School of Neo-Kantianism, regarded ethical idealism as the basis of socialism, and revered Kant as the true pioneer of German socialism. This transcendental idealism, which thinks that social regularity comes from consciousness itself rather than social reality, undoubtedly resonates with Bernstein. He supported the slogan "go back to Kant", tried to treat Marxism with Kant's "critical spirit" and reformed socialism with Kant's thought, which was as the same as belittling the inevitability of the process of social history and denying the dialectics. Since socialism is based on the main requirements of the proletariat and the ethical impulse, its process, ways, means, plans and so on can depend entirely on the good will of the proletariat, which is the main body of socialism. It is obvious that how absurd it is to use Kant to reform socialism.

Labor value theory is the cornerstone of Marxist political economy. Surplus value theory is a great discovery of Marx and is one of the theoretical bases of scientific socialism. Bernstein was deeply influenced by vulgar economics, especially by the theory of marginal theory, and made vulgar explanation of Marx's theory of value. In particular, he followed Eugen Bawerk (Eugen Böhm Ritter von Bawerk), the advocator of Austrian marginal utility theory, and regarded Marx's scientific abstraction of commodity value as an unrealistic fiction. From this point of view, he came to the conclusion that the theory of surplus value was only a kind of unscientific hypothesis, and could not become the scientific basis of scientific socialism. Of course, Marxist theory of socialism is not only based on surplus value as a scientific basis, but the theory of surplus value is undoubtedly one of the main theoretical bases of scientific socialism, because the scientific analysis of capitalist social and economic contradictions and class contradictions is mainly based on the theory of surplus value. The theory of surplus value not only scientifically reveals the deep economic root of the opposition between the working class and the capitalist class, but also explains the historical position of the working class, and points out the inherent contradiction and development trend of capitalist society. Even Kautsky admitted this point. He said that Marx and Engels made socialism from utopia to science, "which is based on this scientifically acquired belief: the development of human society must be determined by economic development, and by class struggles caused by economic relations in societies with opposing classes."[80] Without historical materialism and surplus value theory, scientific socialism cannot be discussed.

What is the essence of Bernstein's revisionist theory? The title of *Social Reform or Revolution,* Luxemburg's famous book, hit the very heart of Bernstein's revisionism. Social reform and social revolution were two segments or processes mutually connected and separately distinguished in the socialist practical movement. The relationship between the two has always been a controversial issue in socialist theory. It can be said that all the theoretical motives and essence of Bernstein's "revision" of almost all fields of Marxist theory focus on formula that "the ultimate aim of socialism is insignificant, and movement is everything". It should be noted here that Bernstein has a variety of explanations for the "ultimate aim". For example, in particular in the defense of others' criticism, the term "aim" is often interpreted as a fantasy to describe the details of the organization of the future society. It is interpreted as some kind of unrealistic faraway and illusory pursuit of the future, or the "ultimate state" of socialism. But from his original intention of putting forward this formula and his whole ideological tendency, his so called "ultimate aim" exactly refers to the "social revolution" as opposed to the "movement", that is, improvement. Luxembourg, Kautsky, Bebel, Plekhanov and others all made outstanding criticisms of Bernstein's mistake of opposing social reform and social revolution. They unanimously agreed that the Social Democratic Party did not give up but attached considerable importance to all the legitimate opportunities offered by capitalist social development for social improvement. However, at the same time, the "ultimate aim" of socialism, namely, the social revolution or the seizure of power through violence has always been kept in mind. "The Social Democratic Party believes that there is an inseparable link between

[80]Kautsky: *Communism vs. Socialism,* See *Bernstein and the German Party,* Page 376.

social reform and social revolution, because, in its view, the struggle for social improvement is the means, while the social revolution is the aim."[81] "The question we are arguing with Bernstein and his disciples is, in the end, not a question of one form of struggle or of that form of struggle, nor of this strategy or that kind of strategy. It is the question of the preservation and abolition of the social democratic movement.[82] The growing socialization of the production process, the increasing expansion of state supervision and the temporary relaxation of labor relations have brought a superstition to the capitalist countries that the socialism can be gradually realized under the precondition of the existence of capitalist countries. Luxembourg also believed that the Social Democratic Party, which insisted on Marxism, was opposed to the Blanquism, which required a small number of conspirators to seize power in the name of the working class. The Social Democratic Party, on the other hand, wants the working class to seize power on its own. As for the question of how to treat the capitalist countries to avoid collapse and peacefully enter socialism, Bernstein's negative attitude toward "collapse theory" was also criticized. Kautsky pointed out that Bernstein's view was not groundless, but was limited to Britain and not found in other countries. We know that Britain is a typical capitalist country, but in terms of its political status and economic development law, it is a totally exceptional country, where labor relations are very relaxed. There is a deeper tradition of "fraternity", where it is possible for workers to gradually gain power on the path of peace without catastrophe. Marx said in 1870s that a peaceful transition from capitalism to socialism was possible in such a country, but it was only possible because the catastrophes were not excluded. Bernstein was too optimistic about the peace situation at that time, which had been mocked by the subsequent world economic crises and the social revolutions caused by world wars.

---

[81]Luxemburg: *Social Reform or Revolution,* Page 1, Beijing, Sanlian Book Store, 1958.

[82]Luxemburg: *Social Reform or Revolution,* Page 2.

Of course, Bernstein has made some contributions to making people to think about reality. For instance, Zetkin believed that: "Bernstein has made great achievements because he has raised a series of questions that need detailed and scientific discussions."[83] In the course of criticizing Bernstein, Kautsky also said that Bernstein's series of articles "explored very important issues and put forward very important issues to discuss. These problems are beneficial to the development of our spiritual life."[84] However, Bernstein gave an incorrect answer on a number of major issues.

In this debate, we should also see that "the orthodox" of Marxism also shows some theoretical inadequacies. For example, the statement of Luxembourg that "the ultimate aim is everything"[85] is suspected of going to the other extreme, and the judgment that "the starting point for the socialist revolution will be a universal and devastating crisis"[86] is also too arbitrary, and so on.

4. Is Marx a Philosopher?

Although some very famous Marxism theoretician in the Second International have made outstanding achievements in the spread of Marxist theory with extraordinary performance in the struggle of opposing revisionism and defending the Marxism, they are inadequate in the understanding of the Marxist philosophy, or they are weak in philosophical problems. Finding reasons from the subjective aspect, the problems lie in that "the philosophical level and the level of understanding of philosophical problems, especially the Marxist philosophical problems of almost all

---

[83]*Bernstein and the German Party*, Page 34.

[84]*Bernstein and the German Party*, Page 44.

[85]*Bernstein and the German Party*, Page 38.

[86]*Bernstein and the German Party*, Page 116.

of the theorists and leaders in the Second International is extremely low."[87] Kautsky is a typical example.

Before betraying Marxism, Kautsky wrote a series of influential books on propagating Marxist ideas, including *The Economic Doctrines of Karl Marx* (1887), *The Class Struggle (Erfurt Program)* (1892), and *On The Agrarian Question* (1899). Lenin thought that these works "will always be a model of Marxism".[88] However, Kautsky's profound insights are mainly in the fields of history, sociology and economics, and in the field of philosophy, and it reveals a superficial nature that is not commensurate with his talent. In his letter to Plekhanov in 1901, he made a frank statement: "Philosophy has never been my specialty."[89]

In 1909, the magazine *Struggle* published a letter from Kautsky to a Russian worker two years ago. The letter said that "You asked: Is Maher a Marxist? It depends on how people understand Marxism. I do not understand Marxism as any philosophy, but as an experimental science, that is, a special view of society... Marx does not declare any philosophy, but declared the end of all philosophy."[90] In his letter of 1901 to Plekhanov, he also said, "I think, even as a Neo-Kantian in a sense, he can recognize the historical and economic doctrines of Marxism."[91] This is tantamount to saying that Marx has no philosophy of his own, that Marx is only a historian, a sociologist, and an economist, but not a philosopher! This almost absurd judgment cannot simply be attributed to ignorance of Marx, because "We cannot forget that

---

[87]Vranicki: *History of Marxism*, Vol. 1, Page 351.

[88]*The Collected Works of Lenin*, Chinese Edition 1, Vol. 23, Page 26, Beijing, People's Publishing House, 1958.

[89]Quoted from Nalski: *Marxist Philosophy in 19th Century II*, Page 244.

[90]Quoted from Vranicki: *History of Marxism*, Vol. 1, Page 351~352.

[91]Quoted from Nalski: *Marxist Philosophy in 19th Century II*, Page 244.

Kautsky is a man who can almost recite Marx's works; from all the works of Kautsky, there must be many wooden boxes in his desk or head, keeping everything Marx wrote in order and making it extremely convenient to quote."[92] In fact, Kautsky had affirmed and explained Marx's dialectics and historical materialism in many works, but he did not regard them as a kind of philosophy. He understood historical materialism only as a sociology and dialectics as a method of social science. In his opinion, Marx's view of history does not depend on a certain philosophy. "The materialistic view of history is not combined with a materialistic philosophy. It can be combined with any world view that uses dialectical materialism, or at least does not conflict with it. Whether this view of history calls itself materialistic or opposes mechanical materialism, it prefers to use the name of realism or monism, positivism or sensationalism, empiricism or empiriocriticism. It doesn't matter." [93] "Materialistic views of history can be conjoined not only with Maher and Avenarius, but also with many other philosophies."[94] Marx's theory is misinterpreted here in two ways. On the one hand, Marxist philosophy is denied as a world view. Historical materialism is treated as an empirical science—sociology. The tendency of historical materialism attestation was more common in the Second International period. On the other hand, the philosophical materialism foundation of Marx's view of history is negated. Since any philosophical view of the world can "get along well" with Marx's view of history, it is natural to use various philosophies to explain the basis of Marx's theory or to "supplement" Marx's view of history. Such logic is not only manifested in Kautsky, but in other Marxists.

---

[92]*The Collected Works of Lenin*, Chinese Edition 1, Vol. 28, Page 215, Beijing, People's Publishing House, 1958.

[93]Kautsky: *The Materialist Conception Of History*, Vol. 1 Part 1, Page 29, Shanghai, Shanghai People's Publishing House, 1964.

[94]Kautsky: *The Materialist Conception Of History*, Vol. 1 Part 1, Page 30.

In terms of the attitude toward Marxist philosophy, Mehring, who was called as "One (almost the only one) of the German Social Democrats who knows philosophy" by Plekhanov, also has a superficial and partial tendency. He did not get rid of the point of view popular in the Second International period, which only regarded philosophy as a kind of ideology. But dislike Kautsky, who simply thought that Marx announced the end of all philosophy; he believed that philosophy was just the manifestation of the class struggle in the ideology, and was a thought form of class struggle. With the elimination of class struggle, philosophy will also disappear. Mehring has been highly praised by Engels for understanding historical materialism as a scientific method rather than a rigid formula and using it to analyze history, but his general understanding of Marxist philosophy, especially the understanding of the philosophical nature of historical materialism is vague and even wrong. In *Kant, Dicken, Maher, and Historical Materialism*, he argued that Marx and Engels cut off the connections with any philosophy, but brought the historical achievement of philosophy (the thought of historical development) into materialism, that is, brought this thought into the field of history first, not the field of nature. The subjective reason is that neither of them is a natural scientist but a historian. This kind of view limits Marx's philosophical transformation to the philosophical view of history and excludes the philosophical view of nature. In other words, Mehring believed that Marx and Engels were still at the same level as the old materialism in their views of nature. And therefore, he concluded: "Marx and Engels always adhere to Feuerbach's philosophy. They only expand and deepen this view by applying materialism to the field of history. To put it simply, they are mechanical materialists in the field of natural science, just as they are historical materialists in the field of social science."[95] On the question of dialectics, both Kautsky and Mehring regarded dialectics as a method of examining social history, or "dialectics

---

[95] Franz Mehring: *On Historical Materialism*, Quoted from Vranicki: *History of Marxism*, Vol. 1, Page 341.

of history". The history here, obviously, does not include nature.

Both the views of Kautsky and Mehring reflect the general tendency of most Marxists in the Second International to varying degrees that Marxism only or mainly includes political economics and sociology, while philosophy is of little importance. This involves the great theoretical question of how to understand the Marxist system. To be sure, apart from the confusion and misunderstanding in terms, it can be said that they generally give full recognition to materialist historical concept, the important component of Marxist philosophy, and even make a good performance. But because of their lack of comprehensive understanding of the nature of Marxist philosophy, their understanding of Marxist philosophy system is quite confused. And therefore, it is inevitable to lack a complete understanding of the internal connection of the whole Marxist theory. It is of no surprise that when Neo-Kantianism and Maherism prevailed for a time, quite a number of Marxists were moved by this fashion and used it to "supplement" Marxism, believing that they were completely compatible with Marxism. Of course, even if there is a lack of a complete understanding of the whole Marxist philosophy, as long as we can really understand the basic spirit of historical materialism, we will be aware of the errors of Neo-Kantianism. Mehring, for example, explicitly criticized Neo-Kantianism in the book *In Defense of Marxism*, even though the philosophical level of such criticism was not high enough.

Many Marxists in the Second International, including Kautsky and Mehring, generally deny that the historical materialism has a general philosophical premise or a general materialistic premise. This problem has aroused more controversy in the study of Marxist philosophy since the Second International. Marx devoted his whole life to the study of the problems in the field of social history, so he expounded many of the basic thought and system of historical materialism. However, this did not affect him from making comprehensive explanations on the general materialistic views of the whole world, including nature and society. Historical materialism or materialist conception of history is by no means sociology in the general sense, but a philosophical grasp of the general laws of social history. The basis of this philosophical grasp is the unity of materialism and dialectics with the core of practical viewpoint. Both Marx's view of nature and the view of history run through the recognition of the preexistence of nature and the objective reality of material existence including social existence and the dialectic of development. At the same time, it also runs through the dialectical viewpoint of the interaction between man and nature with the practical activities as the medium. It is the organic unity of materialism and dialectics that makes Marxist philosophy distinguish itself from the old materialism in the view of nature and history. This is also the significance of the transformation of Marxist philosophy. If we throw away the philosophical premise of materialism, or simply regard Marx's materialism in the view of nature as equal as the old materialism, it is difficult to understand why Marx's view of history is called as "materialism", and is also difficult to understand the scientific nature of historical materialism in solving the problem of the unity of nature and society.

Among the Marxists in the Second International, it was Plekhanov who was able to fully understand Marxist philosophy. When revisionism was rampant in the Second International, especially in Russia, "he was the only theorist who was able to argue with the revisionist representatives of Neo-Kantianism at the time particularly in philosophical aspects (not just in political economics or sociology)."[96] This is because he transcended the narrow understanding of Marxist philosophy over ordinary people. He not only expounded and exerted Marx's view of history in general, but also paid close attention to the explanation of ontology and epistemology of Marxist philosophy. Kautsky and Mehring mainly understood the differences between Marxist philosophy and the old philosophy from the aspect of Marx's historical materialism, whereas Plekhanov emphasized the general materialist philosophy. He thought: "The emergence of Marx's materialist

---

[96]Vranicki: *History of Marxism*, Vol. 1, Page 451.

philosophy is the unprecedented real revolution in the history of human thought, and is the greatest revolution."[97] Plekhanov's explanation of general materialist philosophy is concentrated in his definition of matter: "What we call objects of matter (objects) are objects that do not depend on our consciousness. When these objects act on our senses, they evoke certain sensations, which in turn form the basis of our ideas about the outside world, that is, about these physical objects and their interrelationships."[98] Of course, from today's point of view, Plekhanov's definition is not perfect, and there is no practical point of view, but in the whole philosophy of Plekhanov, Marx's practical viewpoint is understood. For example, he clearly said: "Dialectical materialism is the philosophy of action."[99]

In the history of Marx's development, Plekhanov used the "dialectical materialism" for the first time to express Marx's philosophy system, and thought that "dialectical materialism" was "the only term that can correctly explain Marx's philosophy."[100] It's worth noting that the meaning of the term used by Plekhanov is different from what was later generally understood as "dialectical materialism" (e.g. the current popular textbook juxtaposed it with "historical materialism"). His understanding of dialectical materialism is not part of Marxist philosophy. It is not used coordinately with historical materialism, but refers to the collectivity of Marxist philosophy. "Marx and Engels' materialistic worldview... includes nature and history. Whether in nature or in history, this world view 'is essentially dialectical', but because

---

[97]*Selected Philosophical Works by Georgi Plekhanov*, Vol. 1, Page 374, Beijing, Sanlian Book Store, 1957.

[98]*Selected Philosophical Works by Georgi Plekhanov*, Vol. 3, Page 250, Beijing, Sanlian Book Store, 1962.

[99]*Selected Philosophical Works by Georgi Plekhanov*, Vol. 1, Page 769.

[100]*Selected Philosophical Works by Georgi Plekhanov*, Vol. 1, Page 768 Note①.

dialectical materialism involves history, Engels sometimes calls it history. "[101] This clearly shows that Plekhanov regards historical materialism as an aspect of dialectical materialism. He has clearly expressed his negative attitude towards historical materialism as a whole Marxist philosophy. "Is historical materialism the whole world view? Of course not! It's just part of the world view."[102]

Plekhanov's above views are undoubtedly much more comprehensive and profound than those of Kautsky and Mehring. Although his understanding of the Marxist philosophical system is still worth discussing, it plays a positive role that should not be underestimated in opposing the "revision" of Marxist philosophy by Neo-Kantianism and Maherism.

5. The Battle between Historical Determinism and Non-determinism

About Marx's philosophy, especially the essence of historical materialism, some people have made such comments: "Marxism, after all, belongs to the science of the 19th century. In this kind of science, stiff determinism was the yardstick of all scientific methodologies and theories. It should also be taken into account that his teacher Hegel regarded man as an instrument of objective spirit in his history of philosophy. All this inevitably influenced Marx and sometimes led him to extreme absolute determinism."[103] This view, which is still popular today, is accompanied by Marx's philosophy, and is the main point that many people have always been happy to criticize Marx. This view appears in a more complete form, and can be traced back to the end of the 19th century. Focusing on the essence of historical

---

[101]*Selected Philosophical Works by Georgi Plekhanov*, Vol. 2, Page 311, Beijing, Sanlian Book Store, 1961.

[102]*Selected Philosophical Works by Georgi Plekhanov*, Vol. 3, Page 337.

[103]Stojanovic: *Between Ideal and Reality*, Page 147, Belgrade, 1969. Quoted from Брайович, C.M.: *Karl Kautsky and the Evolution of His Ideas*, Page 93, Beijing, Oriental Press, 1986.

materialism, the Marxists of the Second International mainly involved in how to treat the law of social and historical development, and formed the confrontation between historical determinism and non-determinism.

The proponents of non-determinism hold two main attitudes, one is that Marx's view of history is inherently non-determinism, and the other is that Marx's view of history is determinism with a simple emphasis on the role of economic factors and inevitability, which should be "revised" by Neo-Kantianism. The later view is more common. These views usually take two forms: one is to raise questions and express views directly against the "origin" of Marxist doctrine, and the other is to use opposing dogmatism as the slogan, to open up a new theory aimed at the view of Marxist "orthodoxy", and to expound "anti-tradition" viewpoint.

There are three main arguments in criticizing Marx's view of history as some kind of determinism associated with fatalism.

Firstly, it is believed that Marx advocates materialism, but materialism emphasizes matter rather than spirit, and that matter is always associated with inevitability. For example, Bernstein thinks that: "According to materialism theory, the movement of matter is realized by necessity as a mechanical process. When any process occurs, it must have an inevitable consequence from the very beginning, and any phenomenon must have its material reasons, and therefore, it is the movement of materials that determines the form of the thought and will tendency, and the tendency of thought and will and all phenomena of the human world, are therefore inevitable in material. So, the materialist is an unreligious Calvinist... Accordingly, it means to fundamentally assert the process of all history and the inevitability of its development to explain history by materialism."[104] The premise of Bernstein's viewpoint was wrong. He confused mechanical materialism with dialectical materialism, because in the latter's view, the material movement itself is not just

---

[104]*Speech of Bernstein*, Page 81~82.

about inevitability. He also confused natural materialism and historical materialism and misunderstood historical materialism as the analogy of natural materialism to the field of social history. As we have mentioned above, Bernstein rebuked the principle that social existence determined social consciousness as the absolute opposition between consciousness and existence because he failed to understand the dialectics of Marx's historical materialism. This kind of "determination" obviously means that the material foundation of social consciousness is social existence, and it also acknowledges that social consciousness has active effects on social existence.

Secondly, it is thought that Marx was a pupil of Hegel, and Hegel's dialectics regarded history as the process of developing according to the necessity of strict decision. On the origin of Marxist philosophy, there have been two interpretations of the influences of Hegel on Marx. One explanation is that Hegel's spiritual dialectics led to Marx's attention to the subject consciousness. For example, the founder of Western Marxism holds this view. The other explanation holds that Hegel's view of historical inevitability is undoubtedly a theoretical opportunity for Marx to form a strict or mechanical historical determinism. For example, Bernstein himself regards Hegel's dialectics as "the remnant" of Marxist philosophy, and advocates replacing it by Neo-Kantianism. In fact, Marx's criticism of Hegel's philosophy obtained a double theoretical achievement, that is, to understand human history as an objective and inevitable process in accordance with the law, and to understand human beings as the subjects of creating history consciously, rather than the puppets with no subject consciousness led by historical laws. Marx's investigation of social history runs through the principle of dialectical unity of inevitability and contingency, rather than simply taking a predetermined position. Due to the lack of scientific understanding of the inevitability of historical development, it is thought that any Marx's prediction of historical trends is following some transcendental pattern of determinism. For example, Waltmann believed that: "Marx actually depicts the trends and outcomes of capitalism as a schema before studying the history of capitalism in detail. This is a priori proposition from Hegel's dialectics."[105]

Thirdly, it is thought that Marx overemphasized the determinants of technology and economy in history, and ignored the influence of non-economic factors on the historical process. Although Bernstein and others did not generally declare Marxism as vulgar economic determinism, they regarded Marx in the period of *Das Kapital* as a strict economic determinist. They attacked Marx as a "social fatalist", saying that Marx's interpretation of history was mainly "arbitrariness". When aiming at Barthes' (Roland Gérard Barthes) attack on materialist conception of history that ignores the human factor and sees only the material factor, that is, to deny the role of the people in history, Engels pointed out that he was fighting with the windmill. Bernstein and others were undoubtedly fighting against the windmill, because of what they had accused and describing Marx's view of history as a pure "view of economic history" is completely arbitrary fiction.

The fundamental mistake of the above accusations against Marx lies in the confusion of mechanical determinism and dialectical determinism, and general opposition to determinism advocates "factor theory" or non-determinism. The dialectical determinism advocated by Marx is only to regard material and economic factors as the basis for understanding the whole world or social life. They are by no means seen as the only factors at work. On the other hand, Marx does not advocate the interaction of various factors which generally recognize the social history, because it is common sense and does not help to reveal the nature of social history. An important way to understand the social and historical phenomena scientifically is to grasp the basic, dominant and decisive factors. Without it, the scientific view of history cannot be obtained. There is no necessary connection between the errors of mechanical determinism and the scientific nature of Marx's

---

[105]*Bernstein and the German Party*, Page 243.

dialectical determinism, so it is wrong to oppose determinism in general.

If Bernstein and others understood Marx's view of history as an absolute determinism and tried to replace it with non-determinism, Kautsky, Mehring, Labriola (Antonio Labriola), Plekhanov and others tried to maintain the historical materialism from the standpoint of determinism. However, among these determinists, there is a tendency to vulgarize and naturalize Marx's history. However, some works of Western Marxists often generally refer to Marxist "orthodoxy" of the Second International as vulgar economic determinists, which is also an arbitrary statement. In fact, they echoed the criticisms of revisionists such as Bernstein on the opponents. At the beginning of 1890s, when bourgeois professors and "youth" following them vulgarize historical materialism, many of the leaders of the Social Democratic Party were theoretically immature. Even Bebel, Lafargue (Paul Lafargue) and Mehring have not understood the true content of historical materialism deeply enough that they also have the tendency to vulgarize materialism. But under the influence of Engels' correspondence, many people have deepened their understanding of the essence of historical materialism. In the later period of the Second International, although Kautsky and others still seriously misinterpreted Marx's historical materialism, Mehring, Labriola and Plekhanov made great contributions in defending Marx's historical determinism. And therefore, among the Marxist orthodoxy in the later period of the Second International, basically, people who hold mechanical determinism or vulgar economic determinism are not the majority.

Here, it is worth examining the views of Kautsky on the question of determinism. Vranicki once commented on Kautsky: "The name of Karl Kautsky, in a certain sense, can be regarded a symbol of the Social Democratic Party of Germany in the Second International. The prosperity of this movement is linked to the renowned reputation of Kautsky. Likewise, the decline of the movement meant the bankruptcy of Kautsky, the generally recognized theoretical leader by German socialists and the whole Second International. The movement's theoretical achievements and major shortcomings are best reflected in Kautsky."[106] This "major shortcoming" includes his misinterpretation of historical materialism, which is mainly manifested in his separation of subjective and objective factors in history, the dialectical relationship between freedom and necessity. As a result of this error, he despised the revolutionary activities of Marxist political parties in the struggle for socialism on the strategic and strategic issues.

One of the main theoretical roots of Kautsky's mistake was that he was deeply influenced by Darwinism. He began to study society from Darwinism, that is, to see the society from the perspective of the development of biological organisms and the struggle for the survival of species. When he accepted Marx's view of history, he turned his attention to the development of social economy and the condition of class struggle. However, in his theoretical career, Darwin's theory of evolution hindered his vision, and made him lay too much emphasis on the nature of human and stress too much on the consistent aspects of the law of social development and the law of natural development. As a result, he often used the category of Marx's historical materialism, but expressed a kind of almost mechanical determinism.

Kautsky exaggerated the inevitability of economic development and belittled the active role of people in transforming society. He pointed out in the theoretical section of *The Erfurt Programme* (1891) that the economic development itself, like the laws of nature, would inevitably lead to the victory of socialism. Because of "the inevitability of nature", the working class put forward the socialist task to themselves, and the economic development also led to the realization of this goal because of this kind of natural inevitability. Man is only the product of the environment. In the face of historical inevitability, that is the economic power of ruling people, man is lack of creativeness. This fatalistic view is more obvious in the later works of Kautsky.

---

[106]Vranicki: *History of Marxism*, Vol. 1, Page 344.

Kautsky equated the social law with the natural law, and understood the human nature as the instinct. Both the social development and the movement of nature followed the objective law. This is a basic view of historical materialism. But Kautsky exaggerated the consistency between society and nature, arguing that society is "a special part of nature with special laws, and these laws, if desired, can be called as the law of nature, for in terms of its essence, there is no difference between the former and the latter."[107] This led to naturalism, that is, the naturalization of social relations and the biolization of social processes. In the eyes of Kautsky, not only does the relationship between man and nature depend entirely on the constraints of nature on human beings, but also human nature is rooted in the natural environment. Human nature "does not evolve into human nature through historical development, but it is the nature that man inherited from his animal ancestors at the beginning of that historical process."[108] It can be concluded that the survival struggle of the animal kingdom is the natural continuation of the social class struggle. "Class struggle is only a special form of the general law of the development of nature."[109] Such a superficial understanding shows that if vulgar evolution is applied to historical understanding, it will give rise to historical fatalism. If this historical view is used to guide the proletarian revolutionary movement, it can only provide a theoretical basis for opportunism. For example, in Kautsky's *Questions and Answers for Social Democracy*, he said: "The Social Democratic Party is a revolutionary political party, but it is not a revolutionary party at all. I know that

---

[107]Kautsky: *The Proliferation and Development of Nature and Society*, Page 9, Moscow-Peter Geller, 1923, Quoted from Брайович, С.М.: *Karl Kautsky and the Evolution of His Ideas*, Page 83.

[108]*Kautsky: The Materialist Conception Of History*, Vol. 1, Part 2, Page 51.

[109]Kautsky: *Ethics and the Materialist Conception Of History*, Page 81, St. Petersburg, 1906. Quoted from Брайович, С.М.: *Karl Kautsky and the Evolution of His Ideas*, Page 129.

our purpose can only be achieved through revolution, but we also know that there is nothing we can do to create a revolution, and neither can our enemies stop it from happening. And therefore, we have never thought of launching or preparing for revolution, since revolution cannot be started according to our will. It is also rarely possible for us to talk about when and under what conditions the revolution will take place."[110] This is actually a fantasy that the roasted grouse of the revolution will fly into its mouth.

Similarly taking the advantages of natural science achievements in the 19th century, Marx did not simply absorb Darwin's theory of evolution, nor copied to the social field. However, Kautsky stiffly put Darwin's theory of evolution with Marx's historical materialism, and misunderstood the historical view of Marx as the mechanical determinism, which was a profound theoretical lesson.

Mehring, Labriola and Plekhanov correctly expounded Marx's historical determinism.

Mehring refuted the attack of bourgeois sociologist Barthes on historical materialism and clearly demonstrated his understanding of Marx's view of history. He thought that Marx did not understand the cause and result as the opposite poles, and did not deny the power and significance of thought. Historical materialism always insists on the view that once a certain historical phenomenon is formed because of another and the rooted economic reasons, it will also affect the surrounding environment, and even has react to the cause of it. But Mehring's *The Lessing Legend* has its shortcomings in trying to apply the methodology of historical materialism. Engels, for example, has criticized Mehring for not paying enough attention to the reaction of superstructures such as ideology to the economy.[111]

---

[110]Quoted from Nalski: *Marxist Philosophy in 19th Century II*, Page 241.

[111]See *Karl Marx and Frederick Engels: Selected Works*, Edition 1, Vol. 4, Page 500.

Bernstein used to support Barthes to call the historical materialism as "economic historical view" and opposed the recognition of the dynamic role of consciousness to the recognition of the inevitability of history. Mehring took the lead in criticizing this view, pointed out that Bernstein did not understand the dialectics of historical process and confused materialism with mechanical determinism. Mehring opposed to regard the view of historical materialism as the "view of economic history".

Labriola deeply discussed the essence of Marx's historical determinism. In his two works, *In Memory of the Communist Manifesto* and *Historical Materialism*, he systematically expounded the basic ideas of historical materialism and opposed the erroneous thoughts such as fatalism, social Darwinism and factor theory. He thought: "Human beings are neither creating their own history in the imagined development, nor advancing on a predetermined path of development."[112] While opposing to regard historical events as the process of destiny, historical materialism tries to objectify the explanation of historical process. There are two methods to study the objective historical process: One is the method of factors, namely "abstractly disassembling parts of an organism and breaking them into many factors that make up a unified whole"; and the other one is the method of historical materialism, which is the only way to know the history. "It analyzes and decomposes various factors, just to find the objective inevitability from which they work together to achieve the final result."[113]

The most distinctive feature of Labriola's thought on historical determinism is his three conclusions. Firstly, in the field of historical determinism, it is never possible to directly see the connection between cause and effect. Behind the behavior of will and its causes, the origin of historical determinism is hidden, so historical

---

[112]Labriola: *Historical Materialism*, Page 42, Beijing, People's Publishing House, 1984.

[113]Labriola: *Historical Materialism*, Page 11.

determinism should look for the reasons for the motivation in the material conditions that form the basis of the motive of behavior to transcend the narrow frame of consciousness. Secondly, historical materialism "is not to summarize the whole complex process of historical development as the economic category, but only to explain every historical fact in the final analysis (Engels) with the economic structure that forms the basis of historical facts (Marx)."[114] This requires analysis of social factors and integration. Thirdly, in order to transit from economic structure to various specific historical processes, we must turn to the synthesis of concepts and knowledge. This kind of synthesis, also called as "social psychology", refers to the specific form of social consciousness. It can be clearly seen from the three conclusions of Labriola that Marx's historical determinism should fully recognize the direct or indirect causality, the complex unity of economic phenomena and other social phenomena, and the active role of social consciousness. Although Labriola described historical materialism as making history "naturalized in a certain sense", he stressed that this is only in terms of objectivity. The laws and principles of animal life must not be used to explain human history. He also specially emphasized the social transformation of nature by human beings, and stressed the "artificial environment". "To insist that this environment is only a part and continuation of nature is only too general and abstract, and therefore, in the final analysis, there is no definite meaning."[115]

Plekhanov praised Labriola's *Historical Materialism* as a "rare" "good book". At almost the same time as the publication of the book, Plekhanov wrote an equally excellent work titled *The Development of the Monist View of History* (1895). In this book and other books such as *The Materialist Conception of History* and *Fundamental Problems of Marxism*, Plekhanov expounded the essential difference

---

[114]Labriola: *Historical Materialism*, Page 62.

[115]Labriola: *Historical Materialism*, Page 66~67.

between the monism of historical materialism and the theory of factors, put forward the famous "formula of five factors", and made sharp criticism on vulgar "economic determinism". In his point of view, the fundamental error of the theory of factors lies in staying in the abstract point of view of interaction and avoiding the origin of various social and historical factors. Historical materialism advocates that when examining social history, the factors of social history are not the products of mutual isolation and pure abstraction. In essence, people only create a kind of history, that is, their own history of social relations. However, these social relations are restricted by the productive forces in a certain period of time. Although there were many controversies in the theory of the "five formulas" (productivity, relations of production, political system, social psychology and social consciousness form) put forward by Plekhanov, he insisted on taking productivity as the basis and basic motive force of social development, which should be fully affirmed.

As we know, in the book *Karl Marx's Economic Materialism*, Lafargue called materialism and his position as "economic materialism." Although his understanding of historical materialism is not vulgar "economic determinism", this explanation provided an objective justification for those who attacked historical materialism. Plekhanov thought that even the confusion of terminology was also a serious distortion of historical materialism. "The name of 'economic materialism' is very inappropriate. Marx never called himself an economic materialist."[116] In order to refute the view of vulgar "economic determinism", Plekhanov used a large number of historical facts and the viewpoint of the founder of historical materialism to discuss the reaction of superstructure, especially the role of political factors. In addition, he also analyzed the historical role of the individual and the role played by other accidental factors in history, which cannot be understated. His conclusion was that it was not historical materialism that leaded to "quietism" and "fatalism", but the vulgar "economic determinism".

---

[116]*Selected Philosophical Works by Georgi Plekhanov*, Vol. 1, Page 768.

6. Confusion over Science and Value

In the later period of the Second International, quite a number of theorists made a serious misinterpretation of the scientific nature and value of Marxism, and this kind of distortion mainly appeared among Austrian Marxists.

The word "Austrian Marxism" was originally put forward in 1914 by the American socialist Louis Baudin. It has been widely accepted by many people including members of the school.[117] Austrian Marxists are made up of a number of important theorists from the Austrian Social Democratic Party, including Alfred W. Adler, Rudolf Hilferding, Karl Renner and Otto Bauer. They gathered around *Study on Marx* (a theoretical journal founded in Vienna in 1904 by Adler and Hilferding) to tried to solve the problems put forward by Maherism and Neo–Kantianism on Marxism. Here, we only examine their two main tendencies in dealing with the scientific and value problems of Marxism.

One tendency is to turn Marxist philosophy into positivism. Austrian Marxists, represented by Adler, opposed materialism and historical materialism, and regarded materialism as "metaphysics" and opposed it. They interpreted Marxist philosophy from Kant's transcendental critical philosophy, only understood Marxism as a social science of history or experience, especially emphasized the causality of empirical facts, rejected any value judgment and the impartial "science", or stressed on the "neutrality" separated from ideology.

The other tendency is to ethicize the scientific socialism founded by Marx and Engels. Influenced by Neo-Kantianism, most Austrian Marxists attempted to "supplement" socialist theory with Kant's ethics and replace scientific socialism with ethical socialism, and advocated that socialism is based on the recognition of the general value of human beings and is aimed at ordinary people. And therefore, it is a general moral ideal.

---

[117]See Kołakowski: *Main Currents of Marxism*, Vol. 2, Page 241.

Adler and others held the banner of "Marxism is not dogma" and "We must creatively develop Marx's heritage" with an attempt to find a way of understanding essentially different from that of orthodox Marxists. They believed that it was entirely beneficial to supplement and enrich Marxism with the ideas and concepts of Neo-Kantianism. Their interest was to re-examine the "theoretical basis and epistemology basis of Marxism". As a result, they "found" that Kant's criticism verified the existence of many gaps and vague purposes in Marxism. They argued that Marxism was not logically premised on materialist philosophy.

Adler believed that materialism will make Marxism lose its scientific nature because it was difficult for materialism to explain the relationship between material and spirit, which would inevitably lead to metaphysics. In his opinion, "it's all about the question of the relationship between matter and ideas... Only from the viewpoint of cognitive criticism can we answer this question."[118] That is to say, "The mental things can never be produced from the physical things, and the dependence of the mental process on the physical process is something completely incomprehensible. And therefore, in fact, there is no certainty other than psychological-physical parallelism, so the idea that material conditions have any effects on historical processes, namely, psychological processes, is also inconceivable."[119] Since the historical process is not based on material conditions, everything can be attributed to spiritual things. "Just as economic relations are spiritual relations, productivity is also the power of the spirit."[120] According to this point of view, Adler accused Engels that the basic philosophical issues proposed by Engels were groundless. He advocated that materialism from the first nature of matter should be abandoned and the epistemological theory of consciousness should be adhered to. The latter is

---

[118]Quoted from Vranicki: *History of Marxism*, Vol. 1, Page 404.

[119]Quoted from Vranicki: *History of Marxism*, Vol. 1, Page 404.

[120]Quoted from Vranicki: *History of Marxism*, Page 406.

based on the first thing that is experience, and the question it raises is not the question of which the first between material and spiritual is, but why we can have our experience. For the reason why Marx used the term "materialism", Adler's explanation is due to historical reasons and against the use of spiritualism. In fact, what Marx advocated was "positivist materialism, realistic positivist materialism, and nothing else."[121] Adler's above point of view is to define the standard of "science" by Kant's critical yardstick, that is to say, only by limiting Marxism to the empirical or phenomenal world in Kant's sense can it be scientific. In fact, when people remove the materialistic basis of Marxism, and when people negate the preexistence of the materials, the scientific nature of Marxism disappears fundamentally. From this point we can see that Adler and Kautsky have something in common with each other, which is to wipe out the unique philosophical basis of materialism in historical materialism.

In the eyes of Adler and others, Marxist view of history is a kind of positive science without value judgment, and is separated from ideology. Their science or truth depends entirely on the correct application of the principles of ideological procedure, not on any political attitude or class position. The empirical science they understand is not as the same as the general positivism. The former does not advocate a total objectivism to the facts as the latter. Adler and others believe that Marxism is a complete sense of the empirical scientific theory of society, but this does not mean that Marxism must conform to the standard of knowledge put forward by the empiricists, because empiricists ignore Kant's questions, it is impossible for them to provide an "absolute" basis for science. Adler and others advocate starting from experience and meanwhile seeking to explain empirically the necessary category principles and deductive concepts of social phenomena. They believe that social analysis must be premised on categories associated with subjectivity in the world of experience, which, like Kant's transcendental concept of

[121]Quoted from Vranicki: *History of Marxism*, Page 406.

space-time, come from reason rather than experience, but constitutes the practical experience. Adler opposed vulgar and mechanical materialism, emphasized the reality and significance of consciousness, and believed that the causality of society was mediated by consciousness, that all social phenomena (including economic behavior) were spiritual, not material, and that social scientists must reveal meaningful subjective motivations. While leading Marxism to the "scientific" aspect characterized by subjectivity, Adler and others tried to draw a clear line between "science" and "ideology". They believed that if Marxism was a scientific theory, in order to understand its truth, it was sufficient to apply the generally accepted principles of scientific thought, without firstly accepting any political or class positions. Marxism, like evolution, is acceptable to everyone. Although it also serves the interests of the proletariat, this fact does nothing to explain its ideological content, nor helps people to accept it in logic. In a word, Marxism is only a scientific theory, which is not related to ideology.

The above viewpoint only regards Marxism as an empirical science to explain the world, while neglecting its inherent revolutionary and practical nature. In fact, what Marx thought from the beginning was the interest of the proletariat. Of course, he did not study the social reality and the historical process only from here. When explaining the world scientifically, Marx insisted on taking the objective scientific attitude as the basic principle of his theoretical research, but also ran through the sense of mission of the proletarian. Marx unified the scientific nature and class nature of his theory on the inevitability of historical development. At the same time, Marx had never been indulged in the explanation of "science" of the world, but paid great attention to the transformation of the real world with great enthusiasm. So, in his theory, the proletariat is always regarded as the main body of the transformation of the real society. In a class society, it is hard to say that this view of history is scientific if the real class forces that transform the world are not discovered; whereas something that does not represent the interests of a particular group and does not have revolutionary and purely social "science", is not a characteristic of Marx's doctrine.

Hilferding said: "Marx's political science is like Marxist theory, which has no value judgment." He said that the Marxism "is a kind of objective and free science with no value judgment" in logic.[122] This kind of view reveals a superficial understanding of the nature of Marxism. Of course, there is a strict difference between scientific judgment and value judgment. But when we say Marxism is science, we mean that it is unbiased, and objectively illustrates the laws of the world. Since Marxism is not an empirical science in general, but a theory about liberating all mankind, it does not and cannot rule out value judgment. The problem lies not in the existence of value judgment in Marxism, which is a common sense[123], but in the relationship between scientific judgment and value judgment in Marxism.

In the later period of the Second International, there had been a debate on whether to hold ethical socialism or scientific socialism. The Austrian Marxists were involved in the dispute. Generally speaking, they are trying to combine Kant with Marx, supplementing the scientific socialism with Kant's practical reason or ethics, and advocating ethical socialism.

In their opinion, science and ethics are different, where the former is based on the

---

[122]Quoted from Korsch: *Marxism and Philosophy*, Page 55, London, New Left-Wing Book Club, 1970.

[123]In *Did The Party Go Bankrupted?* (1915) written by Hilferding, it was argued that true Marxism cannot avoid the existence of legitimate or improper problems in reality, nor can it merely derive the concept from causality, but shall acknowledge the valuation. "We no longer merely wish to observe the world, but to change it." This kind of view contradicts his view mentioned above, showing that his acknowledgement of the common sense that there is value judgment in Marxism. See *The Fallacy of the Second International Revisionist about Imperialism*, Page 212-213, Beijing, Sanlian Book Store, 1976.

observation of the facts of objective experience, while the latter is based on the subject's will. As science, Marxism is mainly aiming at its historical view. Marxism as a social phenomenon is morally neutral. However, it cannot answer the questions that "what we should do" and "what is good". If socialism is only regarded as the result of the "natural" development of social phenomena, it cannot lead people to make efforts to realize it, and cannot be regarded as an aim or an ideal, and therefore, socialism should rely on moral judgment. This kind of moral judgment cannot be derived from the description of biological or historical facts, but only from the human will as a kind of self-discipline and capable of creating the principle of conscious responsibility. Kant's moral theory can undoubtedly make up for the deficiency of Marx's socialist theory.

The error of the Austrian Marxists in explaining the socialist theory lies not in emphasizing the need for ethical judgment or value judgment in socialist theory, but in their belief that ethical judgment should be established on the basis of general and abstract human value, without talking about the value requirements of the proletariat, which is the real subject of the socialist movement. They are keen to talk about the universal validity of moral commandments, to affirm Kant's absolute orders in abstract terms, and to regard people's aim as the moral basis of socialism. They accepted the view of Cohen, the representative of the Marburg School of Neo-Kantianism, that historical materialism could not be regarded as the theoretical basis of socialism, and only Kant's ethics can provide a reliable basis for socialism. Because Kant's ethics proves that there is no other purpose than that people are the real value, and this is the principle of socialism. This moral precept has universal adaptability, which can be applied to everyone without exception. So socialism as a moral proposition has nothing to do with social class.[124]

To "reform" Marxism from the Neo-Kantianism, it is inevitable to encounter such a

---

[124]See Kołakowski: *Main Currents of Marxism*, Vol. 2, Page 247.

contradiction: If the theory of socialism is recognized as an integral and organic part of Marxism, where on the one hand, regarding Marxism as an empirical social science, and on the other hand, regarding socialism as based on value judgment, it is hard to say that Marxism itself is the "science" generally understood by Austrian Marxists. Faced with this contradiction, they are often unable to maintain logical consistency in theory. For example, when Hilferding emphasized that Marxism excluded value judgment and adopted a complete "scientific" attitude, he came to such a judgment: "The emergence of socialism is the product of the development trend in the commodity production society... The insight into the inevitability of socialism is by no means the result of value judgment and has nothing to do with actual behavior."[125] Adler also had contradictions. He sometimes thought that what Marxism "had to do seem to be a causal argument to the reality of this historical movement. So any argument in ethics means breaking the scientific method of Marxism, and it means mixing up a completely different view of theoretical experience and practical experience without criticizing it directly according to Kant."[126] However, once the issue of socialism was involved, Adler was bound to be inextricably linked to Kant's ethics. For example, he thought that according to Marx, socialism was based on a purely empirical observation of the chain of cause and effect in history. The historical inevitability of socialism is consistent with its moral values. Adler used the concept of "socialized man" to illustrate this "consistency". The so-called "socialized person" is a person who is driven by social conditions to achieve what he considers to be moral. That is to say, the inevitability and moral value of socialism are united in "socialized people". The scientific nature of socialism is the same thing as the pursuit of the perfect and unified moral ideal of ordinary human beings.

---

[125]Quoted from Korsch: *Marxism and Philosophy*, Page 55.

[126]Quoted from Vranicki: *History of Marxism*, Vol. 1, Page 409.

The proponents of ethical socialism actually portray Marx as a complete moral idealist.

The revisionism of the Second International made a comprehensive "revision" of Marxism, which was vigorously exposed and criticized by the leftists in the Second International, especially by Lenin's destructive blow in theory. However, the controversy between revisionists and Marxists is not over. This is because, on the one hand, the social and historical conditions that breed revisionism have not been completely eliminated, and once the socialist movement has twists and turns or faces a turning point in history, the debate between revisionism and Marxism will erupt again. On the other hand, although Lenin defended and developed Marxism under the new historical conditions and achieved a brilliant victory against revisionism, he did not completely solve the problems raised by revisionism, which was the result of the historical conditions. In the course of the development of the socialist movement, there will inevitably be new twists and turns, and in the face of new problems, revisionism will inevitably appear in a new face or form. In contemporary times, the flood of democratic socialist thought is actually a kind of revisionism replay of the Second International. And therefore, we should sum up and reflect on the gain and loss of the theory of the latter stage of the Second International seriously. It is still of urgent practical significance to study Lenin's experience in opposing the revisionism of the Second International.

CHAPTER 3   "REBUILDING MARX": LUKÁCS, KORSCH & GRAMSCI

The major debate on Marxism emerged in the peaceful environment at the turn of the 19th century and the 20th century seems to get the historical decision due to the victory of the October Revolution that: The socialist revolution is entirely possible through violence. But a new question arises: Why did Marx's prediction of the overall revolution in the capitalist countries of Europe fail? A group of radical intellectuals who accepted Marxism passionately threw themselves into the workers' revolutionary movement in the countries in Western Europe, but were disappointed in the failure of the revolution. The severe reality forced them to think about the experience and lessons of failure. Some famous theorists, such as Lukács (György Lukács), Korsch (Karl Korsch) and Gramsci (Antonio Francesco Gramsci), thought that the fundamental reasons for the failure of the European revolutionary movement lied not in the immaturity of objective conditions, but in the lack of subjective conditions, that is, the "class consciousness" of the proletariat was immature; whereas the emergence of this situation was directly derived from the vulgarization tendency of the main theorists of the Second International to indiscreetly abandon the Marxist dialectics. Accordingly, they advocated "rebuilding" Marxism, tried to reinterpret Marx's theory within a new framework, restored revolutionary dialectics, and awakened the proletariat's consciousness of criticizing the capitalist reality and actively joining in the revolution. They put forward the theories such as principle of collectivity, subject-object dialectics, practical philosophy and cultural criticism, and opened up the first course of Western Marxism.

1. Overall Framework of the "New Interpretation"

The emergence of Western Marxism is the inevitable result of the contrasts between the understanding of Marxism formed by the Second International and the revolutionary reality of Western Europe. An important incentive for the origin of Western Marxism is the strong dissatisfaction with the castration of Marxist dialectics by main theorists of the Second International, such as Bernstein and Kautsky. Although the representatives of this trend differ from each other in terms of specific views, their concerns are common. Their interpretation of Marxism is different from the theoretical model of the main theorists of the Second International in both form and content.

The general characteristics of the interpretation of Marxism of Lukács and others that lies in highlighting the main role of human in the social and historical development process, ignoring the analysis of economic structure and process, turning the focus of research from the economic field to the field of philosophy, and turning the economic factors in the historical development to "the whole society-history process", which is the general characteristic of the interpretation of Marxism of Lukács and others. They were called upon to oppose dogmatism and the vulgar tendencies of Marxism of the Second International. In their eyes, vulgar Marxists abandoned the factor of man as the subject in Marxist philosophy and misinterpreted Marx's social theory as the theory of social law of movement separated from the subject. The concept of historical process is misinterpreted into a single mechanical and deterministic structure, that is, the pattern of scientific or inevitable laws in the sense of natural science. As a result, Marxism became a "withered" dogma, and the history was compressed into a thin economic skeleton. In response to this tendency, they argued to restore Marx's "collectivity" view, to restore the position of historical subject in Marxist philosophy, to comprehensively understand Marx's thought of historical dialectics, and to emphasize the unity of subject and object, and the unity of theory and practice.

In order to realize this theoretical intention, they began with tracing back the theoretical origin of Marx's thought, especially emphasized the theoretical relationship between Marx and Hegel, and used Hegelianism to construct Marxism, which became the main theoretical tendency of the founder of Western Marxism. This is especially prominent in Lukács' *History and Class Consciousness*, which is praised as "the Bible of Western Marxism". Robert A. Gorman, an American scholar, commented on this in the book *New Marxism*: "The movement of reviving the Hegel factor of Marxism systematically and tentatively originated from the sober representatives of orthodoxy and Hegelianism, and finally condensed in G. Lukács' *History and Class Consciousness*."[127] McLellan also believed that one of the main tools Lukács used to generalize the problems of his time was Hegel's philosophy, with all the central concepts in *History and Class Consciousness*, such as the dialectics of materialization, subject and object, as well as collectivity, can be found for their origins in Hegel.[128] Kolakowski compared Lukács and Korsch, and thought that they had made a clear explanation of the Hegel's source of Marx's dialectics, and restored the almost forgotten thought of the unity and practice of Marx in early time.[129] It's not difficult to see that this tendency of Lukács and others is a reaction to the denial of Marxist dialectics by the revisionists of the Second International. Bernstein and others regarded Marx's dialectics as a remnant factor of Hegel's philosophy. However, Lukács acted in a diametrically opposite way, and took Hegel's dialectics as the essence of Marxist methodology. He pointed out that Marx's aphorism that Hegel should not be treated as a "dead dog" was even ignored by many famous Marxists, who only paid attention to the investigation of individual facts, but abandoned the dialectical explanation of social history as a whole. Marxism had been reduced to empiricism or positivism, with its theory and practice having been separated, and its subject and object having been dismembered. In a word, they turned a blind eye to Hegel's dialectic thought, the

---

[127]Robert A. Gorman: *New Marxism*, Page 93, New York, Greenwood Press, 1982.

[128]See McLellan: *Marxism after Marx*, Page 214.

[129]See Kolakowski: *Main Currents of Marxism*, Vol. 3, Page 308.

most vital thing in Marxism, and were completely puzzled about the essence of Marxist methods. And therefore, it is urgent to restore Hegel's dialectics in Marxism.

However, Lukács went to the other extreme. He regarded Marxism as a continuation of the logical development of Hegel's thought, believed that the substantive concepts of Marx's dialectical thought all came from Hegel, and confused materialism dialectics with Hegel dialectics. We advocate studying Marxism from the source of Marxist theory and attaching importance to Marx's sublation of Hegel's dialectics, but by no means restore Marx to Hegel. Anderson once objectively believed: "Lukács turned to Hegel for help, far from being traced back to its roots."[130] Lukács discovered Marx through Hegel to explain Marx, and his essence was undoubtedly to construct a theoretical framework of "New Marxism" on the standpoint of Hegel's philosophy. Not only in Lukács, but also in Korsch's *Marxism and Philosophy*, and Gramsci's *The Prison Notebooks*, we all see a strong Hegel color.

The revolutionary dialectics of "rebuilding" Marxism is not only the aim of "New Marxism" of Lukács and others, but also the theme. In a nutshell, they elaborated Marx's dialectics thought emphatically from the following aspects.

First of all, they thought that Marx's dialectics was the dialectics of "collectivity" about social history. The "collectivity" mentioned here only refers to the collectivity of social history (nature is regarded as the category of society). The reason why they highlighted the principle of "collectivity" was that they regarded it as the supreme principle of Marx's dialectics, and believed that only under this principle can the realistic process of social history be clarified and can the realistic movement of proletarian revolution be explained. This principle is embodied in the organic unity of various factors in social history, and is reflected in the unity of

---

[130]Anderson: *Considerations on Western Marxism*, Page 80.

theory and practice in the proletarian movement.

From the situation of the Second International, it seems that all theorists in form does advocate a comprehensive understanding of social history, but it is difficult to find that some people have clearly advocated that Marx's dialectics was a general method, and described it as the essence of Marxism. It can be said that collectivity is the most important concept in the Western Marxism. Around the principle of collectivity, there are the concepts such as historical subject and object, proletarian consciousness, materialization, ideological criticism and general revolution.

Secondly, they thought that Marx's dialectics was the dialectics of practice and the dialectics of subject. Lukács and others not only opposed the rough attitude of abandoning Marx's dialectics, but also accused the tendency of "naturalism" that summarized Marx's dialectics to the dialectics of object. Both Lukács and Korsch advocated that dialectics can only be the dialectics of subject and object. In the relationship between subject and object, the subject plays a completely dominant role, and the dialectics, which is understood from the subject, only separates the law of social development from the bearer of social and historical activities, which can only lead to fatalism. The dialectics is embodied in the activities of the historical subject, and there is no genuine dialectics other than that. Although Gramsci signified his dissent from Lukács' completely denial of dialectics of nature, and held the idea that there was a contradiction in logic to recognize that the dialectics is the mutual relationship between the subject and object and to reject the subject dialectics out of object dialectics, he also emphasized that the dialectic should be established on the basis of practice. So he always used "practical philosophy" to name Marx's dialectics. They have a common point in describing dialectics, which is showing contempt for the general materialism and believing that Marx's dialectics is beyond the opposition between materialism and idealism.

Finally, they thought that Marx's dialectics was the dialectics of revolution, and the proletariats were the object to master and implement the dialectics. The initial emergence of Western Marxism is inseparable from the attempt by Lukács and others to combine Marxism with the workers' movement in the developed capitalist countries of Western Europe. And therefore, their exposition of Marx's thought was always put forward around the urgent problems of the realistic revolutionary movement. Lukács was concerned with how to establish a general method different from the bourgeois positivism method and guide the proletariat to fully understand the structural nature of capitalist society, and understand the historical status and mission of the proletariat itself, thus creating subjective conditions for the proletarian revolution. Korsch paid attention to how to highlight the revolutionary aspects of Marxism, namely the aspect of dialectics, by emphasizing the inherent connection between Marxism and philosophy. Korsch advocated confirming reality of social consciousness by using the dialectical method and criticizing the "spiritual structure" of capitalist society from the aspect of ideology. Gramsci was committed to taking dialectics as a theoretical tool for the analysis of the new situation, asserted to adhere to the basic spirit of dialectics combining the theory and practice, thought that attention should be paid to the cultural field with full attention on the specific revolution practice characteristics of each country, acknowledged the dynamic role of cultural phenomenon and other superstructure parts, and actively carried out cultural revolution. In a word, they all regarded dialectics as the special ideological weapon of the proletariat to carry out revolution, and understood the direct social function of dialectics as arousing the revolutionary consciousness of the proletariat.

There is no denying that the above ideas have played a positive role in opposing the naturalism or positivism tendency in the interpretation of Marxism and in restoring Marxist dialectics. But it is not difficult to find that Lukács and others exaggerated the role of proletarian consciousness, and transformed the Marx's dialectics into a kind of subjective dialectics. In *History and Class Consciousness*, Lukács undoubtedly had a tendency to deviate seriously from the "origin" of Marxism. Although he made self-criticism later, objectively, he played the role of laying the foundation for the Western Marxism.

2. The Principle of "Collectivity" Relying on Subjectivity

The theoretical framework of "Neo-Marxism" established by Lukács and others is based on the principle of "collectivity", which is regarded by themselves as the most important category against mechanical ceterminism and positivism tendency, and as the principle of embodying the essence of Marx's dialectics of history. The concept was firstly put forward by Lukács and expounded in an all-round way.

Lukács believed that one of his biggest achievements was having restored the collectivity category in *History and Class Consciousness*, and this category occupied a central position in all Marx's works. However, some theorists of the Second International advocated "scientism", excluding this category from Marx's works. "What constitutes the decisive differences between Marxism and bourgeois ideology is not the priority of economic motivation in historical interpretation, but the view of collectivity. As for the collectivity category, the universal superiority of the whole to the part is the essence of the method that Marx took from Hegel and transformed into the basis of the new science."[131] This is what Lukács said in *Rosa Luxembourg's Marxism* (1921), which best reflects the status of the collectivity category.

Lukács' interpretation of "collectivity" began with critical empiricism. He believed that empiricism was the conceptual basis of revisionism and reformism in the workers' movement, intoxicated with the details of society and the analysis of facts, and refused to grasp the whole society as a whole, thus cutting off the overall connection of the society. Empiricism was helpless in the face of the complicated situation of capitalist society and was easily confused by false phenomena. This understanding method, which is contrary to the principle of collectivity, is the result of the reality of capitalist society. Under capitalism, the labor process is divided into many parts because of the separation of workers from the overall

---

[131]Lukács: *History and Class Consciousness*, Page 27, London, 1971.

process of production. As a result, the worker's personality is lost and the social atom is transformed into an individual who produces in a simple and disorderly manner, which will inevitably have a profound impact on the ideology, science and philosophy of the capitalist society. If we only look at the fragmented individual facts of the society, we will regard the economy, politics, culture and other phenomena of the capitalist as insurmountable and eternal phenomena. Empiricism can only bring harm to the proletarian revolution. For example, as Bernstein abandoned the principle of collectivity, it was inevitable for him to give up the starting point and purpose of the revolutionary movement and to abandon the premises and requirements of dialectics. The scientific thought of the proletariat is revolutionary, firstly because its method embodies the priority of the collectivity category.

Lukács explained the general content of the principle of "collectivity" from two aspects. First of all, the whole is better than the part. The essence of Marxism is method, not dogma. This method is not a set of principles of thought and operation in the sense of logic, but a special way of thinking about the world. This method regards society as a whole with "collectivity". The collectivity of society is not formed by the accumulation of individual facts. Facts cannot be explained by themselves, but can only be revealed by its connection with the whole. The whole must be understood before the facts and therefore the whole is ahead of the facts logically. In this respect, Lukács believed that Marx imitated Hegel: "From this, we understand the basic idea of the dialectical method, that is, the theory of Hegel's concrete concept. This theory mainly adheres to the principle that the whole is ahead of the parts, and the parts must be explained in understanding the whole, not the other way around."[132] The essence of Marx's social thought is to advocate the unity of abstract and isolated parts in the whole. "The isolated facts and social

---

[132]Lukács: *Strategy and Ethics,* Quoted from Kolakowski: *Main Currents of Marxism,* Vol. 3, Page 265.

life, as a historical process, interact in a whole. It is only in this connection that the knowledge of the facts is hopefully transformed into an understanding of reality."[133] Secondly, collectivity does not simply refer to the specific aspects of all facts in a certain period of time, but should also be understood as a dynamic reality, that is, including certain trends, directions and outcomes. It is the unity of the status quo, the past and the future. "So the objective forms of all social phenomena change frequently in the course of their constant interaction. The comprehensibility of objects develops in proportion to our mastery of their role in the collectivity to which they belong. This is why only dialectical collectivity can make us understand the reality as a social process."[134]

There is no doubt that naturalism or positivism on the course of social history should be opposed. However, we only need to examine Lukács' concrete views on the principle of collectivity to find out the major differences between him and Marx. Lukács defined the whole of society from the subject. That is to say, it is necessary to understand the society as the process of subject participation and active construction, and to realize the overall understanding in the process of the interaction of historical subject and object. "The dialectical relationship between the subject and the object in the historical process" is the "most important interaction".[135] The principle of collectivity includes not only the relation as the object of cognition, but also the idea of the interaction as the process of cognition. But in the further analysis of the relationship between subject and object, Lukács exaggerated the process of subjective consciousness. Lukács set the principle of "collectivity" against the "priority of economic motivation", and elevated the former as the "decisive" factor in Marxism, thus wiping out many vital scientific

---

[133]Lukács: *History and Class Consciousness*, Page 8.

[134]Lukács: *History and Class Consciousness*, Page 13.

[135]Lukács: *History and Class Consciousness*, Page 3.

CHAPTER 3 "REBUILDING MARX": LUKACS, KORSCH & GRAMSCI | 103

contents in Marxist theory.

Lukács shifted the focus of social cognition from the analysis of the object to the analysis of the subject, which was based on the premise that: "The most important function of historical materialism lies not in the description of pure scientific knowledge, but in the field of action."[136] His mistake was not in the premise of the theory itself, but in his exaggeration of the differences between "the field of action" and the objective scientific analysis of society. Marx devoted his life to the study of social structure and its objective laws, especially the inevitability of social economic processes, because he firmly believed that the activities of changing society must be based on the scientific understanding of society. In the complex overall structure and process of society, the relationship between subject and object runs through it, but the most important interaction between subject and object is reflected in the economic process of society. The proletarian subjective consciousness undoubtedly has various relative independences, but it is essentially restricted by the economic process of capitalism. It is apt to lead people to a simple "theory of interaction" to talk about "collectivity" in an abstract way. While exaggerating subjectivity in the name of "collectivity" can only lead to another division of society as a whole.

The emphasis on the principle of collectivity also exists in Korsch's interpretation of Marxism. Although Korsch did not discuss the concept of collectivity specially as Lukács did, nor did he define Marxism as the principle of collectivity in such a straightforward way as Lukács did, he also regarded the principle of collectivity as the most basic principle of dialectics in *Marxism and Philosophy*. He believed that the principle of collectivity embodied that the ideological movement and the actual revolutionary movement were regarded as a unified historical whole. Furthermore, the principle of collectivity requires taking the ideology as other factors in the

---

[136]Lukács: *History and Class Consciousness*, Page 224.

society, which is the material factors, and refuses analysis on purely economic factors. According to the principle of collectivity, Korsch proposed the ideology criticism theory firstly, advocated the overthrow of the bourgeoisie spiritual structure through thought and action, and regarded this as a premise of the proletarian revolution. Korsch emphasized on putting spiritual criticism in the first place in the "overall" criticism on the capitalist social structure. This is because he thought that Kautsky and others of the Second International created a kind of vulgar Marxism, which resulted in the people's calm and passive treatment on the social reality of capitalism, devoid of people's revolutionary passion, and crisis of Marxist theory on a series of important issues, such as proletarian countries and revolution. Kautsky and others "prior underestimated" the powerful role of bourgeois ideology, whereas Marx's social theory attached importance to the criticism of bourgeois ideology, and emphasized the collectivity of society and the collectivity of criticism of the society. Marxism "is a theory that regards or understands social development as a living whole; or more precisely, it is a theory that understands and practices the social revolution as a living whole... Not only economy, politics, and ideology, but also historical processes and conscious social actions continue to institute a living unity of 'revolutionary practice'."[137]

Lukács highlighted the awareness of the proletariat based on the principle of collectivity; Korsch emphasized the ideological movement of the proletariat, that is ideological criticism according to the principle of collectivity; and Gramsci gave full play to the principle of collectivity by underlining the unity of theory and practice and the cultural revolution.

Gramsci held the idea that Marxism was essentially a kind of philosophy with practice as its core, and it was a unified world view. In the view of practical philosophy, "the unity of theory and practice does not exist as a mechanical original

---

[137]Korsch: *Marxism and Philosophy*, Page 52.

argument, but as a process of historical formation."[138] The "mechanical original argument" here refers to the kind of mechanism that separates theory from practice, which regards theory as an "affix" to practice, as a "supplement" to practice or "minion" to practice. Gramsci asserted that practice should firstly be understood as a whole, that was, the elements of theory cannot be removed from practice. In other words, practice contained theoretical elements intrinsically, and theoretical activities or cognitive activities constituted the forerunner and decisive link of practice. He ridiculed fatalism or mechanical determinism as "nothing more than a kind of clothing that the weak wear it to cover their positive and real wills."[139] In order to break down mechanical determinism, Gramsci inherited the overall description of social and historical structure from Hegelianism to a large extent. That was to portray the spiritual and cultural phenomena of society as the result of behaviors that are independently incorporated into the purpose of the subject. He believed that the dominant social consciousness in a certain society was the objectification of human self-understanding shown as a cultural phenomenon in the society. Culture itself is a substantial part of social relations, in other words, culture is the overall manifestation of society, and it is the sum of social self-reflection and the premise of social progress. From this view of culture, Gramsci believed that the process of social revolution depended entirely on the revolutionary subject, that was, the people's consciousness, which in turn depended on the influence of culture. Consequently, the core content of revolutionary practice is to establish a non-bourgeois culture, and its premise is to overcome the cultural alienation in the reality of capitalist society, and to carry out a cultural revolution. From the overall understanding of social history and proletarian revolutionary practice, Gramsci reached a highly speculative conclusion:

---

[138]Gramsci: *The Prison Notebooks*, Page 16, Beijing, People's Publishing House, 1983.

[139]Gramsci: *The Prison Notebooks*, Page 19.

"Criticism of reality should derive its true content from speculative thinking, that is, it should be made into a means of political thought and practical action."[140]

The principle of collectivity put forward by Western Marxists aims to understand Marxism comprehensively. But since they set the tone from the very beginning for finding the reasons for the failure of Western European revolution from the subjective aspect of proletarian consciousness, and forgot the objective world while obsessed to explain the subjective world, and therefore, it was difficult to realize the overall grasp of social history, which inevitably led to a partial understanding of Marxism.

3. The Dialectics of Historical Subject-Object

Lukács is famous for his book *History and Class Consciousness*. The subtitle of the book is "The Study of Marxist Dialectics." In this symposium, which reflects young Lukács' "new understanding" of Marxism, his views on historical dialectics are systematically presented.

If the principle of collectivity constitutes the basis of his historical dialectics, then the interaction of subject and object constitutes the main contents of this historical dialectics. From the logic of Lukács, the dialectics of subject and object is only the concrete embodiment of the principle of collectivity.

Lukács explained the relationship between dialectics and Marxism according to the principle of collectivity. He pointed out in the preface to *History and Class Consciousness* that Marxism was essentially a method. It was our task to understand the essence of Marx's method and to apply it correctly. Marx's theory and method were the real methods used to understand society and ultimately discover history. This method was entirely historical. In *What is Orthodox Marxism*,

---

[140]Quoted from Holtz: *Some Tendencies of European Marxism*, Page 20, Beijing, People's Publishing House, 1983.

he argued that "orthodox Marxism is only about methods."[141] That is to say, Marxism was essentially a kind of dialectics, and a kind of dialectics of social history. Lukács thought the dialectics was different from the interpretation of Engels in *Anti-Dühring*. Engels "did not even mention the most important interaction, namely, the dialectical relationship between the subject and the object in the course of history...However, without this factor, dialectics would no longer be revolutionary."[142] In Lukács' point of view, dialectics was not the "scientific" method simply used by people to randomly explain of the object, nor was it independent from the subject that utilizes dialectics, so there was no dialectics of nature, but only dialectics of history.

There are two main bases for excluding dialectics of nature from Marxist dialectics. One is that nature is a category of social history, and it is impossible to study nature independently of society. "Nature is a social category. That is to say, whatever is considered natural at any particular stage of social development is related to man; whatever form man takes of nature, that is, the form of nature, the content of nature, the scope of nature and the objectivity of nature, are all determined by society."[143] Secondly, in the pure nature, that is, the nature other than society, man as the subject cannot be combined into the natural process, so it is impossible to obtain the concept of historical process change from the understanding of nature, and to explain the unity of subject and object, the unity of theory and practice, and the origin of thought change. In a word, the dialectics of object or nature is not Marxist dialectics.

Lukács' tendency to deny the dialectics of nature, which was revealed in the *History and Class Consciousness*, conflicted with the general description of his principle of

---

[141]Lukács: *History and Class Consciousness*, Page 1.

[142]Lukács: *History and Class Consciousness*, Page 3.

[143]Lukács: *History and Class Consciousness*, Page 234.

collectivity. He reflected on it in his later years. In the preface to the new edition of 1967 of the book, he pointed out that one of the most obvious features of the book was that it ran counter to the author's original subjective desire, namely, it objectively supported the tendency to "attack the foundation of Marxist ontology". "This tendency regards Marxism only as a social theory, as a social philosophy, thus neglecting and denying that it is a natural theory."[144] Lukács believed that the root of the wrong methodology lied in the neglect of the realistic basis of the material exchange process between society and nature, the narrow understanding of human activities and the elimination of "the natural and noumenal objectivity".

There are mainly three aspects in Lukács' thought on historical dialectics.

(I) Marx's historical dialectics is the continuation of Hegel's thought logic development.

Lukács thought: "If we do not examine Hegel, the founder of this method (refers to Marx's dialectics—Note of the quoter), and his relationship with Marx in details, we cannot treat this kind of concrete and historical method fairly."[145] Contrary to Bernstein, the revisionist of the Second International, Lukács opposed to cutting off the inherited relationship between Marxist philosophy and Hegel's philosophy. Bernstein advocated that the dialectical thought in Marx's works should be abandoned as the remnant of Hegel, whereas Lukács emphasized that Marx's dialectics was the logical extension of Hegel's thought. He greatly appreciated Hegel's theory of "What is true should not only be regarded as entity, but should also be expressed as the subject" in *The Phenomenology of Spirit*. Hegel believed that in the development process of absolute concept, the object was externalized from self-consciousness, formed the movement of interaction between subject and object, returned to self-consciousness through the understanding of object, and

---

[144]Lukács: *History and Class Consciousness*, Page xvi.

[145]Lukács: *History and Class Consciousness*, Page xliii.

thus achieved the identity of subject and object. In Lukács' view, the progress made by Hegel other than Kant, Fichte (Johann Gottlieb Fichte) and others because he ruled out the opposition between subject and object, examined the relationship between subject and object in the course of historical development, and confirmed that there was the same subject-object. However, Hegel had its insurmountable limitation, that is, he can only find the subject from the speculative logic field, and so he cannot find the real historical subject. Marx surpassed Hegel and found the subject of reality in the field of society-history, which was the social class or the proletariat more precisely. The difference between Marx's dialectics and Hegel's dialectics only lies in here. Lukács constructed Marx's dialectics according to Hegel's logical schema. Merely replacing self-consciousness with class consciousness and limiting dialectics of history to the interaction between subject and object of consciousness, this understanding undoubtedly distorts the relationship between Marx and Hegel, and obliterates the essential differences between the two.

(II) The proletariat is both the subject and the object, and their identity is realized in the class consciousness.

Lukács believed that dialectics was a revolutionary factor in social reality, and it expressed the process of history becoming mature and finally being reformed, which was realized by the proletariat, the social bearer. Dialectics was the theoretical consciousness of the proletariat. Why can only the proletariat be the subject of history? According to the principle of collectivity, the subject itself must be a whole, and then can regard the object as a whole; only a general understanding of society can transform the society. "In modern society, only the class can express this view of collectivity."[146] The process of obtaining this kind of overall cognition is the process of the interaction between subject and object. The principle of collectivity includes the interaction of subject and object, and also

---

[146]Lukács: *History and Class Consciousness*, Page 28.

means that the category of collectivity restricts the subject and object. "The category of collectivity not only determines the object of cognition, but also decides the subject of cognition... Only when the subject itself is a whole, the collectivity of the object can be determined; and if the subject wishes to understand itself, it must regard the object as a whole."[147] And therefore, the subject is not an individual, but a group, namely, a class; it cannot be other class, but can only be the proletariat. Only the proletariat can relate to the whole reality in the way of revolutionary practice. Lukács did not seek the object from outside the proletariat itself; instead, he regarded the proletariat as the unity of the subject and the object, that is to say, both the subject of consciousness and the object of consciousness. So he developed according to the consciousness of the proletariat, and described the historical process of the interaction between the subject and the object and tends to be the same.

The identity of subject and object is realized in the maturing consciousness with the development of social and economic conditions. In the pre-capitalist period, it was impossible for people to find themselves as social beings. Social relations on the basis of natural economy made it impossible for people to grasp the "reality as human beings" on the whole. Only in the capitalist society, "man became a social being in the original sense. Society became the reality of human beings. And therefore, only under capitalist conditions can we understand that society is reality in bourgeois society."[148] Of course, even in the capitalist society, the proletariat cannot grasp the "social reality" in consciousness from the very beginning, because the phenomenon of "materialization" is an obstacle for the proletariat to realize the unity of subject and object. In the "materialized" world, the special interests of the bourgeoisie make it impossible to grasp the whole society beyond the

---

[147]Lukács: *History and Class Consciousness*, Page 19.

[148]Lukács: *History and Class Consciousness*, Page 28.

intermediary of "materialization". Only because of its special interests can the proletariat overcome the phenomenon of "materialization", change the fact to be regarded as "the object" in the process of capitalist production in consciousness, and develop themselves from unconscious to conscious consciousness of their own situation. As a result, the proletariat, as a historical subject, develops from the split of subject and object into the identity of subject and object in the process of development of consciousness.

Lukács' view about the proletariat developing from a free class to a conscious class in the revolutionary practice and from its own unconscious to conscious awareness is unblamable. As far as the development process of proletarian revolutionary consciousness is concerned, it is undoubtedly a certain degree of development of Marxism. However, he put the dialectics of the interaction between subject and object of the consciousness as the core of historical dialectics under the guidance of the principle of collectivity, which inevitably distorted the historical materialism. It is easy to ignore the idealistic nature of Lukács. For example, some Western scholars thought that: "Lukács' view on the identical object-subject... did not contain any philosophical idealism, that is to say, there is no physical object but merely a form of masquerade of the spirit in his point of view."[149] This illusion is undoubtedly due to its focus on epistemology, but Lukács' theory focuses on dialectics in the field of social history. Lukács' mistakes can be attributed to two points.

First of all, Lukács violated his original intention of advocating the restoration of the principle of the collectivity of Marxism, and moved towards the unilateralism of separating the unity of practice and cognition. He limited himself to examining the historical subject, establishing the historical subject, but neglecting to examine the

---

[149] G. H. R. Parkinson: György *Lukács*, Page 201, See *Research Materials on Marxism-Leninism*, 1985, Division 4.

historical subject in the process of practice, especially in the activity of material production. The relation between subject and object is the relation of practice and then the relation of cognition and the latter is based on the former. Without this foundation, we cannot explain the relationship between subjects and objects scientifically, let alone the whole picture of social and historical development. Lukács did not deny that social and economic conditions determined people's consciousness. He also stressed repeatedly that the theory should be unified with practice, but as he later admitted, he lacked a correct understanding of Marx's labor thought, and thus made a narrow understanding of practice. Although he emphasized that "nature is a social category", he ignored the material transformation relationship between the subject and object of practice, and confined the object only to the realm of consciousness.

Secondly, Lukács regarded the complete and conscious consciousness as the mark of real human reality, and then ascribed the liberation of man to obtaining the complete class consciousness. The progress of historical development is mainly manifested in the progress of consciousness, and the history of mankind is mainly manifested in the history of the interaction between the subject and object of consciousness, which is the remnant of Hegel's philosophy. As G. Smitt, a professor of philosophy in the Federal Republic of Germany, pointed out, Lukács "regarded human being free from economic enslavement as the same thing as obtaining a complete and concrete historical consciousness. History and class consciousness are the same thing. They not only influence each other, but also have a speculative identity between them: history is the entity, and class consciousness is the subject."[150]

(III) The central task of the dialectics of Marxism lies in the cognition of alienation

---

[150]G. Smitt: *The Reappearance of Spiritual Phenomenology in Lukács' Historical Philosophy*, Published on *Translation Collection of Philosophy*, 1985 (2).

and the elimination of alienation.

Lukács wrote in the preface to the 1967 edition of *History and Class Consciousness*, in terms of social impact, the most important content of the book was the thought of alienation (that is, "materialization" of the original book). The issue of alienation "is regarded as the central issue of the revolutionary criticism of capitalism for the first time after Marx, and its theoretical and methodological roots lie in Hegel's dialectics. Of course, the question was unresolved at the time. A few years later, with the publication of Heidegger's (Martin Heidegger) *Being and Time* (1927), this question became the center of the philosophical debate. Even today, it has not lost its place. This is mainly due to the influence of Sartre (Jean-Paul Charles Aymard Sartre) and his followers and opponents in a debate."[151] McLellan also believed that Lukács' exposition of the concepts of alienation and materialization was the basis for the later Western Marxists to criticize bourgeois culture.[152]

Lukács applied the idea of collectivity to the explanation of capitalist society and gave full play to the analysis of commodity fetishism in *Das Kapital*, thus putting forward the thought of "materialization". In the book *History and Class Consciousness*, Lukács used "materialization" as the word "alienation". He believed that people's understanding of the world was hindered by some "phenomenon", which prevented people from obtaining the overall understanding of the world. This "phenomenon" is called "materialization". Beginning with the division of labor, he explained the relations of production of the capitalism, and the process of materialization caused by political institutions and bureaucracies. He believed that the materialization of workers was a prominent feature of capitalism. Workers were transformed into objects because they became traded goods in the labor market, and lost their emotions and understandings in the social relations between

[151]Lukács: *History and Class Consciousness*, Page xxii.

[152]See McLellan: *Marxism after Marx*, Page 222.

people; the production process (including the goods it produces) was directly controlled by the capitalists and indirectly controlled by the "laws" of supply and demand; and the workers passively carried out orders, and were not productive use value, but production exchange value with no choice of freedom. So in capitalist society, workers become the bystanders unable to control the social forces. Materialization was a necessary condition of capitalism. As long as the workers neglected the life of the real situation, they can endure isolation and the enslavement of the way of life. As long as the workers neglected their real roles in the flow of the whole and future liberated by them, they can endure the exploitation. The capitalist society strengthened this "neglect" through reasonable materialization in all aspects. Capitalism and materialization were only two aspects of the same realistic process. The real subjectivity was no longer the "self" of the individual, and there was no real subject in the materialized world. We must realize the identity of subject and object to eliminate materialization. According to this, Lukács put forward that "the main philosophical foundation for the practical solution to the materialization problem is the realization of its own identity of the subject and object in the historical process."[153] Once the proletariat understood the collectivity of society, they can realize the identity of subject and object and eliminate the phenomenon of materialization.

Lukács' explanation of alienation exactly and partly reflected the analysis of the tragic situation of the working class in the capitalist society by young Marx. At the same time, he also made a new understanding of the capitalist social phenomenon in his own time. However, Lukács regarded alienation as the "central" problem of Marx's criticism of capitalism, which was a superficial and even distorted understanding of Marx's thought.

First of all, Lukács did not really understand the theoretical essence of Marx's

---

[153]Lukács: *History and Class Consciousness*, Page xxiii.

scientific analysis and criticism of capitalism. In his early work *Economic and Philosophic Manuscripts of 1844*, Marx focused on his theory of alienated labor. Through the analysis of the economics and philosophy of labor, Marx pointed out that under the conditions of capitalism, workers were separated from their products and opposed to their own activities, and alienated with human nature. This alienation was manifested in the opposition between workers and capitalists in relations of people. The theory of alienated labor is a transitional theoretical form of Marx from the old theory to the scientific view of history, that is, historical materialism. In many ways, it also had the imprint of Hegel and Feuerbach. Marx did not stop at the analysis and explanation of alienated labor, but broke through the theory of alienated labor, and carried on scientific analysis and criticism to the capitalist society by further utilizing the basic principles of historical materialism such as the contradiction movement of productive forces and relations of production, and by applying the theory of surplus value.

Secondly, Lukács did not strictly distinguish the concepts of "materialization" and "alienation", and ignored that "alienation" was a historical category. Lukács regarded "materialization" (that is, the objectification of labor) as a special phenomenon in capitalist society, which was bound to cause confusion in theory. Although Lukács' explanation of "materialization" mainly referred to the peculiar phenomenon of alienation under the conditions of capitalist society, as he did not understand Marx's strict stipulations on "alienation" (*Economic and Philosophic Manuscripts of 1844* had not been published at that time), and neglected the economic origin of "alienation", it was impossible to explain Marx's early alienation thought scientifically.

Finally, as Lukács cannot correctly understand the profound historical root of alienation, it was impossible for him to put forward a correct way to overcome alienation. He appealed to the understanding of "collectivity" and the "identity" of the subject and object, which could at best achieve the purpose of eliminating the "fetishism" in the concept, but could not eliminate the objective alienation in reality. From the root of his thoughts, Lukács still understood Marx through Hegel on the issue of alienation, making the theory of Marx's critique of capitalist society subject to the speculative formula of "subject-subject alienation-subject return". Even in the early works of Marx there were traces of such kind of formula, which was only the inevitable and immature part of Marx's development from historical idealism to historical materialism. In the theoretical form of scientific historical materialism, there will be no such kind of traces. From here we can see once again that Lukács' desire to restore and expand Hegel's dialectics to restore the revolutionary nature of Marx's theory has not been realized.

4. An Attempt to Get out of the Nadir

Western Marxists claim that their reinterpretation of Marxism is to find a way to get the proletarian revolution in Western Europe out of its nadir. But they confuse Marxism with the Marxism that has been vulgarized by the Second International, and think that it is necessary to firstly get out of the nadir of Marxism development and make Marxism "recovery" revolution to get out of the nadir of revolution. In 1923, the same year that Lukács' *History and Class Consciousness* was published, Korsch published *Marxism and Philosophy*. In this book, he boosted to break through the rigid mode of mechanical interpretation of Marxism, which was popular in the Second International, and "reinterpreted" Marxism from many angles. And therefore, this work has laid down the prominent position of Korsch in the early period of Western Marxist thought. In the eyes of some people, Korsch is "the most outstanding person trying to rebuild Marx's original philosophy", and "is one of the most important representatives of revolutionary Marxism". Their "basis" is that Korsch established a "new" Marxist theme and theoretical framework just as like Lukács did.

It has been pointed out in the above that the Western Marxist trend of thought has a generally consistent academic tradition, which is to rely on Marxist philosophy, especially dialectics; but despise the analysis of economic and political structure. *Marxism and Philosophy* is a book that turns the theoretical focus to the field of philosophy.

From the formal point of view, the theme of *Marxism and Philosophy* is to clarify the relationship between Marxism and philosophy and to highlight or emphasize the philosophical aspects of Marxism; and in terms of the essence, it is to carry forward the subjective dialectics of history and to expound the essence of Marxism as a kind of social revolutionary theory. Around this theme, Korsch firstly reinterpreted Marxism by using Hegel's dialectics, the theoretical system before Marxism.

Korsch believed that the Marxist theorists of the Second International simply abandoned the philosophical problems in Marxism and denied that Marxism had a specific philosophical position. The reason lied in their lack of a correct understanding of the development of history and logic, and that was to say they could not see the influence of Hegel's philosophy on Marxism. Whether for a bourgeois philosophy professor or an orthodox Marxist, despite their different positions, they all agreed that Marxism had no philosophical content of its own. "This purely negative view of the relationship between Marxism and philosophy... is the result of a very superficial and incomplete analysis of historical and logical development."[154] That is to say, if the relationship between practice and theory is cut off, the original meaning of dialectical principle lying in its reflection of the real revolutionary movement cannot be seen, and the inherent relationship between Marxism and philosophy will be inevitably denied. The study of the relationship between Marxism and philosophy must firstly be based on the study of the relationship between Hegel's philosophy and Marxism. Korsch firstly established the investigation principle that: The relationship between the "thought movement" in a specific period and the "revolutionary movement" in the contemporary era is the key to understand German classical philosophy, and is also the key to

---

[154]Korsch: *Marxism and Philosophy*, Page 33.

understand the relationship between German classical philosophy and Marxism. The idealist philosophy from Kant to Hegel reflects the bourgeois revolutionary movement, while Marxist materialist philosophy reflects the proletarian revolutionary movement. Marxist dialectics is an extension of Hegel's dialectics, but the nature of the revolutionary movement reflected by the two is different. The essence of Marxist philosophy lies in that it is the general manifestation of the independent proletarian revolutionary movement, or it is a revolutionary dialectics in essence and a comprehensive and critical method of cognition. Although this understanding of Korsch emphasized the close connection between Marxism and the revolutionary movement of the proletariat, he showed obvious superficial and confusion in such problems as the understanding why Marxism had become the general manifestation of the proletarian revolutionary movement and why Marxist dialectics was revolutionary. First of all, Korsch believed that Marxist philosophy was only the development of German classical philosophy under the new historical conditions, and the difference between the two was only the difference between the class interests they reflected but not the nature of the two philosophies. He thought that there was a natural connection between the two from the common point that both German classical philosophy and Marxist philosophy represented the interests of certain classes, and pointed out that rather than saying that German classical philosophy, "the revolutionary movement in the ideological field, ended in 1840s, it only underwent a profound and meaningful change in nature. The classical German philosophy, which was the ideological expression of the bourgeois revolutionary movement, did not **end**, but **transformed** into a new science which was later manifested as the general manifestation of the proletarian revolutionary movement in the history of thought, that was the 'scientific socialism' theory firstly put forward and established in 1840s by Marx and Engels".①[155] (In Korsch's view, the theory of scientific socialism itself also embodied philosophy,

---

[155]Korsch: *Marxism and Philosophy*, Page 41.

namely, materialistic dialectics.) Marxist dialectics transformed from German classical philosophy was merely the product of the idea of the proletariat—the subject of the revolution, and was not the result of scientific analysis of the whole world, especially the capitalist reality. This kind of excessive emphasis on the Hegel origin of materialist dialectics was merely limited to the view of understanding the revolutionary nature of dialectics with the main interests of the proletariat, obliterated the real significance of materialist dialectics in the reform of old philosophy, and neglected the inherent scientific nature of materialist dialectics. Secondly, while reminding people of the Hegel origin of Marxist philosophy, Korsch ascribed philosophy only to a cognitive method. Anderson once pointed out: "In the whole Western Marxist tradition, the extent to which the subject of epistemology dominates can be seen in the title of his masterpiece. Korsch's *Marxism and Philosophy* has set the basic norms from the outset."[156] The "basic norms" mentioned here means that Korsch is trying to recognize a method of cognition that embodies the collectivity and criticality as the essence of Marxism just as Lukács do. However, the method of cognition advocated by Korsch is mainly a kind of subjective dialectics, which despises the analysis of objective conditions and is keen to explain the subjective conditions of proletarian revolution. He failed to grasp the dual characteristics of Marxist philosophy (including dialectics), which was both a scientific methodology and a scientific worldview, so that he did not pay attention to the materialistic basis of dialectics, nor did him attach importance to the scientific explanation of the objective world. In *Marxism and Philosophy*, his use of the concept of "philosophy" was rather confusing, with no distinction between general philosophy and concrete philosophy. He sometimes said that dialectical materialism was philosophical in nature; sometimes believed that Marx and Engels tried to "overcome and destroy the general philosophy" with scientific socialism (in fact, the concept of "general philosophy" used by Korsch expresses bourgeois

---

[156]Anderson: *Considerations on Western Marxism*, Page 69.

philosophy); sometimes said that Marxist philosophy was the method of scientific understanding; and sometimes asserted that Marxism advocated "abrogation of philosophy" just like abolishing the country, thus equated philosophy with the ideology of a certain historical period. The confusion in understanding and expression of philosophy often made Korsch's argumentation of restoring Marxist philosophy to be self-contradictory.

When discussing the relationship between Marxism and philosophy, Korsch tried to expound his views on the essence of Marxism by criticizing positivism.

In his opinion, the reason why the relationship between Marxism and philosophy was a major theoretical and practical problem lied in that vulgar Marxists treated philosophical problems passively and empirically, thus misunderstood the essence of Marxism, resulting in negative consequences in the revolutionary practice. In *The Current Situation of the Problems of Marxism and Philosophy-- Counter-Criticism* (1930) written by Korsch in response to people's accusations, he thought the most distinctive feature of *Marxism and Philosophy* lied in that it developed a completely non-dogmatic and anti-dogmatic, historical and critical, thus the strictest materialistic view, which was to apply historical materialism to examine materialism itself.①[157] This can be understood from two aspects: Firstly, Korsch tried to illustrate the stage of the development of Marxism itself by the unity of the practice and theory. Secondly, explanation of each stage of the development of Marxism with the Marxist philosophy as the guidance is based on the dialectics with the philosophy and emphasis on the collectivity as the core. The purpose of this investigation carried out by Korsch was to illustrate the epistemological origin of the vulgarization and positivism of Marxist theory. According to his division, Marxism had gone through three stages of development. The first stage began around 1843 (with the theoretical symbol of *Critique of Hegel's Philosophy of Right*)

---

[157]See Korsch: *Marxism and Philosophy*, Page 92.

and ended in 1848 (corresponding to *The Communist Manifesto*); the second stage began with the defeat of the Paris proletariat in June 1848 and ended at the end of the 19th century; and the third stage, started from the 20th century to the time of the writing of *Marxism and Philosophy*, and will continue to the uncertain future. In each of these stages, Marxism embodied the unity of theory and practice (despite the ups and downs of the revolutionary wave), and ran through dialectics. In terms of theoretical form, the theory at the first stage permeated philosophy, which was a theory to understand and practice social development as a living whole, namely, to grasp the theory of social revolution as a whole, and to grasp factors such as economy, politics and thoughts as a whole. With the development of the revolutionary situation in the second half of the 19th century, this initial theoretical form will inevitably change. The theory at the second stage had not changed in essence, and it was still the theory of the overall social revolution. The difference between it and the early theoretical form was only in the different parts of the whole theory of the later stage, namely, its economic theory, political theory and ideology theory were gradually divided, and scientific theory was further separated from social practice (this separation was merely formal). The overall natural umbilical cord of the original theory had been cut off, and the theory of various fields had been developed relatively independently, which was the progress of the theory. However, the vulgar Marxists such as Hilferding and others were completely puzzled, and only understood Marxism as a "science" of economics or politics. They froze this flowing methodology of materialist dialectics into a purely theoretical formula for studying causality in the field of social history, and advocated a purely objective "scientific" research method that rejected value judgment, thus reducing Marxism to the level of empirical science. Against this positivist tendency, Korsch pointed out that Marxism was by no means a "science" in the sense of positivism, and cognition did not reflect reality passively, but actively constituted the complex and interpenetrating world. Marxism is mainly a kind of value cognition. Any purely scientific or purely objective theoretical investigation which is divorced from practice is incompatible with Marxism. Vulgar Marxists made Marxist theory fragmented, split it into isolated and spontaneous branches of knowledge, led to the crisis of Marxism and made Marxism lose its revolution. In view of this situation, Korsch believed that the central task facing the development of Marxism to the third stage was to correct the mistakes of vulgar Marxists in shifting their focus to the outside world, called on them to return to the main body of the revolution proletariat itself, so as to solve the subjective conditions of revolution, or to solve the theoretical basis of revolution in the ideological field.

There is no denying that Korsch's criticism of positivism tendencies has some reasonable factors. Since some theorists of the Second International have vulgarized Marxism, no one had examined the history of Marxism to reveal the epistemological roots of the positivism tendency at that time. But since Korsch had taken an extreme position to analyze the problem, unilateralism was inevitable. Although he admitted in form that Marxism was the unity of scientific cognition and value cognition, he confined the premise of argumentation to the framework of the subject, so it was difficult to correctly reproduce the scientific nature of Marxism. It was difficult to imagine that simply pouring into the contemplation of the subject world will lead to a scientific understanding of the object world related to the subject. Korsch proposed the use of materialist dialectics to analyze the development history of Marxism, and advocated to investigate the theoretical form of Marxism according to the development of proletarian revolutionary practice, which was a meaningful attempt. However, he did not thoroughly carry out this analytical principle, which was mainly manifested in his overestimated evaluation on the early works such as *Critique of Hegel's Philosophy of Right* that were immature and cannot be listed as the scientific and theoretical performance of the proletarian revolutionary movement in strict speaking, and his ignorance of the relative independence of the development of each component of the Marxist theory.

In the process of trying to "rebuild" the subjective dialectics of Marxism, Korsch also put forward the theory of ideological criticism, which was a further display of the principle of collectivity that regarding the ideological movement and the actual revolutionary movement as a unified historical collectivity. According to the principle of the collectivity, ideology should be regarded as the same reality as other social factors, that is, material factors, but not simply as an adjunct to economic factors.

In Korsch's view, in the new revolutionary struggle period, the important question of the relationship between the proletarian revolution and ideology, which had been forgotten by many people, was brought back. According to dialectical materialism, ideology (including philosophy) should be understood as reality in theory and treated as reality in practice. Marx attached great importance to the criticism of ideology from the beginning. Firstly, he criticized religion from a philosophical point of view; secondly, he criticized religion and philosophy from the political aspect; and finally, he criticized religion, philosophy, politics and other ideologies from the economic aspect. The mission of Marxist philosophy was to fight in this particular field of philosophy, and to participate in the revolutionary struggle against the entire existing order. A thorough critique of bourgeois society must begin with the political economy as a particular form of consciousness. And therefore, the criticism of political economy should be the most important both in theory and practice. Korsch also emphasized the consistency of consciousness and reality, which was the characteristic of all dialectics including Marx's materialist dialectics. The logical conclusion of this principle was: The material relations of production in the capitalist era were merely something combined with the bourgeois ideology that reflected it, without which it cannot survive. In other words, the ideology manifesting the capitalist society as a whole in a unique way constitutes the spiritual structure of the society, which supports the economic structure of the society. And therefore, the proletariat must destroy this spiritual structure with thought and action; and the ideological action, as the theoretical criticism and agitation before the proletariat seized power, and the dictatorship of ideology after the seizure of political power, must be carried out to the end in theory and practice.

Korsch emphasized on criticizing the social structure of capitalism in general and criticizing the bourgeois ideology, but he ignored such an important fact that Marx always emphasized that the criticism of practice was higher than the criticism of thought or theory, and the eradication of bourgeois ideology depended in the final analysis on overcoming the capitalist economic system and political system, which were the reality foundation of the bourgeois ideology. If "weapon criticism" and "critical weapon" were juxtaposed indiscriminately, or the criticism of thought was above the criticism of practice, and putting aside the truth that "material power can only be destroyed by material forces" will surely lead the proletarian revolutionary movement astray.

If Korsch's idealistic tendencies were still concealed in *Marxism and Philosophy*, in *The Current Situation of the Problems of Marxism and Philosophy-- Counter-Criticism* (1930), by publicly denouncing Lenin, Korsch showed his contempt for the materialist stance. He thought he had adhered to the line of shifting the center of gravity from materialism to dialectics. Lenin, on the other hand, insisted on turning from dialectics to materialism. In his opinion, Marx and Engels were committed to saving dialectics from German classical philosophy, while Lenin did the opposite and believed that the main task of Marxism was to support and maintain the materialist worldview which no one had ever seriously thought of questioning it. He believed that Lenin's materialism had a serious defect that cancelled Marx's and Engels's reverse on the materialism of Hegel's dialectics, brought the whole argument between materialism and idealism back to the historical stage that German idealism from Kant to Hegel has transcended, that meant to return to the absolute opposites of "thought" and "being", "spirit" and "substance" of the old materialism in the 18th century. In his point of view, Lenin's philosophy of materialism originated from the absolute metaphysical concept of existence, which was no longer dialectical, let alone dialectical materialism. Lenin and his followers unilaterally turned dialectics into the cognition of the object, nature and history, and described cognition as a negative reflection of objective existence in subjective consciousness. And therefore, they not only destroyed the dialectical relationship between existence and consciousness, but also breached the dialectical relationship between theory and practice, abandoned the relationship between the whole of historical existence and all ideology, and replaced it with such narrow epistemological problems as the subject and object of cognition. He also believed that Lenin always treated the real society from an abstract epistemological point of view, had never analyzed the cognition on the same level as other social historical consciousness, nor had viewed it as a historical phenomenon.

Korsch's accusation mentioned above was not only a serious distortion of Lenin's thought, but also showed his deviation from the philosophical position of materialism. In fact, Lenin had made great contributions to the development of Marxist dialectics, epistemology and historical view. Both Lenin's numerous writings and the practice of the October Revolution had irrefutably proved that Lenin was the model to adhere to the unity of theory and practice, and the unity of subjective dialectics and objective dialectics. However, Korsch himself failed to fully understand the essence of Marxist philosophy, refused to explain the basic problems of philosophy both dialectically and materially, consciously or unconsciously separated materialism from dialectics, and criticized Lenin's defense of Marxist philosophy's materialistic stand as a retrogression of philosophy, which fully shown that Korsch was further away from materialistic position.

In the middle of 1930s, Korsch wrote *Why I am a Marxist*, and summarized the essence of Marxism as follows: The whole principle of Marxism was fundamentally special. Even the principles that appear to be universal were the same; Marxism was not positive, but critical; the theme of Marxism was not the capitalist society which was now in a positive state, but the declining capitalist society; and the main purpose of Marxism was not to admire the existing world, but to actively transform it. On the surface, this generalization of Korsch highlighted the particularity, criticality and practicality of Marxism, but according to his specific explanation, he actually revealed the tendency of cutting off the universality and particularity, the scientificalness and criticalness, the theoreticalness and practicalness.

In the universality and particularity of Marxism, Korsch blindly emphasized the concrete analysis and despised the general theoretical generalization, which damaged the scientificalness of Marxism as a universal truth. At the same time, his understanding of science was rather superficial. For example, he accused Engels of treating historical materialism in a non-historical and abstract way, arguing that Engels recklessly recognized the so-called "reaction" between superstructure and economic foundation, ideology and economy and politics, which caused unnecessary confusion to the foundation of historical materialism. For if the actions and reactions occurred cannot be accurately confirmed in number, and the conditions under which one or another occurs cannot be precisely described, the whole Marxist theory of social and historical development will be of no use. It is not difficult to find out from these criticisms that Korsch, who preached the tendency of anti-positivism, is using the model of positivism to set up Marxism, and reduce philosophical analysis to the level of empirical science. He cannot see that Marxist philosophy is scientific because it is a general summary of objective laws (including social laws). It is impossible and unnecessary to describe all the details in the field of social history as precisely as the empirical science. Korsch's understanding of Marxism, both critical and practical, is equally superficial, because it thrown away scientificalness, which is the premise of practicality.

In the early days of his theoretical career, Korsch considered himself a devout believer in Marxism. In fact, his "reconstruction" of Marxism was a deviation from Marxism. However, when Lukács seriously reflected on his early theoretical deviations and declared that he would return to Marxism. Korsch went from deviation to betrayal of Marxism. In 1950, Korsch wrote *Ten Theses on Marxism*

Today[158], and put it bluntly: "To what extent Marx and Engels' doctrine is theoretically effective and practically feasible today, and there is no longer any meaning. ... The first step in reconstructing revolutionary theory and practice is to break up with the monopoly demand of Marxism on revolutionary initiative and leading position in theory and practice." This kind of betrayal of early faith is a tragedy of Korsch's theoretical career, and is also the inevitable outcome of all "Marxists" who attempt to dismember Marxism.

5. Practical Philosophy and Cultural Criticism

Gramsci is a famous Italian proletarian revolutionist and theoretician. In the course of leading the Communist Party of Italy to carry out the proletarian revolution, he devoted himself to combining Marxism with the actual situation in Italy to explore a revolutionary road suited to Italy's national conditions. He put forward new ideas different from the understanding of most Marxists at that time in philosophy, political thought and so on, with theoretical tendencies agreed well with that of Lukács and Korsch in many ways. Between 1929 and 1936, Gramsci wrote the far-reaching *The Prison Notebooks* in fascist prison. In this book, which represents his main theoretical achievements, he focused on the theory of superstructure, among which the thought of practical philosophy and cultural criticism had a great influence on the later Western Marxism.

Gramsci's theory of practical philosophy and cultural criticism was put forward directly against the "economism" and "unionism", which were popular in the Italian workers' movement at that time. In reality, the "economism" and "unionism" constituted the main ideological obstacle of the socialist revolution. Gramsci attributed the theoretical characteristics of economism to three aspects: (I) In the study of historical connections, he did not distinguish necessity from contingency, regarded economic reality as the benefit of individuals or small groups, and ignored

---

[158]See *Marxist Research Materials*, 1983, Division 3.

the main economic classes and all their relationships. (II) He ascribed economic development to the process of technological reform in labor tools. (III) He believed that the development of economy and history was directly determined by the change of an important factor of production, and depended on the use of new technologies and new scientific discoveries. In a word, economism understood economy from a narrow perspective and declared that economy was everything. In a sense, unionism was a kind of strategy performance of economism, advocating that the workers' movement should be confined to the economic field. Both economism and unionism had neglected the superstructure of social development and reduced the political and cultural consciousness of the workers. As a result, the proletarian revolution was delayed. Gramsci stressed that the prerequisite for the success of socialism was not the inevitability of economic development, but the people to truly realize a change of consciousness. The essence of this change was to abolish the cultural traditions carried out by the bourgeoisie in the fields of education, media, law, religion and family, and to establish a new culture of the proletarian masses, that was, to establish the new values of the proletariat so that they can get rid of their subordinate and passive position in spirit. In order to achieve this goal, we must reinterpret the essence of Marxism and correct the mistakes of vulgar Marxism.

Gramsci believed that Marxism was the philosophy of practice, and "the center of unity of the philosophy was practice"[159] His interpretation of practical philosophy included the following contents.

(I) The Essence of Practical Philosophy

Different from the traditional materialism, the practical philosophy is not the materialism understood by positivism or naturalism, nor the idealism in the sense of Neo-Kantianism. The concept of the practical philosophy was inspired by

---

[159]Gramsci: *The Prison Notebooks*, Page 84.

Labriola. In examining Marxism, "it is necessary to revalue the problem as Antonio Labriola has tried to do."[160] "Labriola asserts that the philosophy of practice is an independent and original philosophy with its own elements of continued development. These factors can turn the interpretation of history into a universal philosophy, and it is in this direction that work has to be done to develop the position of Antonio Labriola."[161] As we know, Labriola used to call the core of historical materialism as "practical philosophy" in *The Materialist Conception Of History*, and thought that practical philosophy not only focused on life and labor, but also on thought and abstract theory. "All activities of thinking are an effort, in other words, a new job." Cognition itself is a kind of labor process, which is intertwined with practical labor activities and people's social contacts. Practical activities make thought no longer a "premise or forecast" of things, but "a concrete thing". Cognition and its objects are concretized in practice.[162] Gramsci followed this thought and thought that the true meaning of practical philosophy laid in its adherence to the unity of theory and practice.

How did Gramsci understand the unity of theory and practice? He believed that the unity of theory and practice cannot be based on mechanism. In many works on Marxism, the unity of theory and practice were discussed, but both theory and practice were dismembered. This was mainly manifested in taking the theory as the "appendix", "supplement" and "servant" of practice. "When the two elements of theory and practice were not only divided, but also separated and broken (the process itself was purely mechanical and conditional), the leading role of the element "practice" in the unity of theory and practice should be stuck to, which indicated that the movement was not out of relatively primitive history stage

---

[160]Gramsci: *The Prison Notebooks*, Page 70.

[161]Gramsci: *The Prison Notebooks*, Page 71~72.

[162]See Nalski: *Marxist Philosophy in the 19th Century* II, Page 297~298.

movement, and the movement was still getting through the economic-group stage."[163] The economic-group stage mentioned here refers to the initial or infantile stage of the development of class consciousness. Gramsci went further than Labriola in emphasizing the unity of theory and practice. That is to say, he advocated that the theory should be regarded as an intrinsic element of practice and the theory as the leading factor. As for the unity of theory and practice, Gramsci summarized that: "It is a kind of critical action to unify theory and practice. In such an action, the reasonableness and necessity of practice or the reality and reasonableness of theory are proved."[164] What is the significance of emphasizing the philosophy of practice and the unity of theory and practice? Gramsci believed that in the period of rapid social change, especially in the transitional period when the proletariat reformed the society through revolution, only by unifying the theory and practice directly can, on one hand, ensure the correct exertion of the practical force and make the practical force more effective with expanded influences, and on the other hand, make the revolutionary theoretical program effectively implemented.

According to the spirit of practical philosophy, the will must be carried out into historical inevitability. According to this understanding, Gramsci understood practical philosophy as "dialectics of historical power". This kind of "dialectics of historical power will become the only dialectics". The understanding of historical inevitability of historical dialectics must be understood in the sense of "history-concrete", but cannot be understood in the sense of "abstract-speculative". "When there is a real and positive premise, this premise has been effective and realized by people, has put forward concrete ideas in the face of collective consciousness, and has created a set of beliefs and ideas that have the

---

[163]Gramsci: *The Prison Notebooks*, Page 17.

[164]Gramsci: *The Prison Notebooks*, Page 50.

power of 'people's prejudice', there is inevitability."[165] Only in this way can we historically understand the "reasonableness" of history. Through this understanding, Gramsci aimed to tell people that history was understood fatally. Mechanically treating people's will as a negative thing attached to necessity can only lead to the atrophy of the proletarian revolutionary will.

Gramsci advocated that practical philosophy should be understood as practical monism, and that was to say, practical philosophy was neither material nor limited to spirit, but to grasp the unity of matter and spirit in the course of history in philosophical understanding. "What does the term 'monism' mean? Of course it is neither materialistic nor idealistic. This term will indicate the identity of opposites in specific historical acts. It is a concrete human activity (history-spirit) that is inextricably linked to a particular organized (historicized) 'matter' and the nature transformed by man."[166]

Although Gramsci emphasized the practical characteristics of Marxist philosophy and stressed the organic unity of theory and practice, his understanding of practice itself was too broad, and to some extent confused between practice and theoretical philosophy, the viewpoint of practice, materialism and dialectics were organic and unified. However, when Gramsci emphasized the importance of practice, he had a tendency to antagonize practice and materialism. This practical monism and practical ontology opened the door to idealism through practicalism.

(II) The Origin of Practical Philosophy

Gramsci understood practical philosophy as an element of modern culture. Practical philosophy is premised on such past cultures: Such as the Renaissance and religious reform, German philosophy and the French Revolution, Calvinism and

---

[165]Gramsci: *The Prison Notebooks*, Page 95.

[166]Gramsci: *The Prison Notebooks*, Page 58.

classical political economics of Britain. Gramsci was not content to talk about the origin of practical philosophy from the point of view of general cultural history, but focused on the relationship between practical philosophy and old philosophy to oppose the dismemberment of the understanding of practical philosophy through the explanation of the elimination of opposition between "materialism" and "idealism" contained in the philosophy of practice itself. He thought: "The founder of practical philosophy reinvigorated the whole set of experiences of Hegelianism, Feuerbach doctrine and French materialism in order to restore dialectical unity, but it was already 'a man standing on both feet'. Practical philosophy has also been subjected to the experience of Hegel's doctrine: People have also tried to tear it apart into several parts; there are things that break away from dialectical unity and return to philosophical materialism, while the advanced idealist culture attempts to include in practical philosophy what is needed to produce a new drug."[167] People get what they want, or they explain the old materialism to the philosophy of practice, or to explain modern idealism to practical philosophy. This phenomenon urges Gramsci to pay attention to Hegel's philosophy, which he considered to be the most influential theoretical source of practical philosophy. It seems that the essence of practical philosophy can be truly understood from Hegel.

In Gramsci's view, although practical philosophy comes from three cultural movements: German classical philosophy, English classical political economics and the political works and practice of the French Revolution, the three of them are integrated into an intrinsic new concept, which is based on the German classical philosophy. "The concept of practical philosophy is transformed from the German classical philosophy put forward in its speculative form with the aid of French [revolutionary] politics and Britain's classical [politics] economics into a historical form."[168] So he thought "practical philosophy is equivalent to Hegel and David

---

[167]Gramsci: *The Prison Notebooks*, Page 78.

[168]Gramsci: *The Prison Notebooks*, Page 82.

Ricardo." [169] The significance of Hegel's philosophy lies in helping people understand the reality of history and the unity of human spirit, that is, the unity of history and nature. "The practical philosophy is, in a sense, the reform and development of Hegel's doctrine, is the philosophy of getting rid of (or trying to get rid of) any element of one-sidedness and fanaticism in the system of thought, and is a full understanding of contradictions. Philosophers themselves who are understood as individuals or social groups not only understand contradiction but also regard themselves as a factor of contradiction and raise this factor to the principle of action."[170] With the help of Hegel's philosophy, Gramsci wanted to explain that practical philosophy understood reality as contradiction, as the unity of opposites, and as the unity of the subject itself and the outside world, and promoted the subject and its concept to the basic criterion of practical action. It was undoubtedly a play to Hegel's thought that "man constructs reality according to thought".

(III) The Mission of Practical philosophy

In terms of his subjective intention, Gramsci's understanding of practical philosophy was related to the struggle strategy of the proletarian revolution. He held that practical philosophy was charged with two tasks, one is to "overcome the modern ideological system in the most subtle form."[171] That is, to defeat the bourgeois ideological system and to criticize the bourgeois cultural tradition thoroughly; and secondly, to "form their own independent intellectual group and to educate the masses of the people with medieval culture."[172] In Gramsci's mind, practical philosophy is a worldview that confronts modern idealism in modern

---

[169]Gramsci: *The Prison Notebooks*, Page 82.

[170]Gramsci: *The Prison Notebooks*, Page 86.

[171]Gramsci: *The Prison Notebooks*, Page 74.

[172]Gramsci: *The Prison Notebooks*, Page 74.

culture. This kind of worldview is now confined to the narrow intellectual clique and must be transformed into a conscious understanding of the masses. "Practical philosophy tries not to keep 'ordinary people' from remaining at the level of their primitive common sense philosophy, on the contrary, it tries to guide them to a higher level form of understanding of life."[173] In short, practical philosophy is an important weapon in the cultural struggle of the armed proletariat.

Connected with the social function of practical philosophy, Gramsci proposed that attention should be paid to the role of the proletarian party, because only the proletarian party could guide the proletarian movement with practical philosophy and organically combine the theory and practice. Only when the proletarian movement is at its initial stage, without the guidance of the political parties representing the interests of that class, can the masses act in practice unconsciously. Thus, it is impossible to be politically mature. To get out of this situation, "special emphasis should be placed on the importance and significance of political parties in the modern world in developing and disseminating the worldview, because they basically develop ethics and politics that conform to these worldviews, that is, as special 'experimenters' from these worldviews in their historical activities. The Party makes individual choices from the active masses, and this choice is interrelated both in practice and in theory; moreover, the more vigorous the new worldview itself is in dealing with the old way of thinking, the more aggressive innovation and confrontation are, and the closer the relationship between theory and practice becomes. And therefore, it can be said that the Party is cultivating new, complete and inescapable intelligence, that is to say, the Party is like a crucible, melting theory with practice understood as a real historical process in a furnace.[174] Gramsci emphasized the significance of theory to the revolutionary movement and the important role of proletarian parties in the process of the proletariat's transition from a free class to a conscious class, which was consistent

---

[173]Gramsci: *The Prison Notebooks*, Page 14~15.

[174]Gramsci: *The Prison Notebooks*, Page 17~18.

with Lenin's thought.

From Gramsci's interpretation of practical philosophy, we can see that his theory focuses on the field of superstructure. Specifically, his practical philosophy was but the philosophical foundation of his theory of superstructure. From emphasizing the reality or importance of the theory, Gramsci not only pointed out the important role of political parties, but also pointed out the important role of intellectuals, and put forward the thought of leadership.

McLellan pointed out: "Gramsci has been known as a superstructure theorist. The reason for this is nothing more than the centrality of his mind to the task of intellectuals."[175] Gramsci regarded every man as an intellectual, as he called every man a philosopher. The former means that each person has not only a special worldview, but also a self-conscious code of moral behavior), while the latter means that everyone has a worldview (even a simple worldview or common sense philosophy. They are all engaged in some form of mental labor. "Traditional" intellectuals cannot play their due roles in the proletarian revolutionary movement as such intellectuals lack class self-consciousness with their consciousness deviating from the real society. Whereas "organized" intellectuals can express a clear sense of collective or class consciousness, which is consciously realizing the position and role of their subordinate class in the economic field and the social and political field. Only such intellectuals can play an active role in the proletarian revolutionary movement. The task faced by the proletariat is to bring up its own organized intellectuals quickly. In the process of completing this task, it is necessary to struggle for the ideological assimilation and conquest of traditional intellectuals; the faster and more effective this assimilation and conquest is, the more successful the proletariat is in nurturing its organized intellectuals.

The most important in the work of cultivating organized intellectuals is to enable them to truly and completely master a complete and unified set of worldviews, that is, what he calls practical philosophy. It is in this sense that Gramsci believes

---

[175]McLellan: *Marxism after Marx*, Page 244.

that the political concept of leadership is a development of practical philosophy.[176] The meaning of the leadership given by Gramsci refers to the certain stage reached by the proletarian revolutionary movement, that is, the proletariat constitutes a unified "historical group" with itself as the main body in the aspects of economy, politics and ideology and plays a leading role in the class alliance formed in the process of opposing the bourgeoisie. He placed the morality and knowledge of the proletariat at the heart of this leadership, put culture and ideology at the forefront of leadership, for it is more difficult to achieve ideological domination of the real society. The proletariat must firstly acquire such leadership and then gain and rule the leadership. To get such leadership, we must firstly criticize the traditional culture according to the spirit of practical philosophy, and construct a new people's culture.

Just like Lukács and Korsch who emphasized the overall revolution in terms of overcoming materialization and ideological criticism, Gramsci often used cultural struggle (criticism) to express his understanding of the overall revolution. He used culture to express all the philosophical, moral, religious and other ideological phenomena in the real society, and regarded this kind of cultural superstructure as the same reality as economic phenomenon.

Gramsci regarded the philosophy of practice itself as the core of a new culture. "Advocating that practical philosophy is a new, independent and original theory and is also one of the factors of the historical development of the world is to advocate the independence and originality of a new and mature culture that will develop with the development of social relations." [177] According to the understanding of practical philosophy, the historical action needs certain material conditions, but the material premise "cannot be divorced from a certain level of education, in other words, it cannot be divorced from a certain sum of intellectual behavior, whereas from these intellectual behaviors there is no escape from the

---

[176]See Gramsci: *The Prison Notebooks*, Page 16.

[177]Gramsci: *The Prison Notebooks*, Page 80.

sum of the passions and emotions (as a product and result of them)with a dominant power, because these passions and emotions can force people to act 'at any costs'."[178] "The 'faith of the people' or this type of thought has material power."[179] This realistic spiritual force forms the motive force of the cultural struggle. And therefore, Gramsci actively advocated "allocating" the cultural power of the proletariat from the spiritual point of view. The proletariat must pay attention to overcoming the phenomenon of cultural alienation in the process of creating its own culture. In the capitalist society, cultural products, like other material products, are externalized from the spirit of human beings and are opposed to human beings. The task of the proletariat is to seize these cultural products, so the creation of a non-bourgeois culture is the same historical process as a culture that is truly possessed and alienated in spirit.

Seen from Gramsci's thoughts mentioned above, he pinned his hopes for success on the outbreak of a general revolution based on spiritual practice or theoretical action. Gramsci's philosophy of practice was as the same as Lukács' dialectics of historical subject and object with the power of thought overestimated in its main theoretical tendencies.

From the study of the thoughts of Lukács, Kirsch and Gramsci, it is not difficult to see that their attempts to "rebuild" Marxism is a failure. Many of their views are not conducive to the development of Marxism, and also provide a theoretical "basis" for the dismemberment of Marx by Western Marxism and Western Marxist doctrine.

---

[178]Gramsci: *The Prison Notebooks*, Page 95.

[179]Gramsci: *The Prison Notebooks*, Page 139.

CHAPTER 4   THE MYTHOLOGY OF "TWO MARX"

Controversies are common in the history of thought to find his unpublished works after the death of a great thinker. However, the worldwide long and fierce controversy caused by Marx's *Economic and Philosophic Manuscripts of 1844* is quite rare. The publication of *Economic and Philosophic Manuscripts of 1844* provides a new justification for the thought of "rebuilding" Marxism that already existed. For more than half a century, it has become the so-called "basis" for many Western bourgeois thinkers and neo-Marxists to reinterpret Marxism. The creation of "two Marx's antagonism" is a proof that Marx was further dismembered with impunity.

1. "New Discovery" of Western Marxism

In 1932, a manuscript that was not published during Marx's lifetime and was long hidden by Bernstein and others was published almost simultaneously in the Soviet Union and Germany.[180] The manuscript was referred to as *The Paris Manuscripts* or *Economic and Philosophic Manuscripts of 1844*. The publication of *Economic and Philosophic Manuscripts of 1844* became the most important event in the history of Marxist thought in the 20th century. Such a "special treatment" that the manuscript encountered may have been unexpected to Marx.

---

[180]The Russian translation of the manuscript was published by Riazanov (David Riazanov) in *Karl Marx and Friedrich Engels* (*Архив К. Маркса и Ф.Энгелса*) as early as 1927. In 1932, the Soviet Institute of Marxism-Leninism published the German edition of the manuscript in Volume 3, Part 1 of the international edition of *Marx/Engels Collected Works* (MEGA). The title is *The Manuscripts of Economics and Philosophy of 1844. Criticism of National Economics*. At the same time, two German social democrats, Landshut and Mayer, also published the German edition of the manuscript in *Karl Marx: Der historische Materialismus; Die Frühschriften*, entitled *National Economics and Philosophy*.

The birth of the myth of "Two Marx" and the publication of the manuscript was almost at the same time, because the myth was not created by anyone else, but was exactly one of the original publishers of the German edition of *Economic and Philosophic Manuscripts of 1844*, the Germany's rightwing socialists named Landshut (Siegfried Landshut) and Mayer (J. P. Mayer Herausgeber).

First of all, in the publication preface to *Economic and Philosophic Manuscripts of 1844*, they declared that *Economic and Philosophic Manuscripts of 1844* was a "true revelation of Marxism", "the central work of Marx" and "the only document in which Marx's intellect showed all its power". They also claimed that the coming out of this work was bound to change people's understanding of the "standard concept" of Marxism and thus had "decisive significances" to the argument of "new Marxism".[181]

So what did they "find" in *Economic and Philosophic Manuscripts of 1844*? They thought that the central idea of *Economic and Philosophic Manuscripts of 1844* was that Marx regarded "the full realization and development of human nature" as "the true purpose of history". In *Economic and Philosophic Manuscripts of 1844*, Marx produced the principle of economic analysis directly from the thought of "the real reality of man". "The general title of Marx's contradiction in understanding reality is 'self-alienation'. Marx's central idea is "alienation", so the famous principle of *The Communist Manifesto* is that the history of society is the history of class struggle. It was even rewritten into "the whole history of the past is the history of human self-alienation."[182]

According to the understanding of Landshut and Mayer, the significance of

---

[181] See Landshut and Mayer: *Karl Marx: Der historische Materialismus; Die Frühschriften*, Vol. 1, Page VIII, Page XIII, and Page XXXVIII, Leipzig, 1932.

[182] Landshut and Mayer: *Karl Marx: Der historische Materialismus; Die Frühschriften*, Vol. 1, Page XXIII.

Economic and Philosophic Manuscripts of 1844 was that it opened the way for the "reinterpretation" of Marxism in the spirit of ethical socialism. This ethical socialism negated the "vulgar" idea of depriving the deprived, and preached a subjective necessity to "realize the real missions of the human beings".[183]

Henri de Man (1885-1953), Belgium, another right-wing social democrat, pointed out more clearly in *Newly Discovered Marx* published in the same period (1932) that *Economic and Philosophic Manuscripts of 1844* "is much more explicit than any of Marx's other works in revealing the ethical and humanitarian motives that lie behind his socialist beliefs and the values of all his scientific creations throughout his life." [184] "This kind of motivation is humanitarian, not economic. Marx demonstrated the theory of motivation from the aspects of anthropology and psychology, by the natural pursuit of purpose by the desire generated by passion and need."[185] He thought that "we must never dismiss Marx's work as an 'immature' work of his youth time."[186] On the contrary, "I think, in terms of the quality of his work, Marx's achievements culminated between 1843 and 1848. No matter how highly people think of his later works, these works show some kind of decline and erosion of creativity, even the bravest effort will not always overcome

---

[183]Landshut and Mayer: *Karl Marx: Der historische Materialismus; Die Frühschriften*, Vol. 1, Page XLI.

[184]Henri de Man: *Newly Discovered Marx*, Published in the magazine of *Struggle*, Vienna, Issue 5-6, 1932, Quoted from *Studies (Collection) on Economic and Philosophic Manuscripts of 1844*, Page 348, Changsha, Hu'nan People's Publishing House, 1983.

[185]Quoted from *Studies (Collection) on Economic and Philosophic Manuscripts of 1844*, Page 368.

[186]Quoted from *Studies (Collection) on Economic and Philosophic Manuscripts of 1844*, Page 370.

this."[187]

The main purpose of Landshut and others to raise "Young Marx" and create the myth of "Two Marx" was to "humanize" and "philosophize" Marxism. They said, as long as "taking a comprehensive look at Marx's works of 30 years ago, it will be more clear that: All the rich contents of Marx's spiritual world have been narrowed down to such a narrow scope by the exhibitors of Marx's thoughts so far, and how poor they have been made by 'materialism'."[188] And therefore, it has become a top priority to restore all the rich contents of Marxist humanitarianism.

The myth of "Two Marx" set a humanitarian "Young Marx" against the so-called "traditional" Marxism, that is, Marx and Engels' thoughts in later years. Henri de Man publicly proposed a "dilemma", that is "or if the this humanitarian Marx was regarded as a Marxist, then Marxism of both Kautsky and Bukharin (Nikolai Ivanovich Bukharin /Николай Иванович Бухарин) must be completely revised; or if this humanitarian Marx was note regarded as Marxism, then there will be a humanitarian Marxism that people can use to oppose materialistic Marxism."[189]

We should see that the myth of "Two Marx" was born in the 1930s. This is not the whim of some bourgeois scholars who fabricated in one morning. Its emergence has its profound historical and ideological roots.

First of all, the "humanization" of Marxism by Western bourgeois scholars is a

---

[187]Henri de Man: *Newly Discovered Marx,* Published in the magazine of *Struggle*, Vienna, Issue 5-6, 1932, Quoted from *Studies (Collection) on Economic and Philosophic Manuscripts of 1844*, Page 374.

[188]Landshut and Mayer: *Karl Marx: Der historische Materialismus; Die Frühschriften*, Vol. 1, Page V.

[189]Quoted from *Studies (Collection) on Economic and Philosophic Manuscripts of 1844*, Page 348~349.

reflection of bourgeois ideology. Whether it is Neo-Kantianism, New Hegelianism, life philosophy, Max Weber's interpretive sociology or the phenomenology and existentialism of Husserl (Edmund Gustav Albrecht Husserl), it is mainly characterized by anti-scientism and anti-classical rationalism. As this thought of anti-rationalism is apparently similar to Marx's moral condemnation of capitalism in the early years, some Western scholars try to explain Marx to meet the needs of the bourgeoisie, utilize some humanism factors in Marx's early thought to remodel Marx and to oppose the mature one as a Marxist. Western scholars strongly advocate the "critical spirit" of "Young Marx" and deny the scientific factors in Marx's mature thought.

Secondly, in the first half of the 20th century, the whole Western capitalist world was full of dangers and difficulties. The most prominent was the severe economic crisis in 1920s and the two world wars. In the face of this painful reality, a group of Western intellectuals tried to find a magic prescription from Marx's works for helping the world get out of the predicament of the capitalist system, and the humanitarianism thought of "Young Marx" became a powerful tool for their condemnation of German fascists and for attacking the classical bourgeois management theory and bureaucracy. Of course, there was no denying that there were some unscrupulous scholars who tried to criticize and deny the Soviet regime, the first socialist country that has just been born, with the aid of "Young Marx", and attacked and abused the mistakes of the agricultural collectivization and industrialization development mode during Stalin's reign.

But in general, the myth of "Two Marx" discovered in 1930s mainly used "Young Marx" to oppose "Mature Marx" and used Marx to oppose Engels, thus dismembering the whole Marxism. Since 1950s, with the formation of the confrontation between the two major military blocs of the East and the West and the arrival of the "Cold War" era, it had become the main task of the Western world to attack socialist countries from the angle of ideology. They often based on *Economic and Philosophic Manuscripts of 1844* to attack the dictatorship of the proletariat as totalitarian and autocratic and to preach the so-called "humane" socialism.

Actually, Western scholars cannot deny the strong influence of Marx's later works and their scientific value. Marcuse (Herbert Marcuse) had to admit in 1960s that "Marx's early works are in all respects only the preparatory stage of his mature theory. The significance of these preparatory phases should not be overestimated."[190] They cannot deny that Marx's whole life thought is only a logical development process, nor do they want to give up the "Young Marx" they understand, need and admire.

To overcome this contradiction, they had to say: "Marx spent his whole life rewriting a book, the first draft of which was the *Paris Manuscripts*."①[191] In their point of view, Marx's analysis in *Das Kapital* was not only the content of political economy, but also belonged to the category of philosophical anthropology, which was a continuation of early works. They said that Marx had been answering and explaining Feuerbach's analysis of "the essence of human beings" all his life, thought that in a narrow sense, the late Marx's works changed his early views, and even said that his later works and early works were contradictory; but generally speaking, the development of Marx's thought from "youth" to "old age" is fundamentally consistent, and its core thought is alienation and materialization.[192]

Contrary to the "Two Marx" theorists who wantonly elevated the *Manuscripts of Economics and Philosophy of 1844* and dresses up Marx with humanitarianism, Althusser (Louis Althusser) went to the other extreme when he created the "Two

---

[190]Marcuse: *Reason & Revolution*, Page 360, Frankfurt, 1962.

[191]H. B. Acton: *Karl Marx and Materialism*, Published on *International Philosophical Review*, Vol. 12, Page 271, Issue 45~46, 1958.

[192]See Nicholas Lobkowicz: *Marx and the Western World*, Page 39~40, London, 1967.

Marx Antagonism", and held a completely negative attitude toward "early Marx". He believed that Marx in the *Manuscripts of Economics and Philosophy of 1844* was "Marx farthest from Marx...This Marx is on the verge of transformation, and is standing on the threshold of change at the night before change."[193] That is, "on the threshold of becoming Marx himself through a thorough reorganization."[194] In his opinion, there was a "break in epistemology" between "Young Marx" and "Mature Marx".[195] It was marked by *Theses on Feuerbach* (1845) and *The German Ideology*. Before that, Marx was in the "ideological period" under the influence of Feuerbach and Hegel.[196] After that, Marx gradually entered the "scientific period" when he completely got rid of and abandoned the influence of Hegel.[197] He concluded that the humanitarianism of Marx's early works was opposed to the scientific nature of the mature Marx and even the whole Marxism, and that the "real Marx" is the "anti-humanitarianism" in theory.[198]

In fact, Marx is like all great thinkers. His thought also has a logical historical process of unceasing development. It is non-historical and non-dialectical practice of

---

[193]*Western Scholar's' Comments on Manuscripts of Economics and Philosophy of 1844*, Page 251~252, Shanghai, Fudan University Press, 1983.

[194]*Western Scholar's' Comments on Manuscripts of Economics and Philosophy of 1844*, Page 253.

[195]*Western Scholar's' Comments on Manuscripts of Economics and Philosophy of 1844*, Page 211.

[196]*Western Scholar's' Comments on Manuscripts of Economics and Philosophy of 1844*, Page 212.

[197]*Western Scholar's' Comments on Manuscripts of Economics and Philosophy of 1844*, Page 264.

[198]*Western Scholar's' Comments on Manuscripts of Economics and Philosophy of 1844*, Page 265.

separating the history of Marx's ideological development whether to regard "Young Marx" and "Mature Marx" as "fundamental opposition", to hold a completely negative attitude towards "Young Marx", or to assert that "Young Marx" is the "peak of intelligence" of the whole Marx and "Young Marx is the standard to measure Marxism".

First of all, the propagandists of "Two Marx Antagonism" ignored the historical fact that: Young Marx was in the transition period from idealistic worldview to materialistic worldview. His thoughts during this period were characterized by transitional immaturity.

Like all the great thinkers in Germany at the beginning of the 19th century, Marx also began his ideological process from the starting point of criticizing the alienation nature of religion and trying to reveal the secular basis of religion. In the course of exploring and seeking practical ways to eliminate religion, Marx studied the history of the formation and development of modern countries and the history of modern civil society, revealed the contradiction essence of the binary separation between the state and the civil society, and meanwhile criticized Hagel's philosophy of speculative idealism essence, so as to reach the conclusion of the initial historical materialism that "It is the civil society that decides the state rather than the state decides the civil society". From then on, Marx began a 40-year theoretical study of political economy criticism in order to further understand the essence of civil society. It is in this new field of theoretical research that Marx critically absorbed the alienation theory of Hegel and Feuerbach for the first time, and formed the alienated labor thought, which was the initial understanding of theoretical criticism on the capitalist economic form. With the help of this theory, Marx analyzed and criticized the social relations, class relations and relations of production of capitalist society, revealed the fundamental contradiction between their productive forces and relations of production, and finally came to the conclusion that the development of modern large-scale industry, that is, the development of productive forces determines the development of all social relations and countries, and ideology of capitalism, which is the most fundamental and significant conclusion of historical materialism. So that he made his first great discovery.

It is not difficult to see that the transition of young Marx to historical materialism world view is not only an inevitable logical cognitive process, but also an extremely contradictory and complex cognitive process. Marx went through three cognitive periods, namely, the stage of religion-philosophy criticism, political criticism and economic criticism in just three years. During this period, he was also engaged in a complex and arduous ideological synthesis work with multi-line combat and multi-disciplinary research: He not only studied the history of philosophy, the history of religion and the history of modern political system of the world, but also studied the history of modern civil society, classical political economics and utopian socialism theory; he not only critically inherited the achievements of dialectics and materialism of Hegel and Feuerbach, but also critically absorbed the positive achievements of classical political economics; and he not only borrowed and criticized the theory of utopian socialism in Britain and France, but also struggled against the "real socialism" of the German petty bourgeoisie. And therefore, this complex historical environment determined the contradictory characteristics of young Marx's thought. From his works in this period, we can not only see many of his budding scientific ideas flash, but also his writings with the marks of terms and the influence of thought of Hegel and Feuerbach, which reflects that it is natural for the differences between "Young Marx" and "mature Marx", but this fact is exaggerated and distorted by Western Marxists.

The explanation of "Young Marx" and the "antagonism" of "Two Marx" created by Western Marxists therefrom are totally groundless.

Of course, we do not deny the differences between "Young Marx" and "Mature Marx" in ideological understanding, language style, etc. But this is determined by the continuous changes of Marx's own activity experience, the field of discipline research, the social, political and economic situation of Europe in the 19th century and the situation of proletarian revolution. More importantly, as stated earlier, the transition of Marx's thought from youth to maturity is a development process of logical and dialectical sublation and abandonment. With 1844-1845 as the boundary marker, Marx's view of history made the following series of substantive changes: In terms of the starting point of thought, Marx's understanding with humanism color that "labor is the essence of man" rose to the basic theory of historical materialism that "labor is the basis of social existence"; in terms of the contradiction relationship between individual and society, between human activity and historical law, Marx realized the cognition transition from studying the contradiction between individual and class to discovering the law of society itself, the mechanism of historical law and the inner relationship between human social activities; in terms of the issue of alienation, Marx transferred from explaining division of labor with alienation to exploring alienation from division of labor; and in terms of the issue of communism, Marx developed from criticizing the total alienation of human essence of the capitalist society and believing that the communist society is the comprehensive return and realization of human essence, to think that the communist society is overall development of the human essence and the capitalist society relation is the necessary precondition and necessary preparation for the new social relationship in the future. Thus it can be seen from this that it's all untenable to believe that there is a fault zone between "Young Marx" and "Old Marx", or that the creative wisdom of "Old Marx" is exhausted and the inspiration has dried up and "Young Marx" is the pinnacle of intelligence. The transition from "Young Marx" to "Mature Marx" is a historical process from abstract to concrete in cognition, from moral criticism to scientific analysis, and from founding theory to systematic enrichment of theoretical system.

The viewpoint that "Young Marx" is a humanist, a moral and value critic and a historical subject, whereas "Mature Marx" is a mechanical economic determinist rather than non-critical scientist also lacks historical basis.

Throughout Marx's life, he has never generally opposed or ambiguously denied "humanitarianism". He only opposed the abstract "humanitarianism" that transcends history and class. No matter in his youth time or in the mature period of his thoughts, Marx always hated the cruel exploitation of capitalist private ownership and sympathized with the misery of the proletariat at the bottom of the society. But Marx never denied the great historical progress of capitalism because of its evil. However, Marx's mature works show that: It is far from enough to remain at the stage of criticism and condemnation of this evil reality. It is necessary to materialistically demonstrate the historical inevitability of the emergence, development and extinction of capitalist economic structure from the scientific point of view of the deep study of capitalist economic structure. Human liberation must be based on the rapid development of productive forces and on the realization of proletarian revolution and autocracy. And therefore, Marx's lofty humanitarian ideals throughout his life are not on the basis of some kind of utopia of moral criticism and prophecy, but on the firm belief that "the masses of the people are the subject of creating the history". So Marx's philosophy of history is by no means a kind of mechanical determinism. Although the later works represented by *Das Kapital* emphasized the decisive role of modern capitalist economic development and economic relations on the whole society, Marx never denied that the proletariat was the creator of modern society and the great historical function of the gravedigger of the capitalist system. The objective scientific dissection and analysis of the capitalist economy in Marx's later works did not mean that he abandoned his early sharp critique of the system. On the contrary, Marx never considered science and value to be contradictory. In his viewpoint, any real and thorough criticism should be based on the scientific understanding of certain social and economic facts.

In the course of the formation of Marxism, the *Manuscripts of Economics and Philosophy of 1844* is, of course, a relatively concentrated and systematic work on alienation and humanitarianism. But discussion on this problem of *Manuscripts of Economics and Philosophy of 1844* is not out of the need of abstract speculation but in order to solve the important realistic problems such as the historical position of proletariat and the road of human liberation, and to uncover "the riddle of history". However, different from the scientific socialism demonstration in Marx's mature works, the *Manuscripts of Economics and Philosophy of 1844* were deeply influenced by Feuerbach humanism, both in the way of thinking and in the style of language, even though its ideological theme was basically communist. However, the philosophical argumentation on this subject (that is, the alienation and restoration of human nature, the elaboration of humanitarianism) also had a strong speculative and ethical color. So, what makes the *Manuscripts of Economics and Philosophy of 1844* have the characteristics and particularly interested by the descendants seemed not to be the theme, but the way of expression. "Marxology" found the "basis" of the so-called "ethical socialism" ideology from "young Marx" was exactly the superficial phenomenon. It is groundless to interpret communism as "ethical socialism" in the *Manuscripts of Economics and Philosophy of 1844*, because the demonstration on communism of *Manuscripts of Economics and Philosophy of 1844* is on the basis of economic facts, that is, an analysis of private ownership and the contradiction between capital and labor, rather than abstract human or moral orders. Through the analysis on the alienation of people, the alienation of society, and the alienation of labor, Mark tried to reveal the negative existence status of the proletariat under the capitalist system and the employment nature of labor. In the *Manuscripts of Economics and Philosophy of 1844*, Marx realized that only by actively sublimating private ownership could the alienation be eliminated, and the liberation and communism of human be realized, which was undoubtedly true, but of course its philosophical argument had its limitations.

The contradiction between the theme of thought and the way of expression does not show that young Marx has a kind of ethical socialism which is opposite to the later scientific socialism, nor can it be decided that Marx will be under the influence of humanism in his whole life. Because of proceeding from the analysis of economic facts determines that the future development direction of *Manuscripts of Economics and Philosophy of 1844* is bound to be historical materialism rather than humanism. It is because of Marx's persistent research on political economy that he can overcome the negative influence of humanism completely, and carry out true and scientific demonstration on socialism. And therefore, "Mature Marx" will let "Marxists" feel more and more disappointed, and only the remnants of some old philosophy of "Young Marx" make them have an infinite fascination and enthusing about talking.

Some thinkers in the West created the farce of "Two Marx", not only showing the naked anti-Marxist ideology utilitarian demand, but also showing that their cognitive method of the history of Marx is extremely wrong. They have always used contemporary existentialism, phenomenology or Freudianism to "interpret" Marx subjectively and casually, and put aside Marx's life experience of proletarian revolutionary practice to "read" Marx. In a word, they always ignored the fact that Marx's thought was closely related to the history of European civilization in the 19th century, and they regarded Marx as an eccentric scholar who was lonely, far away from the earth and behind closed doors. But they had never realized that Marx, first and foremost as a revolutionary mentor of the proletariat, would be shining through the ages. In this way, the Marx they needed and imagined was, of course, a man full of "love-talking", full of moral fantasies, drunk and speculative.

2. "From a Travel-Stained Fighter to a Cynical Moralist"

"Marxists" not only "found" the "Marxism" that they need and can accept in *Manuscripts of Economics and Philosophy of 1844*, but also "found" Marx's "standard and ideal mythical image" that they welcomed. Sydney Hook, the famous American pragmatist philosopher, has a vivid passage describing the image of Marx in the 20th century as understood by "Marxists": "Future historians will be surprised and confused by the strange spectacle that emerged in the second half of the 20th century, which is the second birth of Karl Marx. His second birth was not an economist in a dusty tuxedo like the author of *Das Kapital*, nor the sans-culottes of revolution, the inspiring author of *The Communist Manifesto*. Dressed as a philosopher and moral prophet, he brought good news about human freedom in a narrow circle of transcendent classes, political parties, or sects."[199]

In the eyes of "Marxists", the image of Karl Marx is constantly changing, and they think: "In the old European Social Democratic Party, Karl Marx won the honor of a great economist. There he was the author of *Das Kapital*... In the eyes of the Marx and the Communist International activists interpreted by Lenin, Marx firstly appeared as a political thinker. He taught the working class to create their own organizations as the basis for the control of power. In the domination of this kind of view, *The Critique of the Gotha Program* was praised as one of the most important contributions of Marx. However, in the communist worldview of socialism and the development process of the Communist Party, Friedrich Engels and even Josef Dietzgen (Peter Josef Dietzgen) were more significant and influential than Marx... Young Marx as a philosopher was almost unknown and was absolutely ignored before the works of Karl Korsch and György Lukács were published in 1923."[200]

It is not difficult to see that Marx in the ideal of "Marxists" is not the author of *The Communist Manifesto*, *Das Kapital* and *The Critique of the Gotha Program*, but the author of *Manuscripts of Economics and Philosophy of 1844*, as a "philosopher" with the second birth. This "Marx" "negated" the scientific socialist system and the system of political and economic criticism of the capitalist economic system that were built by him laboriously and painstakingly in advance in his youth in form of "future perfect tense".

Existentialist R. Tucker said: "Marx's 'first system', namely, *the Manuscript of 1844*, allowed people to draw the conclusion that: It now seems that Marx was no longer the kind of sociologist and analyst he wanted to be, but, above all, a moralist or

---

[199]Sidney Hook: *The Second Birth of Karl Marx*, Published on *The New York Times Reviews*, May 22th, 1966.

[200]Iring Fetscher: *Young and Old Marx*, See Nicholas Lobkowicz: *Marx and the Western World*, Page 19.

something like a religious thinker, believing that 'scientific socialism' is an old view of a scientific system, which is increasingly giving way to the idea that 'scientific socialism', in essence, is an ethical and religious system of views."[201] "Marxist" Maximilien Rubel said that Marx's theory "is a kind of science of the emergence and destruction of human exploitation way." But it is also, and mainly, "the cosmopolitan Utopia yearned for and strived for by the largest and poorest classes."[202]

It can be seen that it is not "Marxists" who are ignorant or do not know enough about the history of Marxist thought. It was because they could not and would not accept Marx as the founder of scientific socialism and Marx as the greatest political economist. They have never been willing to associate Marx with the proletarian revolution of his time. Their imagination of Marx is the painful existence as a "lonely individual" summarized by existentialist philosophy, a psychopath who is more and more cynical and compassionate because of lifelong poverty and disease, a romantic illusionist who loathes the noise of industrial society and yearns for a golden age of natural economics, and a religious prophet who aims to save all living beings and save the world's poor.

"The second birth of Marx", promoted by "Marxists", is caused by many factors, including the utilitarian needs of ideological criticism, a profound impact of anti-rationalism (existentialism, Freudianism, structuralism, and New Thomas Doctrine) in contemporary Western philosophy, the new problems that the classical Marxism has not met in the contemporary world, and the twists and turns, difficulties and problems of Marxism in socialist practice.

In the name of advocating the humanitarianism of "Young Marx", "Marxists"

---

[201]Robert Tucker: *Karl Marx—The Development of His Thought from Philosophy to Mythology*, Leipzig, 1963.

[202]*Research Materials on Marxism-Leninism*, 1982, Division 5, Page 240.

attacked the socialist system as a highly totalitarian feudal kingdom that stifles human nature and suppresses individuality, and attacked Marxism-Leninism as the illegitimate child of the hybrid of scientism and autocracy, and as a modern religion that Engels, Lenin and Stalin set up by betraying Marx's basic ideas and instilling in the people from the outside. As a result, a series of books entitled "Marx against Marxism" were published at this time (For example, *Marx against Marxism by* Julius I. Loewenstein and *Pathetic Scam: Marx against Engels* by Norman Levine).

In addition, "Marxists", deeply influenced by anti-scientism and anti-rationalism, are particularly "appreciative" of "Young Marx" with a fearless and critical spirit. In their eyes, due to the strong moral condemnation of classical capitalist relations of production and social system, the profound criticism of the overall alienation of human relations in the industrialized society, and the obsessed eulogia and persistent pursuit of the goal of the ideal of "all-round development of the people," "Young Marx" became a modern pioneer of anti-rationalism, existentialism and freudism. Mature Marx, especially the one in *Das Kapital*, adhered to a rigorous, scientific and logical thinking method, and an objective analysis method. So in their view, Marx at this time had lost his unique critical spirit, with his creative intelligence going to exhaustion. And therefore, Marx had "fallen down" in the direction of scientism, positivism, rationalism and determinism that prevailed in the 19th century. Accordingly, only "Young Marx" is the "real Marx" needed in the 20th century.

Seen from the reality, capitalism has a great development in the contemporary era, and is very different from the ear of Marx. But the contemporary capitalism has not become an irresistible "unidirectional" society without sharp class confrontation with high welfare and the people lose their critical power. It is nothing more than explanations of the scriptures and notes and a deliberate misinterpretation of Marx's works to believe that the analysis of capitalism in *The Communist Manifesto* and *Das Kapital* is out of date, to think that what is really meaningful in Marx's works becomes the critical theory of dissimilation of human nature in his early works, and so on.

Obviously, "Marx" and his ideas, which "Marxists" have found through various pretexts, are for the following basic politics and ideologies: (I) the highly developed capitalist society is an eternal social system that cannot be overthrown. And therefore, (II) Marx's thought can only play a partial role in the capitalist system and mainly plays a moral critical role. And therefore, "the second born Marx" must ensure that he cannot claim to overthrow the capitalist system, and must serve for the capitalism to get rid of the current dilemmas and solve the partial problems in the industrialized society. Only such a Marx is "its role beyond the class, political parties or sectarian narrow circle", thus bringing good news to capitalism, not the death knells of capitalism of Marx!

In short, in terms of its ideological source, the so-called "second born Marx" is the product of the explanation of the young Marx's works by "Marxology" with existentialism, philosophy of life, Freudianism, Neo-Hegelianism and even Neo-Thomism. In their eyes, Marx was "the pioneer of existentialism like Kierkegaard (Søren Aabye Kierkegaard)", and an "existentialist", from 1844 to 1845, who opposed Hegel's thoroughgoing "pan-logicism"; some people even compared Marx with Freud, saying that Marx regarded "the liberation of human instinct" as "the starting point of liberation of the whole world" like Freud; others linked Marx's theory of scientific socialism with the Christian philosophy of salvation, saying that the great power of Marx's prophecy was that: although he did not realize it, he returned completely to the original roots of the *Old Testament*, but his prophecy was not in the form of a Christian afterlife, but in the form of the "Millennium Kingdom" of this world. It was believed that Marx regarded the proletariat as the synonym of God in the *Manuscripts of Economics and Philosophy of 1844*, where "the proletariat performs the function of Christ".

Western scholars tried their best to bring Marx into the course of the development of modern European humanism. Fromm (Erich Seligmann Fromm) said: "Marx's philosophy, like most existentialism, is an alienation of human beings, and a protest against a man losing himself or a human being becoming something. Marx's philosophy protested against the dehumanization and mechanization of human beings associated with the development of Western industrialism. ...Marx's philosophy was rooted in the tradition of Western humanitarianism, which began with Spinoza (Baruch Spinoza) and continued to Goethe and Hegel through the French and German Enlightenment in the 18th century. The intrinsic essence of this tradition is concern for people and the realization of their abilities."[203] In their opinion, Marx's theory is not the "heterogeneity" in the Western cultural structure, but a component of it, and thus is the "ally" of bourgeois culture. [204] Of course, this is to prove that Marx's thought is the unique product of the Western (bourgeois) humanistic traditional culture, and is incompatible with "Oriental Marxism", which is the ideology of socialist countries. In this way, it seems that Marx can shake hands with bourgeois thinkers, but opposed to the "Marxists" with each other.

The basic idea of Western scholars is to firstly find some materials from Marx's early works that can be interpreted by humanism, and then carry on infinite exaggeration, put Marx's youth period and mature period against each other completely, and split the unified historical process of Marx's thought development into two parts of diametrically opposite, thus appeared "two Marx". One is Marx as a philosopher and moralist, and the other as a revolutionary fighter and mechanical determinism. As for the two Marx, they think that the philosopher and moral Marx is the real Marx, and this Marx in the contemporary West has been propagated and spread. However, Marx, as a revolutionary "fighter" and "mechanical determinism", is the "depravity" of Marx's thought and cannot belong to the real Marx, but this

---

[203] Fromm: *Marx's Concept of Man*, See *Western Scholar's' Comments on Manuscripts of Economics and Philosophy of 1844*, Page 15.

[204]See Nicholas Lobkowicz: *Marx and the Western World*, Preface, 1967.

Marx is inherited by the orthodoxy today. From this we can see that the myth of "Two Marx" is not merely an academic problem, but a major issue of right and wrong with realistic significance of political struggle and ideological struggle. All the purposes of the Western scholars using "Young Marx" remolded by them to oppose Marx as a scientist and revolutionist lie in fundamentally denying the ideological and theoretical basis of the socialist and communist movements, and making the world proletariat accept their lies and embrace the so-called humanist Marx that is completely distorted and in line with the needs of the bourgeoisie. In fact, "from the dusty fighters to the cynical moralist" is not Marx himself, nor the rational understanding because of the discovery of the *Manuscripts of Economics and Philosophy of 1844*, but is the entirely fiction of the Western "Marxists".

3. Is Alienation the Core of Marx's Thought?

As early as 1930s, Landshut and Mayer concluded that "the general title of the contradiction by which Marx understood reality was 'self-alienation'"[205], and even said that the most basic principles of *The Communist Manifesto* can be amended to "all history so far is the history of human self-alienation"[206]. Henri de Man believed that in the *Manuscripts of Economics and Philosophy of 1844*, "the concept of alienation is of great significance"[207].

In 1950s, Jean Hyppolite brutally advocated: "all the basic concepts of Marxist thought can be said to be the source, and is the concept of alienation borrowed from Hegel and Feuerbach. I believe: starting from the concept, it can best explain the integrity of Marx's philosophy and understand the structure of Marx's main work *Das Kapital* to define the emancipation of human beings as any positive struggle against any alienation of human nature in any form in the course of

---

[205]*Studies (Collection) on Economic and Philosophic Manuscripts of 1844*, Page 289.

[206]*Studies (Collection) on Economic and Philosophic Manuscripts of 1844*, Page 290.

[207]*Studies (Collection) on Economic and Philosophic Manuscripts of 1844*, Page 356.

history."[208]

Karl Weitz, a Catholic philosopher, also believed that Marx's alienation philosophical category received from Hegel as early as his youth, constituted the skeleton of his mature masterpiece *Das Kapital*. "Marx shifted the theme of alienation to the field of political economics. *Das Kapital* is nothing more than a basic theory of alienation, including the field of economic thought"[209]. The basic components of Marxist theory include the analysis of religious alienation on the one hand and the analysis of earthly alienation on the other hand. "In short, it is the thought of revolutionary intermediary as the center of Marxism. This revolutionary intermediary must liberate people from alienation and make it possible for them to reconcile with nature and society."[210]

Another French "Marxist", P. Bonnell, even confused Marx's alienation theory with Hegel's. He said that Marx, like Hegel, argued:" Human life has a dual and internally repressed nature of alienation until history overcomes this alienation and self-destruction; in fact, history only continues until this time."[211] Fisher, a Marxist in the Federal Republic of Germany, also said that Marx's concept of alienation and materialization was the central concept of "humanitarianism", and thus became the central idea of the critique of political economy in *Das Kapital*.[212]

Indeed, we should admit that the concept of "alienation" is one of the important categories of Manuscripts, of later the Manuscripts of Economics from 1857 to

---

[208]Jean Hyppolite: *Studies on Marx and Hegel*, Page 147, Paris, 1955.

[209]J. Karl Weitz: *Karl Marx's Theory*, Page 320, Paris, 1956.

[210]J. Karl Weitz: *Karl Marx's Theory*, Page 601.

[211]P. Bonnell: *Hegel and Marx*, Published on French Magazine *Socialist Comments*, Issue 110, Oct. 1957, Page 318~319.

[212]See Nicholas Lobkowicz: *Marx and the Western World*, Page 39.

1858, and of *Das Kapital*. But the problem is, "Marxists" misinterpreted and used the concept in an extremely wrong way, thus misunderstanding its position and function in Marxist theory system.

"Marxists" confused Marx's concept of alienation with that of Hegel and Feuerbach. They thought that Marx, like Hegel, advocated alienation and materialization, and objectification was the same thing, and regarded the contradiction between human existence and nature as alienation from the angle of humanism, just as Feuerbach did. In a word, as Henri de Man put it that: The simplest formula of alienation was the "opposition between object and subject", which was as the same as "objectification and self-confirmation", "necessity and freedom", and "classes and individuals". "Marxists" regarded the alienation theory of *Manuscripts of Economics and Philosophy of 1844* as the most mature and systematic conclusion of Marx.

Due to the distortion of the concept of "alienation" by "Marxists", it is bound to draw the wrong conclusion of negating materialism, negating the inevitability of historical development, and thus denying the theory of scientific socialism. Accordingly, the Marx they selected, needed and "discovered" "negated" his own historical materialism belief, and "negated" the scientific understanding of the nature of man's sociality, history and class nature. Such a "humanitarian Marx" can only be a "lonely individual" in the sense of existentialist philosophy, "a cynical critic", and "a mad idealist with irrational beliefs", rather than a teacher of the proletarian revolution, a thinker who demonstrated the inevitability of the demise of capitalism and the inevitability of socialist realization on the basis of scientific theory.

The root cause of alienation lies in that they are never willing to accept Marx's idea that overthrowing the capitalist system is the fundamental way to eliminate alienation and realize the all-round development of human nature. They believe that alienation is accompanied by human history and is an inevitable phenomenon of human nature. It seems that the significance of Marx's alienation theory is not to explain the irrationality and inevitable extinction of capitalist system, but to prove its permanence, to criticize and resolve the local alienation contradiction in capitalist society.

To regard alienation as an eternal phenomenon of human society seems to prove the inevitability and universality of alienation under socialist conditions. "Marxists" have never forgotten to blame the mistakes and setbacks in socialist practice. In their eyes, the existing socialist system is an industrial autocratic society and an industrialized bureaucratic society, which is far from Marx's "Utopia". The people living under this system are subjected to a variety of alien domination, including economic, political, ideological, and cultural and so on. Of course, we cannot deny that there are social drawbacks in our social system, such as bureaucracy, but these are not the inevitable phenomenon inseparable from human nature, and shall not be simply attributed to "alienation" phenomenon. They need to be solved by the continuous development of social productive forces and the continuous improvement of education and construction of socialist democracy and legal system.

It is sure that the category of alienation or the concept of alienated labor plays a central role in the *Manuscripts of Economics and Philosophy of 1844*. In this manuscript, Marx defined the connotation of labor alienation from four aspects. That is, the alienation of labor products, the alienation of labor process, the alienation of human nature and the alienation of people. Obviously, as Marx did not have sufficient knowledge of political economy at that time, his analysis of capitalist private ownership was by the means of philosophy much more than economics. Although Marx's theory on alienation in the *Manuscripts of Economics and Philosophy of 1844* has the influence of Feuerbach's humanism, Marx did not only look at alienation from the angle of human nature. In the *Manuscripts of Economics and Philosophy of 1844*, Marx tried to use the concept of alienation to analyze the origin of private ownership, to analyze the root causes of the separation of labor and capital and the separation of capital and land, and to analyze the antagonistic relationship between the asset and the proletarian, which in turn developed into a critical theory of political economy.

To be sure, we admit that the concept of alienation has a very broad and comprehensive nature in the *Manuscripts of Economics and Philosophy of 1844*. In this concept, the contents in economic, social and political, moral, psychological and aesthetic fields are inseparably blended together; even so, Marx has always regarded the fact of economic alienation produced in the process of labor as the premise and foundation of all other alienation phenomena. In addition, in the *Manuscripts of Economics and Philosophy of 1844*, although Marx improperly used the humanistic terminology of Feuerbach's "the restoration of human nature", it does not mean that "Young Marx" adheres to what is called "the eternal abstract theory of human nature". In fact, in the *Manuscripts of Economics and Philosophy of 1844*, on the one hand, Marx criticized the wrong thought that national economists regarded capitalist private ownership as the starting point of history, and revealed the historical stages of the emergence, development and existence of capitalist social formation. On the other hand, Marx did not regard it as the retrogression of history and the depravity of human nature simply because he strongly condemned the inhuman alienation of the most developed private ownership society. On the contrary, Marx also fully affirmed its great historical progress and the role of historical change, and believed that it was an inevitable stage of historical development. Marx never regarded the development of human history as a kind of abstract and eternal alienation and reversion of human essence, just like abstract humanism. The *Manuscripts of Economics and Philosophy of 1844* did not regard any relationship between subject and object as alienation, nor did it equate the materialization and externalization of labor with alienation. Although Marx was somewhat influenced by Feuerbach on the understanding of human nature at that time, it was in the *Manuscripts of Economics and Philosophy of 1844* that Marx put forward the important thought for the first time that practice and labor were the realization of human nature, and the realization and corroboration of human nature.

In *The German Ideology* and his later works, Marx overcame the broad and abstract explanation of the concept of alienation in the *Manuscripts of Economics and Philosophy of 1844*, and mainly limited the concept to a certain state of capitalist production process, the nature of the analysis and regulation. In the *Das Kapital*, the alienation category is mainly used to generalize the capitalist commodity monetary relations, that is to say, the relationship between the things that govern the physical creators, that is, the phenomenon of commodity fetishism. Of course, the category of alienation has never been completely reduced to individual specific economic facts in his later works, and is still a philosophical category.

Fundamentally speaking, Marx opposed to defining the category of alienation from the angle of humanism, and he always thought that alienation was only a special historical form of individual existence in modern society, rather than the eternal essence of human beings. The mistakes of "Marxists" who advocated "the theory of alienation and eternity" lied in the fact that they regarded the alienation phenomenon as one of the basic ways of individual existence in modern society, especially in contemporary society, as the eternal phenomenon of human history, just like the national economists criticized by Marx at that time who regarded the private ownership of capitalism as the starting point of human history and as the eternal phenomenon of human history. But this kind of wrong cognition is the inevitable product of the contemporary Western anti-rationalism ideological trend. Both existentialism and Freudianism understand the nature of human beings by analyzing their biological, psychological and irrational living conditions. And therefore, the way to understand human nature by breaking away from the social and historical nature of human existence is bound to draw the following conclusion: in highly industrialized society, loneliness, anxiety and fear of the human beings seem to be the eternal state of human existence and the eternal essence.

In a word, Western "Marxists" have reshaped a Marx, called "Young Marx". The core of Marx's thought is the theory of alienation. It is completely different from the thought system of materialist dialectics in the mature period, and even opposite. Western "Marxists" greatly extolled the so-called "Young Marx" thought with alienation as the core with the purpose to belittle the scientific and revolutionary Marx, eliminate the scientific and revolutionary Marxism, and dress Marx as a modern romanticist like Rousseau and Feuerbach, a humanist, or a contemporary existentialist.

CHAPTER 5   VARIOUS "SUPPLEMENTS" AND MARX'S
DEFORMATION

In less than 30 years, mankind suffered from two world wars, which aggravated the sense of crisis in Western capitalist society with a large number of practical problems. Marxist theory had once again become the center of people's interests and concerns. In order to save "the world disaster" and "the decline of civilization", many Western scholars began to make a fuss about Marx's theory of human beings, making great efforts to transform Marx's theory into a tool of social criticism in line with their interests. From the end of 1950s to 1960s, a series of obvious changes had taken place in the Western capitalist society. Some Western countries had entered the so-called developed industrial society. People lived for goods and took material enjoyment as the soul of life. Material consciousness suppressed people's revolutionary consciousness, and the ruling class manipulated the popular ideology, extended to all fields of production and life, and distorted people's psychology. And therefore, some Western scholars tried to "rebuild" Marx's theory according to the new historical conditions. Either they linked Marxism with modern Western bourgeois philosophical trends, or "supplemented" Marxism in the way they understood it. As a result, the true Marx was completely unrecognizable.

1. "Psychological Analysis" and "Reflective Revolution"

From the beginning of 1930s to the end of 1950s, around the exploration of the social psychological basic problems arisen from the fascist, Reich (Wilhelm Reich), Fromm, Marcuse and others devoted to the study of psychological tendencies and personality structure, trying to supplement the analysis of political and economic system of classical Marxist theory with social psychological analysis, and exploring the relationship between "psychological revolution" and "social revolution". They believed that in the Western society, which was about to get out of the disaster of war, human nature had been severely suppressed, capitalist democracy was facing a crisis, and state monopoly capitalism was expanding. And therefore, as for the existence of an unjust social system, it was not enough to use the economic and political power of the ruling class as Marx did, only to integrate the cognition of the psychological process with the understanding of the social process, can we establish a complete theory of man and his liberation. And therefore, they clearly put forward that we should use Marx's concept of alienation to explain Freud's theory of sexual repression and make it revolutionized and socialized; and use Freud's theory of sexual repression to explain Marx's concept of alienation to make it biologicalized and perfect. They unanimously agreed that it was the only possible solution to the conflicts between man and civilization to combine Freud's psychology of sexual instinct with Marx's social economics.

Reich pointed out that Marx's historical materialism had two main defects: one was that although Marx correctly explained that consciousness was the product of various economic development processes, he had not effectively explained how the process of economic development actually changed into consciousness; and the other one was that Marx did not explain how consciousness actually reacted on various economic development processes. It was in these two shortcomings that Freud's theory can supplement Marx's theory.

In Reich's view, Freud's theory, especially unconscious psychology, can illustrate how economic factors can be transformed into certain thoughts and actions through internal psychological tendencies; can reveal the consciousness power of social activities, the social impacts on the individuals and the formation of the concept in the psychology; can regard ideology as a kind of labor process between man and nature and between man and society; and can specifically and profoundly show that ideology is not only the force of stabilizing social order, but also the force leading to and exacerbating the disintegration of social structure by making clear the forming process of ideology. Accordingly, in *Dialectical Materialism and Psychoanalysis*, Reich held that the theory of psychoanalysis had a number of important premises in common with that of Marx: (I) Freud's theory was the same as Marx's, which focused on real human needs and experiences, and traced the tragic fates of these instincts when they were repressed by nature and society from the specific material facts of love and hunger. (II) Freud's theory strengthened the attack on the traditional value of capitalism and its system on the basis of Marx's critique of capitalist society and economy, proclaimed the death of everything that was considered sacred in this society, summed it up as an unholy and unreasonable source, opened the way for the exploration of the mysterious unconscious intentions that determined human behavior, laid the foundation for new practice of self-inspiration and self-creation, and provided unparalleled emancipation tools.

According to this understanding, Reich thought that, by combining Marx and Freud together to observe the social revolution, it can be found: (I) the form of class rule imposed on the masses in a repressive society was balanced with the psychological process. It was associated with all the processes of sexual repression imposed on individuals during the initial socialization of patriarchal families. Sexual repression was the main instrument of economic slavery. (II) Although psychological repression was conducive to the perpetuation of rule, it created the root causes of explosive conflicts that Marx ignored. (III) Under the conditions of material scarcity peculiar to the previous historical era, the masses' sexual repressed energy will inevitably sublimate into the endless struggle for survival. Now there will be an explosive clash between human instincts and civilizations that continue to deny them. (IV)

Just as same-sex prohibition was a key component of the general prohibition, the struggle for sexual liberation was also a major step and aspect in the struggle for the overall liberation of mankind beyond capitalist society.

Fromm's view is consistent with Reich. In Fromm's view, the human beings had the instinct and biological needs of pursuing happiness. However, the society was bound to suppress this instinct and desire for the survival and development, and made it sublime to the science creative work to be met. When economic conditions needed the minorities to rule the majorities, it needed to repress the instinct more severely, so that the psychological structure of the masses can adapt to the economic structure and make it consolidate and stabilize as the class relationship. In this way, sexual suffering and sexual repression were disconnected from the external possibilities and internal functions of satisfying this sexual needed, when the sexual crisis was linked to the objective contradictions of the existing society and the decomposition of the existing class relations, the energy of the sexual instinct may then be released and used for new purposes, with new social functions. Then it will no longer serve the preservation of real society, but will help to develop new forms of society. It will no longer be glue, but turned into dynamite. All of these had been ignored by Marx.

Reich, Fromm and others believed that the best medium to combine Marx's theory with Freud's theory was the concept of "character structure", which in their opinion referred to a relatively stable pattern of behavior. This pattern originated from the socialization process of childhood. It represented a special way of one's existence and formed a self-protective device in order to cope with external pressures and threats. This protective device reflected the various repressions, transference, sublimation and fixation of individuals in the development of sexual desire in children and adolescence both in form and content. Although it was a psychological defense mechanism set up against various restrictions of the outside world, it also aimed at the inner harm after maturity, and that was to say, to control one's own various impulses which were not allowed by the society. So, the personality structure was both the product of the interaction between the psychological factors and social factors, and the key to understand the interaction between economic foundation and superstructure. They thought the analysis of personality structure can make people not only pay attention to biological factors and psychological factors of human beings, but also take the external economic effects and historical roles into account, and can even explain the relatively independent ideology. In their view, as the ideology was fixed in the structure of man's personality, the concept system became a material force to strengthen and protect the existing social order, to consolidate the exploitation system and authoritative state that suppressed human nature. Modern capitalist society was based on certain psychological tendency and personality type to a great extent. This psychological tendency and personality type were derived partly from unconscious drive and partly from the basic laws of social existence. For example, Fascism was an authoritative character in the character structure that depended on the middle and lower bourgeoisie. This stratum was between the increasingly rich monopoly bourgeoisie and the increasingly conscious proletariat, tasted the sharp contradictions between the social classes, the blindness and the inhumanity of the social forces, and meanwhile felt anxious and frightened for the decline of their status and the disintegration of traditional values. And therefore, this stratum not only demanded authority to consolidate its old general situation, but also was willing to submit to a more powerful totalitarian state. Reich and Fromm believed that it was because of the structure of character that ideology was able to invade a person's daily life and mode of thinking. In a certain social system, the changes in the economic situation did not necessarily lead to the changes in the ideology of the dominant position. The concept consciousness (especially the concept of the masses) often lagged behind the development of social relations, thus forming certain autonomy. Each society and its political organization had a corresponding psychological tendency and personality type as the basis. In order to extrapolate the viewpoint of personality type to the political and economic field of social life, so that each social group and political system can find the corresponding personality type, Reich further put forward the personality structure model. Fromm, on the other hand, put forward the concept of "social character" to supplement Marx's explanation of how the human mind reflected the material basis. They all thought that the authoritative character in the personality structure was the product of long-term repression, whereas Fascism was a revolt and catharsis of sexual repression and the distortion of sexual suffering. Reich and Fromm stressed that in analyzing the psychological basis for the Nazi regime to come to power, it was necessary to distinguish between two types of people: One type of people who were deeply attracted by fascist platforms and atrocities and connected their own interests with the Nazi regime to adhere to the fascist position was the lower middle class with authority tendencies; while as for the other type of people, although they clung to the Nazi regime without firm resistance, they did not believe in the ideologies and political practices of fascism. Most of them were mainly some workers, peasants and liberals, who were also bewildered and troubled by the reality, feeling worthless and powerless, and renouncing any political actions in the face of the Nazi regime. Reich and Fromm devoted particular attentions to the mentality and personality tendencies of the lower middle class, and thought that they adopted the escape mechanism of "authoritative character" to overcome their psychological inferiority and disillusionment, and gained the strength they lacked by giving up their independence, which the Nazis took advantage of to make it an important force to achieve their own political and economic goals. The Nazi regime strongly demonstrated that the individual was insignificant and that the individual must admit his irrelevance. As long as one melted himself into higher power, he can gain a kind of strength and pride. Fromm stressed that there was a contradiction in modern society that modern people believed that their actions were driven by their own interests. However, his existence was for the purpose of others or superman. The freedom to bring independence and reason to the individual made him isolated and powerless with bewilderment of all day long.

Reich and Fromm also believed that it should be the task of social psychology to make clear the historical development process of human being—Man is the product of history, and history is the product of man. It should not only know how the human passion, desire and anxiety are formed by social processes, but also reveal how people's psychology can become productive forces in a way that changes society. They all thought that fascism was the manifestation of "authoritative character" in the society, and it was the concentrated manifestation of totalitarianism.

Marcuse also strongly advocated the use of Freud's theory to supplement and develop Marx's theory, and used it as a weapon to severely criticize developed capitalism and draw a blueprint for the future civilized society. Marcuse believed that although Freud and Marx had different experiences and discussed different problems, their concerns were basically the same: that was the complete liberation of human beings. They could completely complement each other and melt into a furnace. On the basis of the combination of Marx's theory and Freud's theory, Marcuse put forward his own series of views. First of all, he combined Freud's theory of the essence of love with Marx's theory of human liberation and put forward his own theory of liberation of love. In his viewpoint, in modern civilization, the suppression of human beings was actually the repression of lust. When Marx talked about the emancipation of human beings, he actually referred to the emancipation of lust, but only by combining labor with lust, and realizing that the emancipation of labor was the emancipation of lust, can it fully explain why people in the labor can realize themselves and obtain happiness. Secondly, he combined Freud's view on the suppression of modern civilization's desire for love with Marx's thought on the alienation of labor, and initiated a general criticism of the modern capitalist society. He thought modern capitalist society was a society that suppressed human's lust. In this society, despite the apparent proliferation of sexual freedom, sexual freedom was increasingly used to serve the interests of the ruling community because sexual relations were becoming more and more closely attached to social relations, and sexual life was increasingly becoming a means rather than an aim, and therefore, the sexual repression behind this sexual freedom was more serious, which was mainly manifested in the alienation of labor. With the rapid development of science and technology, people become more and more like a tool to bring people's desires and needs into the whole capitalist order, so that people are deeply alienated and insensitive. As a result, although the modern capitalist society was the culmination of human civilization so far, it was also the pinnacle of the suppression of lust. Finally, he combined Freud's analysis of the repressed social roots of lust with Marx's analysis of the root causes of human suffering and demonstrated the possibility of liberating lust based on a non-repressive civilization. He believed that in the modern developed industrial society, man was faced with the fact that the repression of human lust had not been alleviated and disappeared, but had intensified. Apparently, this was the additional restriction imposed by the operational principles of this society on the desire for love in order to preserve the survival of this particular society. In that case, the elimination of this repression and the complete emancipation of lust will not subvert civilization itself, but will only overthrow the current social order, after which, an unrepressed civilization may be born.

As indicated above, in the eyes of Reich, Fromm, Marcuse, and other Western scholars, what the Freud theory lacked was exactly what Marx's theory had; and what Marx ignored was what Freud fully explained. Fromm had summed up this comprehensive theory as: "Economic forces work, but they must be understood as objective conditions rather than psychological motivations. The role of psychology is at work, but it must be seen as a matter of history. Ideas are influential, but it must be seen that they originate from the entire character structure of a member of a social group. However, apart from the interdependence of economic, psychological and ideological forces, they each have a certain degree of independence."[213] It is clear that this hope of linking Marx with Freud is not

---

[213]See Fromm: *Escaping from Freedom*, Page 162, Harbin, Northern Literature and

successful, as anyone with some common sense knows that Freud's theory is mainly focused on the analysis of the individual from the social environment or the relationship, while Marx's theory focuses on the investigation of social system and social relationship. Furthermore, in Freud's theory, the relationship between individuals and society is only to meet their own needs, but in Marx's view, separated from a certain social relations, there will be no such thing as the need and satisfaction of human beings. It can be seen that it is wrong for Reich, Fromm, Marcuse and others to combine Freud with Marx, to apply Freud to an individual, and to apply Marx to the society. When they lead to different conclusions in the process of leapfrogging, they must choose one of them and follow it, so that it will inevitably lead to the final failure because of double misinterpretation.

Of course, we should also see that fascism appeared in the 1930s, and the Western people suffered a great deal of disaster from it. In the face of this realistic problem, Reich, Fromm, Marcuse and others did not take an evasive attitude, but discussed extensively and meaningfully from different angles on the social psychological basis of the rise of fascism. Although their basic direction of integrating Freud theory with Marx's theory is completely wrong, their detailed analysis of the mechanism of social psychological activity, the dissection of character structure and authoritarian character, the exploration of the relationship between "psychological revolution" and "social revolution", especially the study of social psychology as a medium of interaction between social existence and social consciousness, provided some useful materials and revelations, which is worth studying and thinking.

2. The Misinterpretation of Marxist Criticism: "Critique of Everyday Life" and "Theory of Social Criticism"

Reviewing the critical thoughts of contemporary society, the most striking and powerful is the critique of everyday life and theory of social criticism. Western

---

Art Press, 1987.

scholars who hold this kind of critical spirit believe that the essence of Marx's theory is the critical spirit. In contemporary times, Marxism has become more and more a cultural phenomenon and its influence is not reduced, but expanded, with more and more subjects in the world looking for the basis from Marx. In their view, because of the rapid changes and development in the present world, Marx's theory should not remain on the basis of the original, but should abandon those found out to be outdated, and learn to take a critical look at everything. From this point of view, they tried to use "critique of everyday life" and "theory of social criticism" to "supplement" and "develop" Marx's theory.

The French scholar Lefebvre (Henri Lefebvre) believed that the phenomenon of alienation that Marx said had formed a network of suffocating people in daily life, and the exploration of the problem of alienation must go deep into the daily life, and the abolition of the alienation must start with the transformation of daily life. He tried to transform Marx's theory into "a critique of everyday life" based on the alienation of modern people. In his view, "the critique of everyday life" is to reveal to people: the bureaucratic machine of controlling consumption had penetrated into the depth of everyone's experience, and the idea of eliminating alienation must start from self-reform, so that people can overcome the network influence of social system, remove the shell of the state machine's materialization and mystery, and realize the real origin of the state machine as the way of human behavior to weaken the universality and rationality of modern bureaucratic society. In his opinion, only in the fields of daily life, such as work, leisure, entertainment and consumption, can the masses directly experience the repression of capitalist social relations, feel the ubiquitous alienation, and awaken the consciousness of the changing society.

In Lefebvre's opinion, there were mainly such aspects in "the critique of daily life" as: "The critique of daily life" should analyze it according to the true nature of life, and should not turn it into an ambiguous entity; "the critique of daily life" should study the negative and positive factors of confrontation; "the critique of daily life" should study new conflicts and contradictions in new things; "the critique of daily life" should know how to overcome the internal division and contradictions of human nature, which cannot be achieved overnight or in a decisive moment through simple behavior; and "the critique of daily life" should not simplify the problem of life, but should require higher awareness of criticism and self-criticism. In Lefebvre's point of view, "the critique of daily life" was to break through the falsehood of daily life and to uncover the veil of alienation reality. He thought that in daily life, the economic reality, the political superstructure and various possibilities of the revolution were concealed directly by false ideology, and the mass media was used to wipe out the independent thinking and judgment of the masses. Lefebvre pointed out that the false ideology through abstract concepts, incomplete or distorted imagination, idols, etc. to generalize the interests of a certain class. In daily life, consciousness dominated the actual content of life roughly, and the spiritual force without content functioned abstractly. Here, the basic social relationship was the relationship between isolated consumers and isolated consumer objects. In this process, consumer objects become dynamic and meaningful things. Consumers, on the other hand, become automatic reactor. The modern bureaucratic society that controlled consumption left violence as a reserve, relying more on the inherent self-suppression system in everyday life. In order to avoid contradictions and conflicts, this ultra-repressive society adopted a language system to cover the conflict and ideology, which was a free and democratic system. This system made people feel and experience the omnipresent repression, and tried to take the social control principle as a necessary condition for freedom. Lefebvre believed that the free and democratic system of the capitalist society did not bring freedom and happiness to mankind, but had aggravated the overall depression of human nature than the past, with its social control form more perfect in the progress of the technical organization. The progress of technology led to the disappearance of the traditional way of life and the community, and resulted in the rationality of the bureaucracy and the isolation of the individual. As daily life was organized into the social structure of controlling consumption, although the individual was in the daily experience of socialization, he did not know that he was a kind of social existence. Alienation extended to all life in this way, and no individual can get rid of it. When he tried to get rid of it, he isolated himself, which was the sharp form of alienation. In modern developed industrial countries, the alienation imposed by modern material culture and spiritual culture to human beings was manifested in all fields of daily life. Its symbol was that man existed for the sake of things and for the power of bureaucratic society, and that people were turned into tools or chips.

Similar to "the critique of daily life", "the theory of social criticism" is always concerned about the situation of modern people and its solution, but the difference is that the latter regards the critical thinking of negating reality as the fundamental premise of abolishing alienation. It not only weeps and laments for the ability of creative thinking to be suppressed and forgotten, but also makes unremitting efforts to arouse and restore the subjective initiative of people. Horkheimer (Max Horkheimer), the founder of Frankfurt School, believed that social criticism was the internal power of theoretical development and a powerful tool to transform reality. The criticism of social culture was not to put oneself in the process of specialized social labor, but outside of the process of capitalist reproduction, making people clearly aware of the basic contradictions of capitalism. Its purpose was not to maintain the order of the existing society, but to destroy all the established things so as to prove its irrationality and untruthfulness. Social criticism regarded man as the producer of all historical life.

"The theory of social criticism" mainly focuses on the criticism of the developed capitalist society. Marcuse, a famous social critic, believed that capitalism was developing and stable under the new historical conditions, changed the capitalist structure as defined by Marx and created the basis for new economic and political organization in the Western world. In summary, in Marcuse's opinions in this aspect, there are mainly important points as follows: (I) in the so-called developed society, there are various conditions for the transition from a repressive order to a non-repressive order. The capitalist system does not consolidate itself by accepting technological progress because it absorbs the fruits of the technological revolution in an unreasonable way, so that the so-called "consumer society" is actually an "excessively depressed" society. (II) Technology has become the dominant ideology, guiding progress within a powerful country and creating certain forms of life, and ever since then, the progress of technology is gradually equal to the whole rationality. (III) In order to make the society uniform, this so-called rationality dictates that all social forces must be united. The more likely past revolutionaries were to overturn a system in which they benefited from consumption, the more politically submissive they were.

In Marcuse's view, the developed industrial society was a one-sided society, and the integration of totalitarianism and consumerism and the integration of one-sided society and one-sided thinking had resulted in the overall alienation of modern people. The working class was undergoing a fundamental change and no longer appeared as a living contradiction in the existing society. Today, the power situation and life form established in "the affluent society" defeated the protests and actions that tried to liberate humanity from the bondage, and made people into a single creature that only knew material enjoyment without the spiritual pursuit, just passively accepted without active creativity, and only followed the reality but not to criticize the reality. It was the fundamental characteristics of the developed industrial society to reach an absolute rationality through the technological rationality and consumption control. This kind of absolute rationality was the modern totalitarianism that stifled people's critical thinking. Marcuse pointed out that modern totalitarianism and political democracy were not incompatible, and on the contrary, the mask of democracy can better cover up totalitarianism, making it more effective than in the form of autocracy. Once the individual had fallen into a large number of goods and services provided by the totalitarian society, he cannot demand a new society to replace the existing society; and once an individual passively accepted the thoughts, feelings and desires of the present society, he ceased to think about himself and remold himself. This is because the integration of a developed industrial society limits people's understanding of themselves and the possibilities of the future. However, this kind of integration rule is implemented and consolidated through mass culture.

As a basic ideological tendency of Western Marxists, Lukács, Korsch and Gramsci looked for the reasons for the failure of Western revolution in the immature "class consciousness", while Reich, Fromm and others traced the social and cultural psychological origin of fascism in the psychological "authoritative character". Here, Marcuse (including Lefebvre or other members of the Frankfurt School) took "mass culture" as the main obstacle to the liberation struggle of the developed industrial countries. According to Marcuse, "mass culture", like consumer goods, was produced by totalitarian societies as a form of entertainment and narcotics for people. Guided by this culture, the people were making their master's needs and values become his own, and reproduced the existing society in his own mind, consciousness and feelings. In order to reproduce and legalize the existing society, mass culture made the masses sleep through various media, and thus became a form of domination, which made it difficult to establish a foothold of the "negative power" in the society. The non-critical and one-sided nature of the mass culture made it a magic weapon of the ruling class in developed industrial society.

In Marcuse's eyes, before the birth of industrial society, the traditional culture of capitalism was still bidirectional and critical with an aspect of criticism of reality and transcendence of reality. It centered on asceticism and abstract noble virtues, made people consciously replace contentment and happiness with responsibility and discipline as the purpose of life. It established a whole set of substitutes for satisfying desires: from religion, literature and art, sports to entertainment, this culture provided a channel for Libido to release energy, and continued to condemn the fetishism of the commodity world when it made people comfortable with the status quo. However, the cultural tradition had declined and overwhelmed as a result of the advent of the age of industrial technology. And therefore, one side of modern mass culture in the developed industrial society was the ultimate negation of traditional culture, which deprived the person's personality, creativity and self-discipline, and replaced "unhappy consciousness" by "awareness of happiness", that was to replace the awakening and revolt with numbness and submission. Marcuse pointed out that modern capitalism finally stopped the conflicts between the proletarians and the bourgeois, between possibility and necessity, and between inevitability and liberty in its integration with the working class. In developed countries, the highest stage of capitalism was equivalent to the lowest stage of the revolutionary potential. He was full of pessimism and disappointment at the prospect of the industrial social revolution. The whole social critical theorists expressed strong doubts about the ability of human beings to master nature and control social processes.

The social critical theorists thought that the revolution should not only criticize and reveal the alienation reality of modern society, but should also change the unreasonable existing order facts, and the criticism itself was a kind of practice dynamic social change. In their opinions, human beings were the subject of history and the creator of the culture, who can change the reality of alienation and morbid culture. The past revolutions were all the revolutions which did not touch the subjectivity of human beings and replaced the old forms of oppression with a new kind of oppression. The revolution must appeal to the subjective consciousness and the general dialectics of the unity of subject and object, and put man's subjectivity in the first place of revolution.

At first glance, the critique of daily life and the society criticism emphasize the criticism of capitalist society, which seems to carry forward the critical spirit of Marxism, but in fact, separating the scientific spirit of Marxism from the critical spirit. And therefore, they cannot reach the key point of the contemporary capitalist society, and especially they cannot find a way to critically transform the contemporary society.

3. Dreams and Illusions of Sartre and Habermas

Since 1960s, many Western scholars believed that in order to make Marx's theory truly meet the requirements of the new historical practice, it is necessary to explore, sort out and absorb the contents of various philosophical schools, and to supplement, revise and develop it. The various understandings and comments of Western scholars on Marx and his theory all showed the intention of "rebuilding" Marx to varying degrees. Here we choose two representative "rebuilding" schemes of Sartre and Habermas (Jürgen Habermas) to see their ultimate purposes and fates.

According to Sartre, Marx's theory was basically anthropology, and was a theory of human social activities and practice. He pointed out that, through the practice of human activities, human beings were formed as special social beings in the process of creating and recreating society. "Marxism will degenerate into inhuman anthropology if it does not reintegrate the human being as its foundation... It is because of this rejection of human beings, which excludes people from Marxist knowledge that requires the production of existentialist ideas beyond the historical collection of knowledge. The existentialist concept of human beings is the human basis of Marxist anthropology."[214] Sartre firmly opposed the tendency of the so-called Marx study to ignore the human question. In the view of Sartre, there was a tendency to destroy the individual in order to make Marxist theory form an absolute knowledge system. In Sartre's view of point, in order to make Marxist theory truly full of vitality, people must be restored to Marxism.

Based on this understanding, Sartre brightly raised the issue of human studies and its dialectics. Sartre believed that Marx engulfed man in the sea of society. Dialectics should not be the law of nature but only the law of social history caused

---

[214]Sartre: *Critique of Dialectical Reason*, Page 100, Beijing, the Commercial Press, 1963.

by human practice. Dialectics was only practice and an entirety, authigenous and self-existent, and meanwhile, can also be called the logic of action. "If we do not turn dialectics into a sacred law and a metaphysical destiny, then it should come from an individual, not from what I don't know about super-personal aggregates." [215] In Sartre's view, many Marxists had a fundamental wrong understanding of dialectics, which was not from the internal practice of the individual, but from the natural world outside the individual to find dialectics, making dialectics become abstract, dogmatic and metaphysical formula and fatalism, which were separated from man and lost its richness. In order to have a correct understanding of Marx's theory, it is necessary to guide dialectics to the practice of individuals, and to determine dialectics as the universal method and law of human studies. As for the question of how individual practice constitutes dialectics, Sartre also made lengthy and obscure explanations and arguments.

Sartre believed that the core of Marx's theory was the basic concept of social history, and claimed that the historical materialism of history provided the only reasonable explanation. In fact, he used Aristotle's concept of needs, concept of materials and concept of shortage to analyze the realistic society, and regarded the people in the contemporary social life as the isolated beings of universal loneliness and disappointment. On the one hand, human practice gave meaning to material existence and made it fit for human needs, so as to realize the internalization of externality; and on the other hand, the existence of materials required that man be fully suited to its reality, thus realizing the externalization of immanence. Moreover, the more human beings internalize themselves, the more human beings externalized in materials with the dialectical relationship between human beings and objects of that: the behavior continuously transcends the material, and the material constantly denies the act. In this sense, history is the non-human history of human creation.

---

[215]Sartre: *Critique of Dialectical Reason*, Page 133.

Sartre believed that the lack of means of production threatened each other and made it difficult for people to coexist, thus causing alienation and class struggle, which was the root of all antagonism and confrontation in the past and present, and the initial source of all evils, such as violence and exploitation. Under the condition that most of the basic material needs cannot be satisfied and do not constitute the revolutionary requirements of the ruling class, only by overcoming the needs of alienation can become the basis of a new revolution.

Sartre used the "man" to "rebuild" the assumptions and schemes of Marx's theory, which was far from reality and impossible to realize. Marx thought that man was a social being. To treat an isolated individual as a basic unit was to misunderstand the true personality. True individuality was only possible when communism took the place of capitalism. It is only then that talent may become a man of full development. And therefore, Sartre "rebuilt" the concept of human beings according to abstract humanitarian principles, and his attempt to "revive" Marx was proved to be a failure.

Habermas is another famous figure who tried to "rebuild" Marxist theory. In his thought, the focus was mainly on the relationship between theory and practice. Habermas is different from Sartre in the method of "rebuilding" Marx, which is mainly manifested in his theory of "rebuilding" Marx. Habermas believed that "rebuilding" Marx meant to decompose his theory and reconstitute it in a new form in order to better achieve the goals he set for himself. Habermas' rebuilding of Marx includes two stages: in the first stage, he tried to criticize Marx's position in order to identify the possible serious defects; and in the second stage, he tried to form the best version of Marx by all means of eliminating defects.

Habermas distinguished Marx's theory from science and philosophy. He believed that science was objectivism and science itself had no boundaries. Philosophy was different from science in that philosophy cared about its origin, but didn't care enough to put its own point of view into practice. On the contrary, Marx's theory tried to explain the evolution of society, analyzed both the origin and practice of society, and was different from the usual philosophy in anticipating its own function, which can be indirectly self-tested by a practical inference. But Marx's theory had an important defect that it lacked a possibility of practical inference. Habermas believed that Marx reduced the thinking process to the behavior level of instrumentalism, and turned theoretical thinking into simple strategic practice. The reason for this error was that Marx always understood and thought according to the mode of production. Marx always consciously and unconsciously expanded the mode of production beyond its own scope, which was a mistake to downgrade theory to practice too simply. This kind of view of Habermas is a complete misinterpretation of the essence of Marxism.

Habermas also believed that there was an intransigent dichotomy between Marx's empirical theory on capitalist economy and his critical evaluation of revolutionary practice. In his view, there was a substantive difference between the scope of labor and communication. The former was a rational activity with a purpose to the outside world, while the latter included the communication between the subject and object. Each aspect had its own understanding and mode, and had its own rational judgment standard. He asserted that, in the time today, the question of language had replaced the traditional question of consciousness. In this way, Habermas actually cut off all the connections between the superstructure and the economic base. Compared with Marx's original position, Habermas gave up the idea that Marx regarded thought as the product of social existence, and retrogressed to Marx's previous theoretical ideas. From this we can see that Habermas' so-called "rebuilding" Marx is actually dismemberment of Marx.

By carefully comparing the two "rebuilding" ways of Sartre and Habermas, we can clearly see their differences and unsuccessful points. Sartre's "rebuilding" of Marxist theory is essentially a philosophical anthropology. He tried to add the anthropological elements of his own consciousness to Marx's theory, which he thought Marx's theory lacked it. On the contrary, Habermas was interested in reinterpreting Marx's theory from epistemology, especially its inherent truth. The two ways of "rebuilding" Marx are obviously different, and to some extent they are opposed to each other, because if we insist on the anthropological aspects of Marxism, it is bound to give up the pursuit of absolute truth more or less, for man has become the basis of theory. However, if we emphasize the objective truth too much, we must eliminate the subjectivity of Marxism, for anything with subjective color can destroy the objective truth. As a result, both types of "rebuilding" have failed, and they have failed to fully realize what the essence and fundamental stand of Marxism are. Thus, we can say with certainty that any form of "rebuilding" of Marxism is impossible, and at most can only be an understandable fantasy. Scientific theory can be improved in various ways. However, it is impossible to overthrow the basic principles of the original theory, remodel it thoroughly, and at the same time want to keep inextricably linked with the original theory. Even if it comes from a good motive, it is only an unrealistic hope.

4. The Pursuit of Hope

After the Second World War, when the humanism Marxism was in the ascendant, some Western scholars tried their best to advocate the "objectivity" and "scientific nature" of Marxist theory, opposed the supplement of Marxist theory with various names of "human science", emphasized the complete break between Marx and Hegel, and eliminated Hegel's influence completely from Marx's theory. Among them, the structuralist Marxism, represented by Althusser, believed that there were "interruptions" and "breakages" in the course of the development of Marx's thought. There was no continuity between the early "humanitarianism" Marx and the later "scientism" Marx. The scientific Marxist theory had four characteristics including anti-empiricism, anti-reductionism, anti-historicism, and theoretically anti-humanitarianism. He thought that Marx's early works were only the product of "ideology". They denied Marx's early works, and pointed out that it was necessary remove all ideological impurities from it to make Marx's theory a true science and advocated "pluralistic determinism", which made the understanding of the mystery of human society based on the objective interaction of the various components of the whole social structure. Neo-positivism Marxism, represented by Della Volpe (Galvano Della Volpe) and Colletti (Lucio Colletti), believed that Marx inherited the fruits of Kant's philosophy and Rousseau's political views, and that Marx's dialectics had nothing to do with Hegel's dialectics. They interpreted Marx's dialectics as a general method of scientific experiment. On the question of Marx's thought development, they did not emphasize Marx's early stage and negated his late stage, nor emphasized his late stage and negated his early stage, but confirmed the continuity of Marx's early and late thought development, and put forward the so-called "principle of no contradiction".

However, Althusser believed that when studying Marx's theory, it is required to strictly distinguish the different meanings and functions of ideology and scientific theory. Previous researchers often confused the two, resulting in a lot of confusions and contradictions. In fact, ideology does not give people the proper cognitive tools, and it is only a general term of traditional theory. From the perspective of theoretical framework, there is also a qualitative difference between ideology and scientific theory. The development from the former to the latter requires a thorough adjustment and change of the internal structure of the former, which will inevitably lead to the rupture of epistemology. Following this way of thinking, and after a careful and detailed analysis of the history of Marx's ideological development, Althusser came to a surprising and remarkable conclusion that there were epistemological faults between "Young Marx" and "Old Marx", which belonged to two different theoretical frameworks. Marx's scientific discovery itself was a strong break with the previous historical view, and a theoretical interruption between Marxist science and its former ideological history. According to this understanding, Althusser divided the development of Marx's thought into two different historical periods: before 1845 as the early period that he called the ideological period; and after 1845 that he called the scientific period. According to Althusser's understanding, Marx's theoretical writings before 1845 were basically attached to the theoretical framework of Feuerbach and did not exceed the general concerns of Feuerbach. It was until 1845 when Marx distorted the ideology of reality and discovered the new reality: the organized proletariat, developed capitalism, and class struggle according to his own laws. The delightful double discoveries made Marx the unquestioned founder of Marxism. The important sign of Marx's thought changing from the early stage to the later stage is to criticize human philosophy and old ideology mercilessly, to completely reject them as the old philosophy garbage, and finally established a new theoretical framework and general problem which endowed himself with the characteristics of thought under the keen insight and deep thinking of history and reality.

"Marxism is the theoretical anti-humanitarianism", which is the core content of Althusser's Marxist view that had been through in Althusser's theoretical career all the time, and supported his entire theoretical edifice. The reason why this thought is so important is closely related to its fierce criticism of popular humanitarianism in the Western world. Althusser believed that before Marx broke away from Feuerbach in 1845, he regarded humanitarianism as a theory, with liberal humanitarianism in his earlier thought and later Feuerbach's humanitarianism of community that occupied the predominant position. It was only after Marx had made a thorough critique of the theoretical foundation of his youth-the philosophy of man-that his theory reached the state of science. Without a complete break with theoretical humanitarianism, there would be no scientific Marxism. Accordingly, Althusser asserted that Marxism was theoretical anti-humanitarianism.

Althusser pointed out that, since 1845, Marx had completely broken away from all theories that attributed history and politics to the essence of man. Marx's break with philosophical humanism or philosophical humanitarianism was by no means a minor detail, but Marx's great scientific discovery, which meant that Marx abandoned the theoretical framework of previous philosophy and adopted a new theoretical framework, a new systematic way of asking questions to the world, and some new principles and new methods. This new discovery was integrated with Marx's historical materialism. In Althusser's view, it was just because Marx eliminated the concept of human being as the subject of history that it was possible to study all concrete problems in the course of history scientifically.

How to treat the relationship between Marx and Hegel and Feuerbach, especially the differences between Marx's dialectics and Hegel's dialectics, has always been a controversial topic in Western academic circles. Althusser held that Marx's dialectics and Hegel's dialectics had completely different structures and fundamental differences. He firmly opposed the metaphor that Marx's dialectics was the reverse of Hegel's dialectics. He pointed out that the essential differences of Marx's dialectics and Hegel's dialectics lied in their different understandings of the whole society. In Hegel's viewpoint, society expresses a unity in all its aspects or fields at a certain stage of development, and it is a simple inner spiritual principle. Marx, on the other hand, does not admit that there is any simple initial essence in the social foundation that dissimilates and expresses oneself in different fields, and thinks that it is necessary to admit that any object is a complex structure from the beginning.

Althusser also put forward the famous "reading method according to the symptoms" for reading Marx's works in the process of studying Marx's thought and criticizing the thought of "humanitarianism Marxism" by combining the structuralism method. That is, when reading Marx's works, it is required to regard what is seen in words as a surface structure, and to find out the deep structure hidden in it. He believed that reading Marx's works not only to see the writing of black and white, it was more important to see the silent thought, which was not clearly stated but hidden in the original text. Only by grasping it can we grasp the theoretical framework and the essence of the problems in Marx's theory and touch the essence of the ideas that are active in Marx's works.

To sum up, it can be seen that Althusser's analysis and evaluation of Marxist theory has its positive and reasonable factors, including a certain grain of truth, but he completely denied Marx's early thought and any sense of humanitarianism, which is biased and partial. It is wrong and unsuccessful to understand Marx by means and principles of structuralism, to try to link structuralism with Marxist theory, and to revive Marx's scientific thought.

Della Volpe and Colletti, the representatives of Neo-positivism Marxism, believed that the failure of the proletarian revolution was mainly due to the incorrect interpretation of modern capitalism, and the replacement of scientific decision-making with vague humanitarianism and Hegel's doctrine. For this reason, they advocated reexamining Marx's basic works and analyzing and studying the history and present situation of the proletariat in order to draw the correct conclusions from it, to make Marx's theory become a decisive cognitive tool for real class analysis and prophecy again, and to emphasize that Marx's theory should make empirical analysis and scientific foresight on the development of history. In their view, in quite a long time between 1920s and the Second World War, it was the Marxism of the Soviet model and the humanitarianism Marxism from Lukács to the Frankfurt School that dominated the stage of Marxist thought and theory. Although they were quite different, they shared the same philosophical source and basis: they shared the same Hegel matrix. Both versions of Marxism assumed the continuity of "dialectics" between Hegel and Marx, but the former emphasized Hegel's "dialectics of matter", whereas the latter emphasized Hegel's "collectivity" and "alienation". They all regarded the real proletariat as a philosophical category and ideological citation, as the embodiment of the law of dialectics, or the subject-object, rather than as a concrete, active, and empirical entity, to study its specific internal structure, its practical actions and theoretical forms and its historical model of self-activity throughout the world. In this way, the critical and scientific potential of Marxism disappeared into dialectical and methodological speculation.

Della Volpe and Colletti claimed to re-evaluate and supplement Marx's theory. The focus was on dialectics, particularly the attempt to explain the relationship between Marx's theory and Hegel's dialectics. Della Volpe thought that there was no continuity between Hegel's dialectics and Marx's dialectics. In his opinion, Marx provided us with the method of using the logical structure, abstract way, concept and philosophical assumptions of dialectics with idealism to critically identify all the elements of this dialectic essence, at the same time, Marx also provided us with a new exposition on dialectical methods, which made us pay attention to the profound epistemological wealth of historical materialism and general experimental methods. Della Volpe pointed out that Hegel's dialectics went back to abstract dialectics by moving from abstraction to concrete, and confused the development process of the concept and the development of the actual thing. Marx's dialectics, on the other hand, contained epistemology with the establishment of scientific laws from concrete to abstract to concrete. He said: "We think that Marx's method is the way to make abstraction to be continuously historicized, is the means of revealing abstract historical prescriptions, and revealing abstract historical prescriptions is the practical meaning of circular movement (concrete-abstract-concrete)."[216]

Colletti, a student of Della Volpe, continued to develop his teacher's point of view, and advocated more radically that the dialectical materialistic dialectics of matter, which was now popular, was copied from Hegel. Because materialist dialectics was Hegel's dialectics of matter in a strict sense, just as this kind of material dialectics presupposed the total breakdown of the conflict of reality into logical opposites or contradictions, it also very consistently presupposed rejection of materialism, which was to refuse the objective reality to be outside of man but not depending on man.

Della Volpe believed that what Marx described as a contradiction in the real world was actually a real opposition, not a contradiction opposition. Colletti further developed this view, and pointed out that the real opposition was the opposition without contradiction, and it did not violate the law of "law of identity" and "law of

---

[216]Galvano Della Volpe: *Marxism and Hegel's Dialectics*, Published on the Soviet Union Magazine—*Problems of Philosophy*, 1957 (3).

contradiction", so it was compatible with formal logic, whereas the opposition of contradiction was contradictory, and it gave rise to a dialectical opposition. He held that, in the opposition of contradictions, the opposing parties were interdependent rather than isolated, and if there was no contradiction with it, this contradiction would lose its condition of existence and its significance, and vice versa. In real opposition, the opposing parties were not interdependent, but can exist in isolation. Even without the other side, this side will not lose its condition of existence and significance.

In Colletti's view, the basic principle of materialism and science was the law of contradiction. It cannot contain dialectical contradictions, but can only contain "real contradictions", conflicts and oppositions between forces. There was no contradiction in the real opposition. It was not a dialectical contradiction, but a non-contradictory opposition. Colletti also believed that although Marx also continuously talked about contradictions, that is, contradictions existing in nature and society, for science, contradiction was always and should be "subjective errors" that need to be ruled out, and science contained "the principle of no contradiction". For science, there were no objective contradictions, and science only admitted the contradiction in theory. When the theory itself contradicted itself, science will immediately declare Marx's dialectics as the materialistic logic of modern experimental science and dialectical materialistic material dialectics as copied from Hegel, then use Kant's "real opposition" to replace the "contradictory opposition" in real life, and put forward the principle of no contradiction, all of which was originated from Della Volpe, and inherited and brought into play by Colletti.

CHAPTER 6   THE PLOT TO SPLIT THE "DIOSCURI"[217]

Marxism was founded jointly by Marx and Engels. Engels' outstanding scientific contributions and his friendship and cooperation with Marx are of key significance to the establishment of Marxism. It will inevitably develop from dismemberment of Marx to the creation of the opposition between Marx and Engels to misunderstand Marxism. It is exactly this path that Western Marxism and Marxology took. They denigrated the friendship between Marx and Engels, tried to put the giants like the "Dioscuri" against each other, quibblingly found the differences in Marx's and Engels' thought theory, and described this differences as contradiction and opposition. The so-called opposition of Marx and Engels' is just another way to dismember Marx.

1. The Myth of "the Opposition between Marx and Engels"

Lenin pointed out: "to correctly evaluate Marx's viewpoint, we must undoubtedly be familiar with the works of Engels, who is his closest comrade and friend. If we do not know all the works of Engels, we cannot understand Marxism, and therefore, we cannot fully expound Marxism."[218] In other words, Engels' works are a part of Marxism, and Engels is indisputably one of the founders of Marxism. It is because of the joint efforts of Marx and Engels that Marxism is presented to people as a complete theoretical system and becomes the scientific theoretical weapon of proletarian revolutionary practice.

---

[217]Dioscuri are the twin brothers in ancient Greek mythology, and the crystallization of the love between Zeus and Leda. They are inseparable and regarded as the protector of Sparta. See Marx's Letter to Engels dated April 24th 1867.

[218]*The Collected Works of Lenin*, Chinese Edition 1, Vol. 21, Page 72, Beijing, People's Publishing House, 1959.

However, in the middle of 20th century, the comparative study of Marx and Engels became fashionable. Among the Western scholars, the "new discoveries" of Marx and Engels emerged one after another, and the myth of "the opposition between Marx and Engels" was also faked out. Numerous papers and publications wiped out the friendship between Marx and Engels and the consistency of their thoughts and ideas, and regarded the activity of Marx and Engels to jointly establish a scientific worldview as a "sad scam".[219] In their eyes, there had never been a unified Marxism, and the so-called "Marxism" and "Engels" were two completely different doctrines. Not only bourgeois Marxists thought so, but some "Neo-Marxists" also participated in this kind of chorus of the opposition between Marx and Engels, and acted in concert with "Marxists". In this "chorus", there was no consistent tune and no unified command, and they just understood and forged the relationship between Marx and Engels from their own point of view. Despite there were various contradictions between them with no unanimous conclusions, there was a common voice to declare that Marx and Engels were opposed against each other.

The scholars who made the argument of the opposition between Marx and Engels did their utmost to belittle Engels and deny his status as one of the founders of Marxism. They believed that in the history of Marxist thought, Engels was only a propagandist, or at most an "illustrator." Engels was portrayed as a man who simplified and vulgarized Marx's theory, as if Marx's true thought and his theories about social history were "modified" by Engels with Darwinism and philosophical mechanism, so all kinds of insults and censures overwhelmed Engels. They attacked Engels for explaining Marxism superficial and arbitrarily, and deviating from the philosophical line formulated by Marx. They believed that Engels was the first revisionist in the history of Marxism, the plagiarists of Hegel's dialectics, and an

---

[219]Norman Levine, an American scholar, discussed the so-called overall opposition between Marx and Engels specifically in the book *Pathetic Scam: Marx against Engels* published in 1975.

idealist looking for a substitute for God in nature. In short, they thought that there was a "fundamental difference" between Marx and Engels, and this difference was not only expressed in details, but in the most fundamental problem of the development of nature and society. That was to say, Marx and Engels were opposed to each other on fundamental theoretical issues.

In fact, about the myth of opposition between Marx and Engels is not the "patent" of Marxists in the middle of 20th century, but is something that has been emerged since the birth of Marxism. Engels once pointed out: "Since 1844, there had been numerous essays about the vicious Engels deceived virtuous, and they alternately appeared with another type of essay about Ahriman-Marx's seduction of Ohrmuzd-Engels from the right path."[220] From the very beginning, the opponents of Marxism took it as a magic weapon in attacking Marxism to search for materials on the differences between Marx and Engels, and to create the opposition between Marx and Engels. From *The Historical Philosophy of Hegel and Hegelians including Marx and Hartman* published by Barthes in 1890 and *The Historical Philosophy as Sociology* published in 1897 in arguments with Engels, we can clearly see this. Of course, different from contemporary Marxists, Barthes was not familiar with Marx's early works. By comparing Marx's *Das Kapital* and Engels' *Anti-Dühring* and *The Origin of the Family, Private Property and the State*, Barthes asserted that Marx and Engels represented two different sociological tendencies respectively, saying that Marx's *Das Kapital* represents social statics, while Engels represents the tendency of social dynamics.[221]

In Russia, the views of opposition between Marx and Engels found a market among

---

[220]*Marx/Engels Collected Works*, Chinese Edition 1, Vol. 36, Page 14, Beijing, People's Publishing House, 1974.

[221]See Gorshkova: *The Development of Historical Materialism by Engels in 1890s*, Page 53~54, Beijing, People's Publishing House, 1981.

populists. In 1907, Chernóv (Víktor Mikháilovich Chernóv) published the *Essay Collection of Philosophy and Sociology*, advocating that Marx's thought in *Theses on Feuerbach* is completely different from Engels' thought and saying that Engels stands for "the crudest materialism of arbitrariness". In *Marxism and Transcendental Philosophy*, Chernóv "attempted to antagonize Marx and Engels from the very beginning". Lenin gave a powerful critique on this in *Materialism and Empiricism*.

While Chernóv was attempting to antagonize Marx and Engels, Burchowski of Poland was working hard on the book *Anti-Engels*, which was published in 1910. It was a theoretical "liquidation" of Engels that he had taken years to complete. At the time, it was a book that more systematically expounded the opposition between of Marx and Engels. In this book, Burchowski seriously attacked Engels under the guise of preserving the purity of Marx's theory. He believed that Engels' *Anti-Dühring* was a betrayal of Marx's theory, and that Engels' "positivism" developed in *Anti-Dühring* was very different from Marx's "Humanism", whereas this difference indicated that Marx and Engels were fundamentally opposed to each other in their philosophical thinking.

In Italy, as the Marxist Labriola did not completely get rid of his early historical views, he opposed positivism and philosophy systematization, and meanwhile showed a certain tendency of setting Marx and Engels against each other. Whereas Benedetto Croce openly accused Engels, saying that "Engels' views are completely different from Marx's." In his view, "Marx and Engels are just private friends."[222] Jin Tilai, another Italian philosopher, believed that Engels had misinterpreted Hegel and led to different views from Marx. "Engels' *Anti-Dühring* has never reached the true understanding of Marxism, and has never touched the philosophical part of his

---

[222]Croce: *Historical Materialism and the Economics of Karl Marx*, Page 82. See Jacoby: *Failed Dialectics*, Page 54, Cambridge, 1981.

friend and teacher."[223] During this period, there was also a heated discussion of the opposition between Marx and Engels in Italy. In *The Letter to Croce*, Surell wrote, "It is sure to say that Engels has completely deviated from Marx." He did not grasp a broad philosophical background, and obviously lacked a clear idea of Hegelianism. To a large extent, he led historical materialism into the orbit of evolution and made it an absolute dogma."[224] Odrel also criticized Engels as "the first to reproduce Marxism not only as an economic dogma, but also as a complete system of philosophy". He thought that Marx used "class itself" as the motive force of the revolution, while Engels replaced it with productive forces, saying that Engels was full of "a spirit of industry".[225]

It is Lukács' *History and Class Consciousness* that has the greatest influence on contemporary Western Marxists or "Neo-Marxism". In this book, Lukács held that Engels wrongly "extended and applied dialectics to nature, but the key determinant of dialectics, namely, the interaction between subject and object and the unity of theory and practice... was not in our understanding of nature."[226]

In his opinion, dialectics exists only in the field of social history. And therefore, he accused Engels of "dialectics of nature", which was mechanical nature theory with positivism tendency and an essential difference from Marx's humanitarianism thought. As Lukács is regarded as the ancestor of "Neo-Marxists", especially due to the publication of Marx's early work *Manuscripts of Economics and Philosophy of 1844* in 1932, some of his views in *History and Class Consciousness* have been confirmed. Thus some of Lukács' misconceptions are widely spread.

---

[223]Jin Tilai: *Marx's Philosophy*, Page 125~126. See Jacoby: *Failed Dialectics*, Page 54.

[224]Surell: *The Letter to Croce*. See Jacoby: *Failed Dialectics*, Page 54.

[225]See Odrel: *A Study Manuscript on the Division of Marxism*, Page 59, 70, 74~75. See Jacoby: *Failed Dialectics*, Page 55.

[226]Lukács: *History and Class Consciousness*, Page 24 Note .

The "Neo-Marxism" grown up in the middle of the 20th Century is directly influenced by Lukács, such as the Frankfort School, Existentialist Marxism, Practice School in Yugoslavia and the "New Left School" in Europe and the United States, which make a fuss on the opposition between Marx and Engels, and further exert the wrong ideas of Lukács, Korsch and others in this aspect. Even Scientism Marxism, the other school of the "Western Marxism" with little influence of Lukács and others, also advocate the opposition between Marx and Engels. For instance, Althusser, Colletti and others all discussed the so-called contradiction and opposition between Marx and Engels from their own standpoint.

Schmidt (Alfred Schmidt), one of the representative figures of Frankfurt School, put forward a variety of criticisms to Engels in his book *The Concept of Nature in Marx*, saying that Marx's view of nature is fundamentally different from Engels' view of nature. In his opinion, The Concept of Nature in Marx is a humanized nature, the product of social labor that has been processed and reformed by human labor, and is a social and historical category; whereas Engels believed in the pure nature of Feuerbach and put nature and social history against each other, making them as two separate parts, thus deviating from Marx's theory on nature and regressing to an arbitrary metaphysical stance. He believed that it was a true unity that Marx unified man and nature in the practical category, while it was an idealistic proposition that Engels tried to emphasize the unity of the world in the material category, because there was only concrete material form in the real world, and there was no abstract material form at all. To regard abstract matter as the ontology of philosophy was to establish philosophy on some fictional principles, which was a mean idealism. As a result, Schmidt opposed Marx and Engels on some basic theoretical issues. Other representatives of the Frankfurt School, such as Adorno (Theodor W. Adorno), Horkheimer, Marcuse and Fromm have demonstrated the opposition between Marx and Engels to some extent.

The Yugoslavia Practice School philosophers Markovich, Peter Lovic, Vranicki and others also thought there were "essential differences" between Marx and Engels in the interpretation of some basic philosophical problems. In his famous *History of Marxism*, Franitzki regarded Marx as a "philosopher of revolutionary practice", while Engels was "the creator of dialectical materialism" and the believer of the dialectical concept of "naturalism", and accused Engels for artificially opposing materialism with idealism by supporting "metaphysics of materialism" and separating existence from thought, material from consciousness, and object from subject.

Western Marxism was established by some bourgeois scholars who claimed to "study the history and theory of Marxism objectively without any prejudice". Among them, except for a few scholars such as McLellan and Gould Na, the vast majority of Marxists regard the opposition between Marx and Engels as an important discovery in 20th century for demonstration.

Lichtheim (George Lichtheim) was highly praised by modern Western Marxists such as Levine for his first clear and systematic demonstration of the opposition between Marx and Engels.[227] He demonstrated the "differences" between Marx and Engels in social history and socialist theory in a series of works such as *Marxism: An Historical and Critical Study*, *The Origins of Socialism*, *From Marx to Hegel* and *Marxism*. In the book *Marxism*, he specially listed a chapter "'Scientific' Tradition of Engels and Marxist "to fabricate the opposition between Marx and Engels. Lichtheim believed that what Marx represented was a critical theory emphasizing "real man", while Engels represented a kind of scientism theory which emphasized "objective" and "fact". Thus, he described "dialectical materialism" as an "innovative" worldview founded by Engels in late 19th century.

L Lander Graber, the Neo-Thomas, thought Engels' "interpretation of materialism

---

[227]See Norman Levine: *Anthropology in Marx's and Engels' Thoughts*, Published on *Journal of Comparative Communist Studies*, Omnibus of Issue 1-2, Vol. 6, 1973.

was carried out according to the old tradition of mechanical materialism." [228] In his point of view, Engels tried to save dialectics, but the rescue was unsuccessful. On the contrary, the "old traditional factors" which Marx has overcome, namely, the factors of mechanical materialism, were brought into Marxism, so Engels did not know how to grasp the relationship between man and reality in an abstract way. Instead, he concretely and empirically explained the relationship, thus stiffening and dogmatizing the Marxist view. And therefore, he declared that Engels had put an end to Marxist philosophy.

J. Fisher, another Neo-Thomas, thought Marx integrated Hegel's dialectics with Feuerbach's humanism, and came up with the theory of self-emancipation of man and man, which was the essence of Marx's philosophy, and was quite different from dialectical materialism, because the concept of ontology established by the natural theory of dialectical materialism can only lead to metaphysics. Fisher believed that Engels was the founder of dialectical materialism, because after Engels created the dialectical materialism, he "brought the dialectical into individual philosophy department", which combined with modern natural science, so that his departure from Marx's on the road was farther and farther.[229]

I. Fetscher of the Federal Republic of Germany pretended to objectively regard the opposition between Marx and Engels as a reasonable change of Marxist philosophy. He thought that Marx's early works represented true Marxist philosophy. For young Marx, attention was focused on the necessity of eliminating alienation in theory, but when Marx later discovered the proletariat as a social force, and believed that when the revolutionary actions of the proletariat can eliminate alienation, he no

---

[228]Lander Graber: *Dialectic Problems*, Published on *Studies on Marxism*, Division 3, Page 57, Tubingen, 1960.

[229]See J. Fisher: *Materialist and Positivism in the Present Age*, Page 66, Gratz, Vienna. Altoting, 1953.

longer paid attention to the theoretical argument about the necessity of eliminating alienation. Since then Marx had not contributed much in philosophy. It was only in *Anti-Dühring* and later works that Engels developed the world view of the proletariat, namely, dialectical materialism.[230] Fetscher held that Engels should take primary responsibilities for the development of Marxism into an ideological system. He also pointed out that because Engels overemphasized the factor of scientific determinism and equated the natural process with the social process, it destroyed the dialectical unity of theory and practice and ignored the consciousness component in the social process.

De Vries also said that we had seen all the principles of the dialectical materialist cognitive theory only in Engels' works wrote in the 1970s and 1980s. He believed that "because Engels' philosophical activities deviated from the philosophical point of view in Marx's early works, the initial central idea of Marx became very vague between the workers' movement and later Marxist philosophers. All attention had been paid to the process of the emergence and demise of capitalist societies, as if the social movements, like those of nature, must have moved in accordance with a certain law."[231]

Maximilien Rubel was the first French Marxist to put forward the concept of "Marxism". In his view, Marx was "a pioneer of a complex humanitarianism", who did not leave behind a complete system of scientific and social thought. As a proletarian world view, Marxism was organized according to Engels' works, with "subtle relation with Marx's basic doctrine". But in fact, Rubel still made a fuss about the relationship between Marx and Engels. He thought that Marx's theory of

---

[230]See I. Fetscher: *From the Philosophy of the Proletariat to the World View of the Proletariat*, Published on *Studies on Marxism*, Division 2, Page 44.

[231]J. De Vries: *The Cognitive Theory of Dialectical Materialism*, Page 15, Munich, 1958.

revolutionary history was transformed by Engels into an automatic historical process determined by economic structure and class confrontation, and the dialectical unity between revolutionary action and the cognition of the social and economic constraints of historical process disappeared.

Like Rubel, another Marxist scientist Michel Henry in France thought that Marxism was not related to Marx's own ideas, and it was a kind of philosophical system founded by Engels after Marx's death, which was incompatible with Marx's will and did not conform to Marx's thought. And therefore, he thought with regret that Marx had not been understood all the time. In his opinion, all Marx's basic philosophical works (*Critique of Hegel's Philosophy of Right*, *Manuscripts of Economics and Philosophy of 1844*, and especially *The German Ideology*) had not been understood by those who founded Marxist ideology and built their own world according to it. It seems that only they understand Marx, but what we see from the Marx they understand is Fichte, or they understand Marx from Fichte's standpoint, because, according to their understanding, Marx only emphasized the dynamic function of subjective consciousness, and the whole history (including natural history) was the self-realization of human beings in the process of self-alienation. So, in their eyes, Marx broke away from materialism while Engels preserved materialism and expounded the view of evolution on the basis of the inherent contradiction between nature and social history. And therefore, they accused Engels of "materialist theory of evolution", who cannot understand how consciousness is generated and its position in the history, and run counter to Marx's thought of "initiative".

Since 1970s, Kolakowski, Levine and others have stolen the limelight in preaching the opposition between Marx and Engels.

Kolakowski, a Polish philosopher in exile in England, devoted a great deal of time to taking about the so-called "fundamental differences of thought" between Marx and Engels in his book *Main Currents of Marxism*, which are summed up in four aspects: (I) the differences between naturalistic evolution and the anthropocentrism; (II) the differences between the technological view of knowledge and the epistemology of practice; (III) the differences between the view of the "decline of philosophy" and the view of the integration of philosophy and life; and (IV) the differences between infinite progress theory and revolutionary eschatology. He particularly emphasized the opposition between Marx and Engels on dialectics. In his view, Marx regarded dialectics as the interaction between subject and object, which ultimately led to the unity of subject and object; whereas Engels' dialectics was put forward under the influence of the discovery of Darwinian Theory and Darwinism, and explained various phenomena of society and history from the viewpoint of naturalism. And therefore, it will affect the objective historical law to deny the individual's activities. So Kolakowski said that there was potential of transcendentalism in Engels's dialectics of nature, which was fundamentally different from Marx's view of "anthropocentrism". He said that *Dialectics of Nature*, Engels's book, was full of obsolete illustrations and groundless speculative reasoning about philosophical cosmology. He even found the differences between them from the learning methods of Marx and Engels, saying that Engels was lack of specialized philosophical accomplishment, and was an amateur enthusiast of philosophy.

The American scholar Norman Levine is dedicated to collecting ideas about the opposition between Marx and Engels. The purpose of his book, *Pathetic Scam: Marx against Engels*, is to try to prove the complete opposition between Marx and Engels. He claimed that these oppositions were manifested in philosophy and sociology, in the view of nature and history, in the interpretation of the basis of the future communist society, and in the understanding of the ways and tactics to realize communism. In his opinion, Marx based his philosophy on the concept of practice. Man was the existence of practice, and man changed the nature through his own activities (practice), making the nature become the nature of humanization. Man gave the nature people's nature in the transformation of nature at the same time, and reflected the purpose of man in the nature. Engels, on the other hand, ignored the meaning of human premise, considering the free matter and movement as the basic force in the universe. Engels was a metaphysical materialist because matter and motion produced man and nature. Levine believed that the differences between Marx and Engels in the view of social history lied that Marx did not regard history as an inevitable process, did not think that the development of history was a single line and was driven by the forces of the macro universe to move in one direction. Whereas Engels regarded history as a single line of development and believed that there was a kind of macro cosmic force that determined the inevitable path of history. In a word, behind the unique curved lens of Levine and others, Engels became the sinner who dogmatized the creative Marxism, and transformed Marxist dialectics into philosophical mechanical theory and social positivism. They believed that after Engels, the viewpoints understood by Marxist researchers (including Plekhanov, Lenin and others) did not belong to Marxism, but to "Engels". Marxism and Engels belong to different ideological systems.

Due to the formation of a strong academic trend of thought in Marxology in the West, the bourgeois scholars have realized that it is necessary to compile a large encyclopedia to summarize all the strange theories in the study of Marxism, so *Marxism, Communism, and Western Society: A Comparative Encyclopedia* came into being. Carl Balestrrem wrote a lengthy entry about Engels for it.[232] In this article, he summarized the Western views of the opposition between Marx and Engels on the following three points. Firstly, Engels believed that history was an objective process determined by the economy, developing in the inevitable direction of its nature; Marx, on the other hand, regarded history as a process influenced by concrete action subjects in revolutionary practice. Secondly, Engels demonstrated a dialectical philosophy of nature in detail, namely, dialectics of nature; Marx, on the other hand, only envisioned the nature by connecting with

---

[232]See *Marxism, Communism, and Western Society: A Comparative Encyclopedia*, Vol. 3, New York, 1972.

human beings, and conceived nature as the alienated object of human labor, which must be restored to its original state. Thirdly, Engels contributed to a comprehensive ideological system through his discourse on dialectical philosophy of nature, epistemology and historical philosophy. Marx, however, emphasized the rationality of his whole theory, made it have the nature of experience, practicality and criticism, and opposed the transcendental, abstract and dogmatic form of ideology system.

Balestrrem did not put forward any questions further more: that is why Western scholars put forward the opposition between Marx and Engels in these three aspects. Of course, even if Balestrrem raised this question, he could not answer it, for he himself had the same prejudice on the opposition between Marx and Engels. In fact, the Western scholars put forward the opposition between Marx and Engels to split the relationship between Marxism and the proletarian revolutionary movement, to portray Engels as a vulgar and ideological man of Marxism, and to believe that the proletarian revolutionary movement was only associated with this vulgar ideology, so that they can criticize the successors of Marxism in an imposing manner, saying that they inherited Engels' "vulgar ideology", not "Marxism".

Although Western Marxists appeared as scholars, and claimed to study Marxist history and theory objectively without prejudice, in fact, the deep-rooted influence of bourgeois ideology on them permeated all the time into their research work. They tried to put Marx and Engels against each other, which seemed to be an academic problem, but by actually aiming to achieve the goal of destroying the complete scientific theoretical system of Marxism by splitting the theoretical relationship and historical inheritance relationship of Marx, Engels and the successors. Rather than glorifying Marx, they are isolating Marx.

2. The Fiction of "Humanism Marx" and " Scientism Engels"

Early believers of the opposition between of Marx and Engels just found some words in the classic works of Marxism as the basis to prove the differences in the thoughts of Marx and Engels, then exaggerated indiscriminately, and generalized the conclusion of the opposition between Marx and Engels, thinking that it can wipe out the revolutionary friendship between Marx and Engels and prove the inconsistency of the thoughts of Marx and Engels, thus negating Marxism. Marxists in the 20th century put emphasis on Marxist theory system when making the opposition between Marx and Engels, and proved the lies of "the overall opposition" between Marx and Engels from all aspects of Marxism history and theory. The so-called "Humanism Marx" and "Scientism Engels" they greatly exaggerated was a kind of fiction with ulterior motives.

Lander Graber said Engels was different from Marx in that the nature described by Engels did not exist to Marx. Marx advocated the anthropocentrism of philosophy, which was contrary to Engels' view of the "inherent comprehensibility" of nature. He believed that Marx always insisted on the speculative unity of matter and spirit, while Engels let man's own production and reproduction depend on "matter and free nature", thus undermining this unity. So he accused Engels of "demanding a study of the real world" as the "root of the dogma of Marxism".[233]

In *Marxism, Communism, and Western Society: A Comparative Encyclopedia*, Balestrrem quoted the views of Lander Graber, Fetscher and others, saying that Marx and Engels had completely different views. Marx did not pay attention to the new discoveries of natural science from the angle of philosophy and methodology. Engels, on the other hand, overemphasized the natural science and stressed the factor of scientific determinism, and equated the natural process with social process, thus destroying the dialectical unity of theory and practice and ignoring the consciousness component in social process.

Kolakowski described Engels as a naturalist, and an admirer of evolution. In his view,

---

[233]Lander Graber: *Dialectic Problems*, Published on *Studies on Marxism*, Division 3, Page 58.

Engels moved the laws of nature into the realm of history, explained man with the laws of nature and evolution, and believed that man was governed by the law of evolution, which is absolutely contrary to Marx's viewpoint that nature we know is an extension of man and an organ of practical activity. Based on this viewpoint, Kolakowski also proposed that there were two different centers between Marx and Engels, which Marx advocated "human center", and Engels advocated "natural center".

Fiction, however, is always fictional. It says that "Marx wisely ignored (outside of man) the natural world"[234], with no "interest" in nature at all[235]; and says that Engels only recognizes the "independent existence" of nature, neglects the initiative of man, and regards man as "the passive object of the ruthless external force". However, the historical fact of Marx's and Engels' thought development is not so at all.

The fact is that Marx showed a clear interest in the philosophy of nature as early as when he began his philosophical research, because he realized that without a deeper understanding of nature, there can be no real understanding of man and society. And therefore, natural science is the foundation of human science.

In 1837, during his rest and recuperation in Straw, Marx read all of Hegel's works, including *Science of Logic* and *The Philosophy of Nature*. In 1839, before writing his doctoral thesis, Marx wrote three plans[236] for the outline of Hegel's *The Philosophy of Nature*, which basically reflected the main contents of Hegel's philosophy of nature. Marx himself also said that in 1837 he spent a lot of his brain studying natural science.

---

[234]Lichtheim: *Marxism*, Page 247, London, 1964.

[235]Petrovich (Ivan Petrovich Pavlov): *Marx in the Middle of 20th Century*, Page 28, New York, 1967.

[236]See *Marx/Engels Collected Works*, Chinese Edition 1, Vol. 40, Page 176~182.

During the period of *Rheinische Zeitung*, Marx was also a Hegel idealist believer, but he had tried to deduce such a conclusion from objectivism of Hegel's idealism that social institutions should be based on the natural laws of the outside world. He insisted that legislators should not put their whims above the nature of things, because legislators did not actually "create" or "invent" laws, "just as those who are good at swimming do not create or invent the nature of water and gravity."[237]

In *Manuscripts of Economics and Philosophy of 1844*, Marx pointed out more clearly that the science of nature, like science of man, was part of the world view of communism, whereas the biggest flaw in the previous philosophy was "alienation" of "increasing materials" as suggested by natural science, "even history took the natural science into account, and only regarded it as a factor of enlightenment, usefulness and some great discoveries".[238] At the same time, Marx pointed out more deeply that man's profound understanding of nature was a practical force to promote social progress, and that natural science "entered human life and changed human life" through the development of industry. Although it still constituted the basis of human life in the form of alienation, on the other hand, it provided conditions for "the liberation of human beings".[239] Marx added: "Science is the science of reality only from nature."[240] However, Western Marxists regarded *Manuscripts of Economics and Philosophy of 1844* as the basis of Marx's emphasis on man, negation of nature or "with no interests in nature". Surely, Man occupies

---

[237]*Marx/Engels Collected Works*, Chinese Edition 1, Vol. 1, Page 183.

[238]*Marx/Engels Collected Works*, Chinese Edition 1, Vol. 42, Page 128, Beijing, People's Publishing House, 1979.

[239]*Marx/Engels Collected Works*, Chinese Edition 1, Vol. 42, Page 128, Beijing, People's Publishing House, 1979.

[240]*Marx/Engels Collected Works*, Chinese Edition 1, Vol. 42, Page 128, Beijing, People's Publishing House, 1979.

an extremely important position in the *Manuscripts of Economics and Philosophy of 1844*, but *Manuscripts of Economics and Philosophy of 1844* never denied the reality and priority of nature. Marx thought that the basic content of labor was objectification. That is, workers condensed their essential power in products, and the objectification of labor must be based on the objective reality of nature.

In *The German Ideology*, Marx and Engels believed that history contained two aspects, namely, the natural aspect and the human aspect were "closely connected"[241], thus resolving the problem put forward in *The Holy Family* when ridiculing the idea that if "the theoretical and practical relationships between man and nature are excluded from the historical movement, and the natural sciences and industry are excluded"[242], even the most preliminary cognition of historical reality can be obtained.

Later, Marx studied mathematics meticulously in the course of heavy political economic research, and left behind the famous *The Mathematical Manuscripts of Karl Marx*. His *Das Capital* made extensive use of mathematics, mechanics, mechanology, technology and agronomy. In November 24th 1859, after Darwin's *On the Origin of Species* was published, Marx quickly read the book and talked for months with Liebknecht about Darwin and the revolutionary forces of his discovery, and highly appraised Darwinian theory for providing the basis of natural history for their views. Even in his later years, Marx attached great importance to the development of natural science. In 1882, at the Munich Electric Exhibition, French physicist Marcel Deprez showed off his first experimental transmission line between Miesbach and Munich, and Marx paid particular attention. As Engels said, "every

---

[241]*Marx/Engels Collected Works*, Chinese Edition 1, Vol. 3, Page 20 Note ①, Beijing, People's Publishing House, 1956.

[242]*Marx/Engels Collected Works*, Chinese Edition 1, Vol. 2, Page 191, Beijing, People's Publishing House, 1957.

new discovery in any theoretical science, even if its practical application is not even foreseeable, it makes Marx feel hearty joy, but when it comes to the discovery of an immediate revolutionary impact on industry and the general development of history, his joy is completely different"[243], because Marx "regarded science first as a powerful lever of history and as a revolutionary force in the highest sense".[244] Marx regarded gunpowder, compass and printing as three great inventions that predicted the arrival of bourgeois society, and pointed out clearly that "science is also included in the productive forces", that the great industry integrated the huge natural force and the natural science into the production process, and that in the social big machine production, the production process had become the scientific application, and the science had become the production process function.

From the correspondences between Marx and Engels, we can see Marx's attitude towards natural science more clearly. At least, we can see that Marx is supportive of Engels' study of natural science. As long as we just take a look at the exuberance of Engels' discussion of natural science with Marx in those letters, we can conclude that Marx has the same interests in natural sciences.

In a letter to Marx dated July 14th 1858, Engels asked Marx to send him Hegel's *The Philosophy of Nature*, and spoke at length about the progress of natural science, which can provide facts "from all sides" for Hegel to enrich his dialectical ideas.[245] In Engels's letter to Marx dated June 16th 1867, Engels talked about the chemical works of Hoffman, and said that although the author's point of view was a

---

[243]*Marx/Engels Collected Works*, Chinese Edition 1, Vol. 19, Page 374, Beijing, People's Publishing House, 1963.

[244]*Marx/Engels Collected Works*, Chinese Edition 1, Vol. 19, Page 374, Beijing, People's Publishing House, 1963.

[245]See *Marx/Engels Collected Works*, Chinese Edition 1, Vol. 29, Page 324, Beijing, People's Publishing House, 1972.

mechanical theory as a whole, but it showed that the atom "once depicted as the separability of the limit" actually was just a kind of relationship. In each stage of material segmentation, there was a change from the quantity difference into a qualitative difference, which was one of the basic laws of dialectical movement. In his reply to Engels, Marx said, "you are absolutely right about Hoffman. In addition, you can see from the end of Chapter III of my description that the craftsman has become a capitalist because of **pure quantitative change**, that in the body of the text I quote **the law of conversion from pure quantity to qualitative change** found by Hegel., and regard it as an equally valid law in both history and in science. In a note to the text (I had ever listened to Hoffman's speech at the time), I mentioned molecular theory." [246] It can be seen that Marx not only has a strong interest in nature, but also regards nature and society as a process of historical development which is unified and obeys the common objective law.

Because of this, once Engels had new thoughts and ideas about natural science, he always let Marx share his excitement first. On May 30th 1878, Engels wrote to Marx, describing "some dialectical ideas about the natural sciences" that appeared in his mind that morning (in *Dialectics of Nature*, Engels gave a more detailed explication of these ideas). In this letter, Engels discussed with Marx: "because you are at the center of science, you are in the best position to judge what is right."[247] Marx replied to Engels: "I am very happy to have just received your letter. But I do not have time to seriously think about it and discuss it with the 'authorities'. So I dare not venture to express my opinion."[248] As Marx was thinking about economics at

---

[246]*Marx/Engels Collected Works*, Chinese Edition 1, Vol. 31, Page 312, Beijing, People's Publishing House, 1972.

[247]*Marx/Engels Collected Works*, Chinese Edition 1, Vol. 33, Page 86~87, Beijing, People's Publishing House, 1973.

[248]*Marx/Engels Collected Works*, Chinese Edition 1, Vol. 33, Page 86~87, Beijing, People's Publishing House, 1973.

that time, and even so, Marx recommended Engels' letter to Carl Schorlemmer, one of what he called "authority". It is thus clear that he attached great importance to Engels' study of natural sciences.

From the letter from Marx to Engels dated July 4th 1864, it can be seen that Marx not only had a strong interest in Engels' study of natural science, but also had once cast himself into the research of natural science. He said: "you know, first of all, my understanding of everything is slow, and secondly, I always follow your footsteps. So lately I may have to study anatomy and physiology seriously, besides, I will also go to the lecture (where the object is displayed and dissected)."[249] Of course, it is also due to those well-known reasons, that is, the need to formulate the revolutionary strategy of the proletariat, the need to study the political economy, and the need to formulate some of the more basic principles of Marxist philosophy, Marx did not devote more time to the study of nature, but to "do sporadic, intermittent and piecemeal research"[250]. However, this is enough to show that the facts are not as hypothetical as the contemporary Marxists fabricated. Marx did not deny the objective existence of nature, but showed a strong interest in exploring the objective laws of nature from his attention to natural science.

Just as a great deal of historical material proves that the so-called claim that Marx "is not interested in nature" of the Western Marxists is pure fiction, it is also groundless to say that Engels neglected the study of man. The reason is that, Engels, like Marx, fully affirmed the active role of human beings in understanding and transforming nature. Engels has repeatedly criticized the one-sidedness of the old materialism on the relationship between man and nature, clearly pointing out that the essential difference between human beings and animals lies in: "Animals only

[249]*Marx/Engels Collected Works*, Chinese Edition 1, Vol. 30, Page 410, Beijing, People's Publishing House, 1974.

[250]*Karl Marx and Frederick Engels: Selected Works*, Edition 1, Vol. 3, Page 51.

use external nature to change nature simply by its own existence; man, on the other hand, uses his changes to enable nature to serve his own purposes and to **dominate** nature."[251]

As early as his youth, Engels said: "We value history more than any school of philosophy, even than Hegel." Moreover, there are essential differences between the emphasis on history and the history in the eyes of Hegel, because Hegel's history is the track of "self-consciousness" movement, which contains the historical materialism of the end point in the starting point. As a materialism , Engels did not put his focus on the dead "thing" as the old materialism, but put it on the creation activities of a realistic man, **"history does not do anything**...It is human, realistic and live human, who have created these things. 'History' is not a particular personality that uses people as a tool to achieve its own purposes. History is nothing but the activity of those who pursue their own goals."[252]

The German Ideology, jointly wrote by Marx and Engels, clearly demonstrates their common views. In this work, Marx and Engels profoundly criticize Feuerbach's intuitive materialism, noting that he did not understand the revolutionary significance of practice, thus did not understand the relationship between man and his surroundings. Feuerbach "did not see that the perceptual world around him was by no means something that had existed ever since the beginning of the world, but a product of industrial and social conditions."[253] "This kind of activity, constant sensual labor and creation, and production is a very profound foundation for the whole existing perceptual world, which as long as stops for even a year, Feuerbach will see that not only will great changes take place in nature, but the whole human

---

[251]*Karl Marx and Frederick Engels: Selected Works*, Edition 1, Vol. 3, Page 517.

[252]*Marx/Engels Collected Works*, Chinese Edition 1, Vol. 2, Page 118~119.

[253]*Karl Marx and Frederick Engels: Selected Works*, Edition 1, Vol. 1, Page 48.

world and his (Feuerbach) intuitive ability, even his own existence, will not exist."[254]

In Engels' view, man does not reflect the objective world around him passively, but positively influences it, modifies it, changes it, and even creates new things, resulting in a new process. If in the early days of human history, people still unconsciously and spontaneously adapt to the objective laws of nature, then, in the social practice, people gradually understand these laws, use them to serve themselves, and lay foundations for their own production and labor process. Because "man's living conditions are not readily available as soon as he differentiates from animals in a narrow sense; and these conditions can only be created through subsequent historical development."[255] The most representative passage is: "the natural science, like philosophy, still completely ignores the influence of man's activities on his mind till today; one of them only knows the nature and the other only knows the thought. But the most essential and the closest foundation of the human thought is **the change of the nature caused by the human being**, instead of the nature itself alone; human intelligence develops in accordance with how one learns to change nature. Accordingly, the naturalistic view of history (for example, Draper and some other natural scientists have this kind of understanding more or less) is unilateral, holding that only nature acts on man, that only natural conditions of everywhere determine man's historical development, and that it forgets that man also reacts on nature, changes nature, and creates new living conditions for himself."[256] Is it can be said to "ignore human beings" to pay so much attention to people, people's initiative, and creativity? We could hardly imagine that if Engels did not put man in the relationship with nature

---

[254]*Karl Marx and Frederick Engels: Selected Works*, Edition 1, Vol. 1, Page 49~50.

[255]*Marx/Engels Collected Works*, Chinese Edition 1, Vol. 20, Page 535, Beijing, People's Publishing House, 1973.

[256]*Karl Marx and Frederick Engels: Selected Works,* Edition 1, Vol. 3, Page 551.

and in the course of historical development to affirm his initiative and creativity, how he could affirm man and man's value!

It's true that in the historical background of the prevalence of idealism, Engels stressed the objectivity of nature too much, but did not deny the initiative of human beings. On the contrary, both Marx and Engels had made dialectical affirmation of these two aspects. And therefore, there is no such case that Marx "is not interested in nature" or Engels "negates man". As Western Marxists themselves do not understand the dialectical relationship between nature and human beings, they think about this problem in the metaphysical way of thinking, so they set Marx and Engels against each other. In the 20th century, when appraising the Italian Marxist researchers, Jacoby thought that the reason why they would put Marx and Engels against each other and criticized Engels was that they were based on Feuerbach's point of view, "to ask for a reconsideration of the connections between Hegel, Feuerbach and Marx." [257] So it is with contemporary Marxists who understand Engels from Feuerbach's point of view (or simply from the point of view of "old philosophy"). As a result, they regarded Engels as Feuerbach, criticized Engels, and did not see the essential differences between Engels and Feuerbach, because Feuerbach's philosophy of nature emphasizes the objective reality of nature, and meanwhile regards man as a part of nature, and regards the relationship between man and nature as the relationship between two natural things, as between nature and itself. Although Feuerbach calls his philosophy humanism, man does not have the characteristics of real man. He believed: "without nature, personality, self and consciousness will be nothing. In other words, it becomes an empty and non-essential abstract thing."[258] Feuerbach understands human beings only from the perspective of nature, but Engels is different, he not

---

[257]Jacoby: *Failed Dialectics*, Page 56.

[258]*Philosophical Writings of Feuerbach Anthology* Vol. II, Page 122, Beijing, The Commercial Press, 1984.

only from the perspective of nature to understand the human beings, but also from the perspective of human beings to understand the objective reality of the nature, and therefore, nature and man form a dialectical unity and the foundation of Marxist philosophy through the intermediary of society and practice.

However, Western Marxists are trying to destroy this unity and shake the foundation of Marxist philosophy. The "humanist Marx" they fabricated actually took away the basic contents of Marx's thought and "revised" this exclusive scientific theory of the proletariat into a universal human philosophy that is abstract humanistic philosophy. And accordingly, they exaggerated the significance of Marx's early works with no limits, especially for the over-praise of *Manuscripts of Economics and Philosophy of 1844*, which was described as "the apocalypse of human studies". But they failed to understand that Marx, in writing the *Manuscripts of Economics and Philosophy of 1844*, was looking for a way to thoroughly criticize private ownership with sympathy for the status of workers. The human beings that Marx was talking about were the proletarians at the bottom of the capitalist society. It was in the interests of the proletarians, Marx attacked capitalist private ownership, capitalist production and labor.

Any thorough philosophy cannot but express its theoretical position on the fundamental issues of man and nature, subject and object, substance and spirit. Like Marx, Engels did not avoid these important theoretical problems when he expounded his thought on historical dialectics. He started from the relationship between man and nature, subject and object to solve a series of major philosophical problems of man and history. He was opposed to any naturalistic and mechanistic tendencies towards history, and to the old philosophy advocating that nature was acting only on man, and that it was only natural conditions that determined the development of human beings everywhere, forgetting that man also reacted in nature, changed nature, and created new living conditions for himself. Engels focused on practice and the labor on which human beings depend for survival, and put the study of human beings on the basis of this reality all the time. It is a kind of nothingness and rootless person in the real world to talk about people without practice. It is Engels' famous theory that "labor creates man itself" that captures the essential differences between human beings and animals, and scientifically reveals the origin of human beings as a major subject of philosophical anthropology. Labor not only creates man, but also is the requirements of human development. It is not only the foundation of man's material existence and development, but also the basis of human's spiritual ability development. It is labor that truly distinguishes man from animals. Animals only adapt passively to nature, and simply change nature with their own existence, and man makes nature serve his own purposes through the changes he makes, and dominates nature. The whole history of man is his own creation. Western Marxists ignored Engels' argument about man's initiative in creating history and reforming nature, used the so-called "iron-faced" law to misinterpret Engels unilaterally, described Engels as a mechanical determinist who only acknowledged the objective laws of the world, and named it "scientism", which was different from the "humanism Marx" fabricated by them. In the academic research, these ideas put forward by Western Marx seem to be novel and unique, dazzling people's eyes and ears, but they cannot stand further scrutiny and examination, for they are fiction completely divorced from the historical facts of Marxism.

3. The Difficulties of Materialist Dialectics

On the fiction premise of "Humanism Marx" and "Scientism Engels", the opposites of Marx and Engels made a comprehensive distortion of each part of the Marxist theory system. Western Marxists launched an attack firstly on the field of materialistic dialectics. They split the unified theory of the materialistic dialectics into two opposite parts of the social dialectics and the dialectics of nature, and think that Engels only talks about the dialectics of nature, while Marx only talks about the social dialectics. They said that Marx himself never talked about dialectics of nature; Marx's dialectics is mainly applied to human history and society, and therefore, Marx's dialectics is "human-centered" dialectics of human studies, rather than the universal law established by Engels and applied equally to human society and nature. They hold a positive attitude towards the so-called "social dialectics" and "the dialectics of human science", but seem to have no tolerance for the "dialectics of nature". Almost all opposites of Marx and Engels are devoted to critics of dialectics of nature, especially Lukács' *History and Class Consciousness*, which symbolizes that the negation of dialectics of nature constitutes a theoretical tendency of Western Marxism and an academic consensus of Western Marxology.

Lukács' *History and Class Consciousness* interprets dialectics as deviating from Marxist philosophy. He holds that the essence of dialectics is the overall category, the dialectical interaction between subject and object, the unity of theory and practice, and is the decisive element of dialectics. Dialectics always revolves around the overall understanding of history. It can only be confined to the field of history and society, but there is no such interaction in nature, so there is no so-called dialectics. Lukács said: "It is extremely important to recognize that this approach applies only to the historical and social fields. Engels misinterpreted dialectics mainly because he wrongly followed Hegel to extend this method to nature. Whereas some basic decisive factors of dialectics, such as the interaction between subject and object, the unity of theory and practice, and the realistic historical change as the basis of various categories are the fundamental reasons for the change of thought, do not exist in our knowledge of nature."[259]

Although Lukács did not base his views on the opposition between Marx and Engels in criticizing dialectics of nature, his criticism of dialectics of nature became the theoretical start of the Western Marxism opposition between Marx and Engels. In fact, the views of Western Marxism in the future are only a restatement and play of Lukács' views. Bloch (Ernst Bloch) understood dialectics as the relationship between subject and object. Lefebvre believed that the real basis of dialectics was not in

---

[259]Lukács: *History and Class Consciousness*, Page 24, Note ⑥.

nature but in human practice and in the relationship between man and nature. These are the restatements of Lukács' viewpoints that the so-called dialects are "the dialectical relationship between the subject and the object in the course of history." Gramsci, Korsch, Sartre and the representatives of the Frankfurt School all express this roughly the same view in their own way, that is, to admit only the historical dialectics and the relationship between subject and object in the social field, but to deny the objective existence of dialectics in nature, which is actually consistent with the denial of the objective existence of nature by Western Marxism.

If the old materialist philosophy still believes in the objective reality of nature, then contemporary Western Marxism inherits the tradition of idealism in the history of philosophy. They doubt the objective reality of nature, declare that "nature is a social category", or pretend to acknowledge the objective existence of nature, but to say that this objective existence of nature is meaningless to human society and should be put out of theoretical research. What they want to study is the nature of man and the nature of subjectivity. Lukács thought that sensual and natural things could not be separated from rational and social things. Of course, there was no problem in emphasizing the unity of sensual and natural things and rational and social things, but the key was that Lukács put this unity on the basis of the rational and social things, so he opposed the objective study of nature, and criticized Engels' study of nature as plain realism and metaphysical materialism. In his view, nature is meaningful only as a product of transformation which has been included in social relations.

Schmidt of Frankfurt School once correctly found the differences between The Concept of Nature in Marx and Feuerbach's concept of nature, and pointed out the primitive directness of Feuerbach's worship of nature, which regarded nature as a primordial pure nature. But that is all, for when Schmidt elucidated his understanding of The Concept of Nature in Marx, there were some important distortions involved. He saw the differences between Marx's and Feuerbach's concepts of nature, but did not see the connection between them. He regarded The

Concept of Nature in Marx as the one that taking everything natural having been processed by human labor and as the product of social activities with a "social and historical nature." Based on this distortion of The Concept of Nature in Marx, Schmidt could casually criticize Engels, saying that the nature that Engels understood was the "pure nature" of Feuerbach, which "goes beyond Marx's interpretation of the relationship between nature and social history, and goes back to arbitrary metaphysics"[260], namely, "retrogression into plain realism".[261]

Indeed, before the emergence of Marxist philosophy, there were two kinds of views of nature. The materialists in the 18th century tried to explain the world from the world itself, and negated the theological view of nature that attempted to explain nature by virtue of some supernatural force. It is correct for them to admit that nature is an objective and independent entity. But they did not see the connection between nature and man and society, and did not understand nature in the course of historical development. The German classical philosophy saw this defect of materialism in the 18th century, but they went to the other extreme. From Kant's half-conceited inclusion of nature into the category of "self-consciousness", to Fichte's introduction of "non-self"(nature) from the "self", and to Hegel's regarding nature as a part of the movement of "self-consciousness", they all tried to find answers to explain nature outside nature. And therefore, although German classical philosophy can look at nature from a historical perspective, although the intrinsic link of the development of nature's movement has been revealed, the process and internal link are placed in a hypothetical and illusory bearer (Fichte called it as "self", while Hegel called it as "absolute spirit"). When Marx and Engels founded Marxist philosophy of nature, they accepted the viewpoint of materialism in the 18th

[260]Schmidt: *The Concept of Nature in Marx*, Page 44, Beijing, The Commercial Press, 1988.

[261]Schmidt: *The Concept of Nature in Marx*, Page 50~51.

century trying to explain the world from the world itself, and also absorbed the historical spirit of the latter, thus established the dialectical materialist view of nature, to grasp the relation between nature and human, society and history on the premise of affirming the objective reality that nature is independent of human beings. Lukács and others called nature as a social category, which in fact aimed at denying the objectivity of nature, denying that nature existed before human society, and formed the foundation of human society, and denying the primacy of nature. They overthrew the relationship completely, instead of regarding the natural world as the premise of the society, but regarded the society as the premise of the natural world, and regarded human practice as the basis of the real existence of nature. Moreover, they also strongly imposed this understanding on Marx.

For example, Schmidt asserted that Marx regarded the decisive factors in the process of social history in the final analysis as the forms and methods of production and reproduction of people's direct lives. What Marx called "nature" was only the element of human practice, and was the subject itself. Marx "by no means understood this kind of person beyond reality in the sense of objectivism without intermediary."[262] Schmidt believed that it was a rigid metaphysical view of nature to admit the "free nature" that existed without man's activities. He accused Engels of "the more natural view is the vivid practice of separating nature from human beings, the more criticized by *Theses on Feuerbach*. In Engels' view, nature and man are not combined by historical practices of primary significance, and man is the product of evolution of natural processes, is just a moving speculum of a natural process, not productivity."[263]

In fact, Schmidt 's negation of nature's preexistence is merely a clearer statement of the viewpoints of his teacher—Adorno and Horkheimer. Adorno accused Engels of

---

[262]Schmidt: *The Concept of Nature in Marx*, Page 14.

[263]Schmidt: *The Concept of Nature in Marx*, Page 50.

"making materials and nature undialectically become the first existence."[264] In his opinion, the real "first existence" should be the subject, and the subject has a higher universality than the object. "One can never think about the object outside the subject, but can think about the subject outside the object.[265]" Of course, he also claimed that he acknowledged the existence of "object" in principle, and even admitted that the object had a certain "primacy" to the subject, but he also made various restrictions on the object, and thought that the object was only the physical and mental power of human being. And therefore, there was only one thing in Adorno's place, which was "subject". But Adorno regarded this as a true understanding of Marxism, and criticized Engels for deviating from the viewpoint of "Marx". Horkheimer selected the same angle with Adorno to distort Marx, and then denied Engels with the distorted Marx. In Horkheimer's opinion, the objective thing that Marx insisted was nothing more than subjective things, namely alienated and idolized things. He openly opposed the "worship of the so-called objective material world." He held that real materialism was a developing process involving the interaction between subject and object. "The interaction between subject and object" that he understood was in fact that man, through his practical activities, absorbed nature itself and made it a part of society. Compared with Schmidt, the expression of Adorno and others is more philosophical because they described their thoughts with abstract concepts such as subject and object, whereas Schmidt restored them to concepts such as nature and man. In this way, we can clearly see Schmidt's negation of the nature of the essence of idealism, and understand that Adorno and other Western Marxists emphasized the principle of subjectivity was to negate the preexistence and objective reality of nature. Since the objective reality of nature and its first status are denied, it is a matter of reason to deny the dialectics of nature.

---

[264] Adorno: *Negative Dialectics*, Page 143, Frankfurt, 1974.

[265] Adorno: *Negative Dialectics*, Page 188.

If Adorno and others distorted the dialectics of Marxism by playing a game of the subject and the object, Sartre was opposed to the dialectics of dialectics by "human dialectics", and defined dialectics with "collectivization" and "comprehensibility". Of course, his "collectivization", like the collectivity of Lukács, is the collectivity of historical phenomena. No matter what the topic of dialectics is, in his opinion, it always revolves around the question of an overall understanding of historical phenomena. Without man and his society, the objectivity of nature is incomprehensible, and only in the social history, dialectics is real and understandable, but the dialectics of nature is inconceivable. He thought that Marx revealed the historical dialectics for the first time in the history of human thought, that "the key to opening up the historical dialectics is a famous saying in Marx's *The Poverty of Philosophy*: The relations of production form a whole"[266]. However, dialectics is the activity of collectivization, and the constantly developing activity of understanding history and creating history.

However, Sartre's concept of collectivization is different from that of Lukács, because Lukács' collectivity is only a social whole confronted with nature, whereas Sartre's collectivity is not only the confrontation with nature but also the individual confronted with society, "that is, man himself, also the biological individual is a whole", and "the whole of economic reality or production fact ultimately depends on the overall human body of each individual. "[267] The individual is the collectivity, and the creation, cognition and the grasp of the individual to the history collectivity is the collectivization and dialectics. It's obviously a typical idealistic statement of dialectics. However, Sartre always suggested that it was consistent with Marx's thinking. So when he criticized Engels's *Dialectics of Nature* based on this view, it

---

[266]Sartre: *Science and Dialectics*, Cited from *Foreign Philosophy*, Division 1, Page 156.

[267]Sartre: *Science and Dialectics*, Cited from *Foreign Philosophy*, Division 1, Page 154.

appeared in the face of opposition between Marx and Engels. He believed that the nature did not possess the "comprehensibility" of human beings and their creation-social history, thus the dialectics of nature did not exist. If there was dialectics in nature, it was only the dialectics in which people introduced.[268] The dialectics of nature only indicates that people construct a dialectics from the outside according to the model of dialectics and according to a kind of constructive hypothesis. It is the dialectics that man gives to nature, so how can the objectivity of dialectics be started? In Western Marxism, it is very typical like Sartre to use Fichte to understand Marx and deny the objective law in nature.

However, what Sartre did not summarize after he had made a lot of elaboration in negating dialectics of nature was done by Merleau-Ponty (Maurice Merleau-Ponty), who said: "It is true that Engels accepted the adventurous claim of dialectics of nature from Hegel. The question that dialectics of nature is the most vulnerable part of Hegel's legacy will not be discussed here, but how can dialectics of nature avoid idealism? If nature is nature, and if it is outside us, we cannot find the necessary matrix in nature to form dialectics. If nature is dialectical, it is because it is perceived by man, and is inextricably linked to human activity." [269] Merleau-Ponty's criticism of Engels is even more intense than that of Sartre. He accused Engels of "putting dialectics into nature" and of "bringing man's way of being into nature, the magic of it". He said that because Engels "added a dose of naturalism to dialectics," and "immediately disintegrated dialectics."[270]

In addition, Neo-Positivism Marxism and Structuralism Marxism adopt a way of cutting off the link between materialist dialectics and any previous thought in the

---

[268]Sartre: *Science and Dialectics*, Cited from *Foreign Philosophy*, Division 1, Page 158.

[269]Merleau-Ponty: *Sense and Non-Sense*, Page 274, Evanston, 1964.

[270]Merleau-Ponty: *Adventures of the Dialectic*, Page 387, London, 1974.

denial of materialist dialectics. Della Volpe believed that Hegel's approach was inextricably linked to idealism, so we cannot reject Hegel's idealism and save his dialectical approach as Engels said in *Ludwig Feuerbach*. In his opinion, Marx's dialectical method was fundamentally different from and had nothing to do with Hegel's dialectical method, because Marx's dialectics of science was to oppose the general uncertain abstract of idealism with special definite abstraction. It was only an experimental method, was the materialistic logic of modern experimental science, and its symbol was "concrete-abstract-concrete cycle". So, Colletti, a student of Della Volpe, could assert that because of Engels, Marxism was theoretically responsible for the mistakes for almost a century. This is material dialectics, a plagiarism from Hegel. Colletti accused Engels of 90% of *Dialectics of Nature* was a desperate concession to Hegel's original and romantic philosophy of nature, and was composed of rough positivism and evolution. Different from the every rigorous and comprehensive page of Marx's works, Engels' works have a tendency of vulgarization.

Althusser had a similar point of view with Della Volpe School on this issue. He believed that we can never imagine that Hagel's ideological system had not put its dialectics defiled, nor can we imagine that dialectics may be hidden in Hagel's system, like a kernel inside its shell. Althusser believed that in order to liberate dialectics, it was not enough to peel off the first shell-Hegel's system, but also to strip the second shell attached to it., whereas the second shell was Hegel's dialectics itself. Marx opposed the mysterious form of Hegel's dialectics with his own reasonable form, while Engels was annotating Hegel, and providing the materials proof of the natural sciences for Hegel. So the dialectics represented by Marx is fundamentally different from the dialectics annotated by Engels.

The vast majority of Western Marxists tampered with Marx's dialectic thought and denounced dialectics of nature from the standpoint of subjectivism. Almost all the scholars who wanted to squeeze into the followers of Lukács were eager to show their negative attitude to dialectics of nature. Bloch believed that dialectics itself was the relationship between objects and subjects in the world created by human beings, besides, nothing else. Lefebvre said that the human practice with the function of changing "objectivity" was the core of Marxist dialectics, so it should not be in nature, but in practice to look for the basis of dialectics in the relationship between man and nature. The Yugoslavia "Practice School" accused Engels of not following these early analyses of Marx in his own late works, but following Hegel's point of view. Predrag Vranicki thought that the principles and laws of dialectics "were determined by Hegel, and Marx applied them to analyze bourgeois society concretely. However, although it was not Engels' original intention to address the issue systematically and comprehensively, his approach also contained a major flaw, as there was no significant measure of human history, no complexity of the historical situation and the historical practice of mankind, and the dialectical problem only obtained its full meaning and explanation from the historical practice of mankind."[271] Polish philosopher Kolakowski criticized Engels for creating a basic method applicable to both natural science and social science based on the discovery of natural science at that time and regarded social science as an extension of natural science to reveal the dialectical laws that apply to all areas of research. In his opinion, on the issue of dialectics, Marx focused on subjective dialectics, while Engels emphasized objective dialectics. Marx considered dialectics to be the interaction between subject and object, which ultimately led to the unity of subject and object, while Engels' philosophical conclusions based on the science and mathematics at that time are now out of date.

In short, in the eyes of Western Marxists, only Engels described the laws of nature as dialectical, whereas Marx himself never did. It seems that to Marx, dialectics does not exist in nature itself, but in the relationship between man and nature. It should be noted that this nature is not the original sense of nature, but a social existence as a social category, and belongs to human beings. The connection

---

[271]Vranicki: *History of Marxism*, Vol. 1, Page 254.

between man and nature is the connection between man and man himself. Dialectics exists in this connection or relationship, without which there is no dialectics. They believed that as Engels did not put dialectics in the specific social and historical field, and in the relationship between man and himself for investigation, but made a mistake of putting the concept of dialectics into the objective nature as an objective law of nature. This mistake has nothing to do with Marx's thought, or even is completely opposite to Marx's thought.

In fact, Marx, like Engels, always firmly believes the objective existence of dialectics of nature, and tries to reveal it. Since the writing of *Manuscripts of Economics and Philosophy of 1844*, in Marx's theory study of 40 years, Marx always put the dialectical development of the material nature as the certain premise. As we have pointed out many times above, in the process of founding Marxism, there is an undeniable fact that there is a division of labor between Marx and Engels. Marx devoted his whole life to the study of social history and economics, so he had more expositions on historical dialectics. However, discussing historical dialectics does not mean negating dialectics of nature. It has been proved that Marx expressed his positive opinions on dialectics of nature in many places. On June 22nd 1869, Marx made it clear in his letter to Engels that the law of dialectics existed in both nature and society, and specially pointed out that the law of mutual variation of quality was equally effective in history and natural science. In addition, Marx also tried many times to study the natural science personally, expounding his viewpoints on dialectics of nature.

It is even more a subjective idealistic assumption to create the opposition between Marx and Engels on the dialectical issue. Lenin once pointed out that Engels' exposition on nature in *Anti-Dühring* was "totally based on Marx's materialist philosophy" [272],believing that "Marx has repeatedly called his world view as

---

[272]*Selected Works of Lenin*, Edition 2, Vol. 2, Page 581.

dialectical materialism, and it is this world view that Engels' *Anti-Dühring* (Marx has read all the manuscripts) states[273]. Engels himself said in his preface to the *Anti-Dühring* in 1885: " It can be said that Marx and I are the only person who saved conscious dialectics from German idealism and turned it into a materialistic view of nature and history."[274] Especially in the ten years after Marx's death, Engels not only devoted himself to the study of dialectics of nature, but also made outstanding contributions in the field of historical dialectics.

It is worth pointing out that Lukács, Sartre, Bloch and other Western Marxists all emphasize the category of "collectivity" of philosophy. But in fact, they just do not understand the meaning of the collectivity or the entirety in the study of Marxist philosophy. The collectivity that they understand is only the social and historical collectivity which contains the interaction of the subject and the object, or like Sartre, who understands the collectivity as an individual, which is essentially different from Marx and Engels' regarding the whole world including nature and social history and its development process as a systematic whole.

When the Western Marxists talk about the relationship between man and nature, they always limit the category of nature, which is to say, they regard nature as a social category, while forget the other relation between nature and society, so they couldn't understand dialectics beyond the limits of social history. However, Marx and Engels are standing in a very high point to understand the world, and therefore, they not only see the nature belonged to people in real life as a social category, but also see the nature independent from people and society, objectively existing, and possibly or going into the society every time and every day with a major influence on the social movement and the development of the nature. In other words, Marx and Engels not only transcend social history, but also transcend nature to expound

---

[273]*Selected Works of Lenin*, Edition 2, Vol. 2, Page 252.

[274]*Karl Marx and Frederick Engels: Selected Works*, Edition 1, Vol. 3, Page 51.

the dialectical laws that are universally applicable to the unified large system of nature and society. As for Marx and Engels, dialectics of nature and historical dialectics are a unified whole. Although they hold the world from different angles, their common point is to reveal the inevitable law behind the complicated phenomena in the objective world. Of course, dialectics of nature and historical dialectics have their own characteristics because of their differences in the object of study, but Marxists should not break the relationship between them by emphasizing their characteristics at any time, nor should they deny the dialectics of nature by emphasizing the historical dialectics, for only when dialectics of nature and historical dialectics exist as a whole in the minds of thinkers can the nature of materialism be guaranteed. To talk about dialectics of nature without historical dialectics is at most only natural evolution, but it is difficult to avoid the entanglement of idealism once entering the field of social history. On the contrary, it is difficult to grasp the basic characteristics of social history to merely talk about historical dialectics without dialectics of nature, let alone grasping the essence of the world. Western Marxism has abandoned the dialectics of nature and unilaterally talked about the relationship between subject and object, thus turning historical dialectics into idealism.

4. Historical Dialectics and Social Development Outlook

In the history of human epistemology, the field of history is like a swamp of thorns. Once many thinkers dabbled in this field, they fell deeply into the quagmire. In their eyes, history is a secretive and shy new bride, whose true face is always unwilling to be exposed to people. Almost no field of science has as much subjective speculation and far from reality as it does in historical science, which is entirely due to the special nature of the field of history. Because history is the stage of human activities, and history records the footprints of human activities. And therefore, what people see in the field of history is only those phenomena that appear on the surface, that is, the conscious activities of human beings. But the objective law, which is hidden deep in history, is wrapped in the thick crustacean of human consciousness. Only Marx and Engels stripped this thick shell, revealed the deep mystery of history, and established true historical science. But the scientific historical outlook of Marxism has been unable to be understood by scholars and thinkers with the prejudice of old philosophy, as a result, it has been attacked and blamed as much as ever. When creating the opposition between Marx and Engels, Western Marxology and Western Marxism did not give up the distortion and tampering with Marxism in the field of history.

For Marxism, it is self-evident to admit that there is an inevitable decisive factor behind the historical development. However, in the contemporary Western Marxism and Marxology, the word determinism has absurdly become a derogatory term linked to bureaucracy. Not only were they ashamed to admit that they were determinists, but also showed a rare good intention: to try to dress Marx as an indeterminist, and to distinguish the so-called "voluntarist" Marx and the "determinist" Engels. They believed that Marx was inclined to moralism, idealism and voluntarism, while Engels was inclined to behaviorism, materialism and determinism. For example, Balestrrem believed that what Marx emphasized was the historical autonomy of the individual in action. But Engels talked about his economic process and regularity. Fetscher thought that Engels put too much emphasis on the factors of scientific determinism and equated natural process with social process, thus destroying the dialectical unity of theory and practice, and ignored the consciousness in the social process. Rubel said that Marx's theory of revolutionary history was transformed by Engels into an automatic historical process determined by economic structure and class confrontation, and the dialectical unity between the revolutionary action and the understanding of the social and economic constraints of the historical process disappeared. Levine thought that Marx's historical theory focused on practice and on man's creativity and initiative, and regarded the creative activity of man as the birthplace of history, while Engels committed the mistake of idealizing the material and applying metaphysical materialism to the field of history, taking history as being governed by deterministic material forces and claiming that only material things are realistic, thus slid into dogmatism.

Western Marxists also play the same tune as Western Marxist scientists, or similarly, tried to portray Marx's image on a nihilistic canvas in a non-deterministic way. They thought that the third article of Marx's *Theses on Feuerbach* proved that Marx was a non-determinist. Engels, on the other hand, was a determinist opposed to Marx. But in fact, as long as we turn over all Marx's basic works on social history, we can know that determinism is precisely an important aspect of Marx's own thoughts.

Taking *Das Capital* as an example, Marx not only revealed the inevitable law of the operation of capitalist society in this magnificent work on the law of the development of capitalist society, and pointed out that capitalist production "took effect on the inevitability of iron", but also obtained the objective inevitability of the natural historical process of the whole human social movement from the analysis of the typical form of capitalist society. The sum of the main relations between production and its formation in the process of production is the decisive basis of human history progress and the essence of all social history. Marx said: "The unique economic form of extracting unpaid surplus labor from direct producers determines the relationship between domination and subordination, which is directly derived from the production itself, thus has a decisive reaction to production. However, the whole structure of the economic system produced by the relations of production itself, as well as its unique political structure, is based on the above economic forms. At any time, we always have to find the deepest secrets and the basis for concealment for the whole social structure, and thus for the political form of sovereignty and dependence relationships, and in short, for any particular form of state at the time, from the direct relationship between the owner of the conditions of production and the direct producer, any form of which is always naturally adapted to the mode of labor and to a certain stage of development of the productive forces of the labor society."[275] If we look at this relationship in the dynamic historical process, then Marx "regards the social movement as a natural historical process governed by certain laws, which are not only subject to the will, consciousness and intention of man, but determine man's will, consciousness and intention."[276]

Without more citations, the arguments casually taken from *Das Capital* are enough to show that Marx is a determinist. Of course, Western Marxists and Marxist scientists will say that Marx's determinism thought in *Das Capital* is only suitable for the capitalist society he analyses. This is completely wrong, for the method used in *Das Capital* shows that although this work of Marx is based on the capitalist society as the object of its analysis, the basic principles expounded in the analysis of this society are universally applicable to all social forms. To Marx's theoretical research, analytical capitalism is only his starting point, and it is from this point that Marx can look down at the whole history by standing at the summit of historical development, find the key to solve the riddle of all history and reveal the inevitability of history.

Of course, the determinism of Marx is essentially different from the determinism in the past philosophical thought, which is a kind of negative "intuitionistic" one-sided determinism. This determinism does not recognize any accidental factors at all, does not see the dynamic side of social history, and is bound to lead to fatalism, so Marx settled this determinism in Article 3 of *Theses on Feuerbach*. Marx said: "There is a kind of materialism that people are regarded as the product of environment and education. It is thus assumed that the changed person is the product of another environment and of changed education-a doctrine that forgets that the environment is changed by man, and that the educator himself must be

---

[275]*Marx/Engels Collected Works*, Chinese Edition 1, Vol. 25, Page 891~892, Beijing, People's Publishing House, 1974.

[276]*Marx/Engels Collected Works*, Chinese Edition 1, Vol. 23, Page 20.

educated. And therefore, this theory is bound to divide the society into two parts, some of which are high above society." Marx then pointed out that: "The change of environment is consistent with human activities, which can only be seen and reasonably understood as **revolutionary practice**." [277] Obviously, what Marx criticizes is the kind of incomplete determinism which must divide the society into two parts, while Marx's own determinism is understood through "revolutionary practice", because there are also basic determinants in social history, which are hidden in "revolutionary practice" and at the same time shown with the help of "revolutionary practice". Western Marxists and Marxist scientists always think that Marx's aphorism can become a proof of non-"determinist Marx", however, on the contrary, "revolutionary practice" must be first of all material practice. In social history, "revolutionary practice" must be manifested in the form of production, which is shown as the relations of production formed in production and production. "The practice of revolution" cannot be the abstract initiative expression of a single person at any time. Only the activity of actively transforming the objective world in social history can be called as practice, and is "revolutionary" practice. Western Marxists and Marxist scientists always start from the "individual" angle when they understand Marx, in which practice becomes the expression of abstract initiative, and a manifestation of will, so it was not surprising that they described Marx as a voluntarist and a non-determinist.

Western Marxists and Marxist scientists deny that the determinism of Marxist philosophy is mainly influenced by the trend of non-determinism since the late 19th century. Since Dilthey (Wilhelm Dilthey) declared that the society can only be understood by intuitive introspection instead of taking advantage of causal necessity, Windelband (Wilhelm Windelband), Rickert (Heinrich John Rickert), Croce and others had criticized determinism, saying that the history of inevitability was rooted in Newton's popular prejudice of 19th century. The American historian Aaron

---

[277] *Karl Marx and Frederick Engels: Selected Works*, Edition 1, Vol. 1, Page 17.

Nivens asserted that the theory of history, which regarded historical events as inevitable results, was a logical simplification and cleansing of complex history. As a result, they "underestimated the importance of luck or accident in history", while in fact, "unexpected diseases, climate change, and the loss of a document, and a sudden madness of a man or woman had ever changed the face of history."[278] And therefore, Croce believed that the way out of historical research lied in "abandoning determinism, which is transcending nature and its reasons. It is to advocate an approach contrary to the one traditionally adopted, which is to give up the category of cause and take another category. The other category can only be the category of purpose, which is an external and transcendental purpose, and opposite corresponding to and similar to the cause. The purpose of seeking transcendence is' philosophy of history'."[279] Driven by this trend of thought, Western Marxists have abandoned the search for the historical inevitability based on economy from Lukács, but were dedicated to annotating social history in the context of possibility and chance. They will knock down all the "stiff" historical necessity, let the historical subject get rid of all the material entanglement, remove the obstacles of necessity to freedom and practice, carry forward the subject consciousness, change and create all the subjectivity. However, when they regarded themselves as Marxists, they cannot directly throw the "sewage" in their hands on Marx's head, so they put their own painstakingly woven clothes on Marx's body, and let Marx appear as indeterminism.

The distortion of Marx in the field of history also comes from the complete denial of the development subject of history—man has any position in the social structure, like Althusser. They thought that Marx's history was based on a series of concepts

---

[278]*Selected Works of Modern Western Historiography*, Page 282, Shanghai, Shanghai People's Publishing House, 1982.

[279]Croce: *Theory and Practice of History*, Page 49, Beijing, The Commercial Press, 1982.

such as "social formation", "productive force", "production relations" and "superstructure", but man has no status because the mode of production is incompatible with the concept of man. Any production is characterized by two inseparable elements-the labor process and the social relations of production. The labor process is a combination of some simple elements, that is, the individual activity of human beings, the object of labor, and labor tools. This combination defines the essential characteristics of the labor process: the conditions of the labor process are material and natural. The production tools play a dominant role in the process of labor. Labor is "to transform material nature into a product, thus the labor process as a material structure is determined by the physical laws and techniques of nature. The labor force is also included in this structure."[280] The relations of production are the relations between producers, but this relationship is based on the material means adopted by the producers in production and their material relations. And therefore, "the social relations of production must not be reduced to relations between people, and to relations only contained among people... In Marx's view, the social relations of production do not bring people to the stage alone, but bring the parties in the production process and the material conditions of the production process, which are 'combined' in a special way to the stage."[281] According to Althusser, society is combined according to this structure, and history is only the operation or extension of this structure. And therefore, the initiative of man, the purpose of practice and the chance of history are completely gone. In this sense the understanding of Marx is not only Marx himself but also the old materialist philosophy criticized by Marx in *Theses on Feuerbach*.

Among the Western Marxists and Marxist scientists, the main purpose of the distortion of Marx is to oppose Engels. In their opinion, Engels is not only a

---

[280]Althusser: *Reading Das Capital*, Page 171, London, 1967.

[281]Althusser: *Reading Das Capital*, Page 174.

determinist, but also a unilateral "economic determinist." John Tenneh said that Engels "clearly placed particular emphasis on the determinant role of the economy, even considered race itself as an economic factor, and thus clearly highlighted the concept of economic factors. It gave meaning to the determinism of human history, which held that human history had gone through the same stage of development, while ignoring all other factors other than economic conditions." ①[282] Indeed, since the writing of *The German Ideology*, Marx and Engels had repeatedly stated their common view that, under the existing relations of production, social processes were very similar to natural processes. Many ostensibly accidental events were actually dictated by an order governed by the laws of economic processes. The subjects of social activities often do not really consciously realize the value of themselves or their actions., and the work they have accomplished is an involuntary result. This kind of thought is clearly expressed in Marx's Preface to *Critique of Political Economy*. In this respect, Engels and Marx are in complete agreement. On the other hand, it is not only Engels who is ignoring "factors other than economic conditions", on the contrary, it is exactly Engels who, in his later writings, emphasizes the comprehensive interaction of various factors in social life.

In view of Barthes' misinterpretation of historical materialism, description of historical materialism as "economic materialism", saying that it only recognizes that economic factors play a role, while all the other diverse elements of social life were simply the results, Engels pointed out: "Although the material living conditions are the original cause, this does not exclude the realm of thought works on these material conditions in turn."[283] In Engels' view, historical phenomena are not the sum of isolated factors, as Barthes thinks, but exist as part of a unified social organism that interact and influence each other, and take the development of the

---

[282]John Tenet: *The Challenge to Karl Marx*, Page 220~221, New York, 1941.

[283]*Marx/Engels Collected Works*, Chinese Edition 1, Vol. 37, Page 431~432, Beijing, People's Publishing House, 1971.

material life relationship as the ultimate basis without exception in the final analysis. In order to understand the whole social life, it is far from enough to find out the economic reasons. Marxism, in the final analysis, regards economic relations as the decisive basis of social history, but does not directly and simply attribute all historical phenomena to economic relations, nor denies the reaction of superstructures such as politics to the economic base. And therefore, Engels said: "If Barthes thinks that we deny the politics of the economic movement and so on reflects any reaction to the movement itself, he's fighting with the windmill."[284] He also pointed out that all that these gentlemen lack was dialectics. They always saw the causes here and the results there. They never saw that it was an empty abstraction. This metaphysical bipolarity existed in the real world only in times of crisis, and the entire historical development took place in the form of interaction. Although the forces of interaction are very uneven, the economic movement is much more powerful, the most primitive, and the most decisive.

Similarly, when Ernst vulgarized historical materialism into mechanical determinism, Engels gave a sharp critique: "There he straightly repeated the absurd conclusion he had learned from the metaphysical Dühring, saying that history was formed entirely automatically in Marx, without the participation of people (who made history), and saying that economic relations (but they themselves were created by man!) is playing with these people like playing a chess piece. This man could confuse the distortion of Marx's theory by enemies such as Dühring with the theory itself."[285] Engels stressed that in the study of history, we must pay attention to "the study of the whole history, must study the conditions of the existence of various social forms in detail, and then try to find out the corresponding viewpoints such as politics,

[284]*Marx/Engels Collected Works*, Chinese Edition 1, Vol. 37, Page 490.

[285]*Marx/Engels Collected Works*, Chinese Edition 1, Vol. 22, Page 97~98, Beijing, People's Publishing House, 1965.

private laws, aesthetics, philosophy, and religion from these conditions."[286]

It can be seen that Engels attached great importance to the "interaction" of the superstructure such as economic relations and politics, law and ideology. He not only criticized the view of denying that the politics has independence and economy play a role in the final analysis. Moreover, he and Marx also admitted the defects of theoretical interpretation in the process of founding historical materialism, that is to say, they emphasized the role of economic factors and ignored the discussion of the role of superstructure and ideology. He stressed the need for a dialectical and comprehensive understanding of the interaction between the various factors in social development, neither of which could be ignored, nor should the role of one factor be exaggerated or reduced, and the balance between them should be well grasped.

There is no doubt that Engels was a determinist , but Western Marxists and Marxist scientists had to say Engels as an "economic determinist" , saying that Engels applied the inevitability of the material boundary in natural science to explore the same inevitability in the social sciences, which could only explain their distortion and ignorance of Engels' writings and ideas .

The view on historical development is completely different whether to admit the objective inevitability of historical law, or whether he is a determinist. The historical development view of non-determinists emphasizes the accidental factors and randomness in history, while the deterministic view of history regards the development of history as an objective and inevitable process. Marxist view of history is dialectical determinism, so it affirms the objective and inevitable trend of historical development, and meanwhile acknowledges the complex situation in the process of historical development, that is to say, the social and historical development outlook of Marxism is a dialectical view of development, which

---

[286]*Marx/Engels Collected Works*, Chinese Edition 1, Vol. 37, Page 432.

recognizes the unity of subjectivity and objectivity in the historical process, the unity of necessity and contingency, the unity of singularity and diversity of the way of historical development.

However, the Western Marxists and Marxist scientists created the opposition between Marx and Engels on the issue of singularity and diversity. In their view, Marx did not admit that there was a kind of history, which can be predictable in advance with single linear and phased development, while Engels dogmatically insisted on the theory of single-linear development. Levine believed that, according to Marx, the historical process was not single-linear and undeveloped, but multi-linear and developing. For example, Marx distinguished four main types in world history: Asian, Greek-Roman, Germanic and Capitalist, and within these four types of relationships, there were also many small types. He said that Marx thought it was necessary to pay attention to the individuality and uniqueness of each society. Marx's theory of development did not focus on the sequence of time or on the inevitability of history, but on the changes within the social structure. However, Engels conceived that, no matter at any place, with the development of economy and along the single line of development route, human history would go through primitive society, slave society, feudal society, and capitalist society and develop into the communist society in proper sequence. So Levine said that Marx's view of social development was anatomical, while Engels' view was criticized as physical.

British anthropologist Maurice Bloch said, Marx believed that "the path of evolution is not only one, which has been seen in *Anthropology Notes*. If we pay our attention only on *The Origin of Family, Private Property and the State*, this kind of flexibility will seems to be extremely dull. In the book, Engels told us more or less that the revealed laws of evolution may not be changed by the new discoveries. What he offered us was still a very strict linear evolution theory"[287]. Engels

---

[287] Maurice Bullock: *Marxism and Anthropology*, Page 107, Beijing, Huaxia Publishing House, 1989.

"provided a single and fixed route to the evolution of society", which Marx did not. [288] So, Bullock criticized Engels for simplifying Marx, saying that in Engels's view, "human history, to a great extent, is regarded as the continuing development of natural history, which is subject to the biological principles of evolution and the principles of natural selection."[289]

American anthropologist Lawrence Krader also believed that "Marx, in view of the different forms of family evolution among ancient Romans and Jews, firstly criticized the single-linear development of society. This kind of criticism cannot be found in the view of Engels or that of Kovalevsky, who followed him", "Engels believed that the origin of a nation can be ascertained without having to rely on such external factors as conquest or subjugation... Marx pointed out that it was simplistic to exclude the factors of conquest as a theoretical possibility for the formation of a state..."[290]

Tunayf Skaya believed that: "Marx and Engels have different attitudes towards Morgan, that one of them takes a critical attitude, while the other one takes an uncritical attitude. Their conclusions from Morgan's works are also different. Take the issue of the transition from one period to another for example, Marx pointed out that in one transitional period, it was believed that the emerging duality indicated the beginning of various confrontations; Engels, on the other hand, always felt that antagonism only existed at the end of a transitional period, and it seemed that class society would almost reached its peak after the form of communes was destroyed and the private system had been built up. Engels

---

[288]See Maurice Bullock: *Marxism and Anthropology*, Page 108.

[289]Maurice Bullock: *Marxism and Anthropology*, Page 109.

[290]Lawrence Krader: *The Ethnological Notebooks of Karl Marx*, Published on *Proceedings of the National Academy of Sciences*, New York, Category 2, Vol. 35, No. 4.

believed that history was a straight line of development, but Marx thought it was a dialectical development from one stage to another, pointing out that there were various ways from the primitive commune to a different world."[291]

Whether Marx is described as a "multi-line theorist" or Engels as a "single-line theories", it is serious distortion of the social history outlook of Marx and Engels. For there were no questions of "single line" or "multi-line" in the works of Marx and Engels. "Single-line theory" and "multi-line theory" are only concerned with the way in which the social formation in the surface layer of world history is replaced, so the two formulations themselves have metaphysical color of either this or that. The social and historical development outlook of Marx and Engels requires that the replacement of social forms be examined on the basis of the general laws of the development of world history. While Marx and Engels revealed the general laws of the development of world history, they grasped the particularity and diversity of the development of various countries and nationalities. The special law of the development of each country and nation is the premise of the general law of the development of the world history, and the general law of the development of the world history is in these special laws. So, the history of the development of human society is the dialectical unity of singularity and diversity. In terms of the overall outline of the development of world history, it is manifested as singularity, which is once embodied in different countries and nations, there will be great distinctions and differences in their special ways, and it will be shown as diversity.

In the works of Marx and Engels, there is a difference in the division of historical development stages. In *A Contribution to the Critique of Political Economy*, Marx divided the whole world history into "Asia, ancient, feudal and modern bourgeois production methods." In the *Manuscripts of Economics from 1857 to 1858*, Marx

---

[291]R. Tunayf Skaya: *Marx's "New Humanitarianism" and Dialectics of Women's Liberation in Primitive Society and Modern Society*, Published on *International Practice*, British Magazine, 1984 (1).

divided the development of human history into three stages of greater span according to the development degree of social productive forces, namely, various forms of precapitalism dominated by natural economy, a society dominated by commodity economy with capitalism as a typical and main body and a communist society dominated by public ownership economy in the future. In fact, these two kinds of division are consistent with the division of the five stages of the primitive society, the slave society, the feudal society, the capitalist society and the communist society, which are shown in turn. Seen from the development history of Marxism, with the deepening of Marx and Engels' research on the history of human society, the division of the stages of social formation development becomes more detailed and clear. But Marx's theory on the succession and development of social formation in turn is a logical summary of the general process of human social development in the whole world history, which, in his own words, is "super-historical", which does not regard this kind of division as a specific mode of historical development of a nation or a country, nor to require all nations and countries to develop according to this model, regardless of their historical environment. And therefore, when Marx began to study the ancient society and the oriental society, he highlighted the problem of historical development diversity outside of Europe and backward social organism as an important theoretical aspect, and thought that Russia and the Eastern countries can transcend the "Kaftin Canyon of the capitalist system", or greatly shorten the process of capitalism, and quickly transit from feudal society to communist society.

Western scholars described Marx as a multi-line theorist based on Marx's theory of Russia and eastern society. They simply did not understand the relationship between the assertion on the analysis of specific social regions and the general conclusions on the study of the whole human history. They saw the differences, and turned the differences into opposition, but did not see the connections between them. In the final analysis it is an old saying, "these gentlemen do not understand dialectics", they "see only white or black". In fact , Marx's analysis of the Russian society in his later years cannot prove that he is a " multi-line theorist " opposed to the so-called Engels as a "single-line theorist". On the contrary, Marx did not deny that the Russian society followed the historical evolution of human society from lower to advanced. He only conceived that Russia may take a special way based on the real social historical conditions of Russia. The way was different from Western Europe, nor did it follow a certain kind of stereotype, but had its own uniqueness. What we see from it is that Marx did not treat Russian society dogmatically according to some fixed model, but analyzed the reality of Russia concretely, and concretized the theory of social formation into the understanding of Russian society, which was completely consistent with Engels' repeated emphasis that historical materialism was only a guide to the study, but cannot replace any specific studies. Marx followed this principle and made his analysis of the Russian commune an indispensable part of his dialectical view of history.

Moreover, in Engels' research, Engels does not blindly emphasize the universal and general aspects of social history. Instead, when his research enters a specific scope, he never neglects the study of the particularity within this scope. For example, in *The Origin of the Family, Private Property and the State*, Engels paid enough attention to the special aspects of this social form when analyzing the primitive state. He believes that in this initial stage of development of human society, kinship is the basis of the whole social structure, that is, kinship is the relationship that plays a decisive role in all the savage and barbaric nations. Moreover, this relationship constitutes the differences between the content of prehistoric history of mankind and the content of literary history. In the discussion of the transformation from primitive society to slave society, Engels also considered the change of the internal structure of the clan as an important content. He clearly saw that the improvement of the production level of materials alone could not lead to the change from primitive society to private ownership society, in this process, primitive kinship also played an important role, and the improvement of production level itself must be combined with the specific social reality of kinship. All these fully illustrate Engels' flexible use of dialectics in the study of historical science, which unifies generality and particularity organically. Of course, most of Engels' works focus on the general theory of philosophy, so what he emphasizes is the general laws hidden in the deep behind the phenomena, as well as in his study of social history. However, it is not possible to conclude that Engels is a "single-line theorist", on the contrary, it is Engels' revelation of the singularity in the general sense of social history and Marx's analysis of the diversity in the concrete meaning in his later years constitute the dialectical unity of Marxist social history theory.

CHAPTER 7 THE DISCOVERY OF "THE THIRD MARX": THE FINAL MANUSCRIPT

In 1930s, the publication of Marx's *Manuscripts of Economics and Philosophy of 1844* aroused controversy about "two Marx"-"Young Marx" and "Old Marx" in Western academic circles. In 1970s, after the publication of *Anthropology Notes* in Marx's later years, some Western scholars claimed to have discovered a "third Marx"—a cultural anthropologist Marx, and a Marx in his later years who ended the general subject of criticizing capitalism and turned to eulogize the "sublime" of the ancient human civilization about to be destroyed[292]. It is an important issue whether the third Marx exists or not in the fierce debate in the field of contemporary Marxist research.

1. The Fiction of "The Third Marx"

The fiction of the "Third Marx" by Western scholars is mainly based on Marx's *Anthropology Notes* in his later years, which reflects the Western scholars' attempt to interpret Marxism's ideological tendency with humanism. In fact, the Western academic circles have already done this for a long time. But in the past, they could only base on Marx's early works to find the basis for portraying Marx as a "humanist" or "anthropologist." In order to achieve the goal of humanizing Marx, they adopted the method of setting "Young Marx" against "Mature Marx" and putting Marx and Engels against each other. But, this practice also caused suspicion and controversy even within the Western academic community. So, Western scholars are always looking for new ways to convince people of their lies. The publication of Marx's *Anthropology Notes* in his later years seems to satisfy their needs. However, does *Anthropology Notes* really provide a new basis for the Western scholars to humanize Marx?

---

[292]See T. Botmore: *A Dictionary of Marxist Thought*, Page 23~24, London, 1983.

Marx's *Anthropology Notes* in his later years mainly include notes and abstracts he made during 1879-1882 when he read the anthropological works of Kovalevsky, Morgan and so on.[293] It is made up of excerpts from large sections and fragments of Marx's expression of some new ideas. In 1972, the famous American anthropologist Lawrence Krader was the first to compile and publish four core notes from Marx's *Anthropology Notes* in his later years (notes on Morgan, Lubbock, Maine, and Phear) with the title of *The Ethnological Notebooks of Karl Marx*. There is no doubt that Krader did a very meaningful work for the study of Marx's thought, but the controversy has gone far beyond the *Anthropology Notes* of later life.

In the prologue to *The Ethnological Notebooks of Karl Marx* and *The Asian Production Mode*, and in *Karl Marx As Ethnologist*, Krader believed that Marx's later study of anthropology was to return to a philosophical humanism represented by *Manuscripts of Economics and Philosophy of 1844* in his earlier years on a higher basis. He summed up Marx's philosophical exploration throughout his life as a shift from early philosophical anthropology to later empirical anthropology. His disciple Silile Levitt expounded his viewpoint in detail in *Marx's Anthropology and Evolution,* and held that Marx's *Anthropology Notes* in his later years was a major breakthrough and development of Marx's early philosophical humanism.

Marx spent a lot of time and energy to study the anthropology works of European and American anthropologists in his sickly old years. Is it really a return to the early philosophical humanism represented by *Manuscripts of Economics and Philosophy*

---

[293]*The Anthropology Notes* generally refers to: *The Abstracts of The System of Commune Land Ownership and the Cause, Process and Result of Its Disintegration by M. Kovalevsky, The Abstracts of Ancient Society by Lewis Henry Morgan, The Abstracts of Lectures Delivered by Maine for the Inns of Court were the Groundwork of Ancient Law by Sir Henry James Sumner Maine, The Abstract of The Origin of Civilization and the Primitive State of Man by John Lubbock and The Abstract of The Aryan Village in India and Ceylon by Phear John B.*

of 1844? The answer is no.

It is true that the question of human beings is an extremely important theoretical issue in historical materialism. Marx, as the founder of historical materialism, not only paid close attention to this issue in the course of establishing a new philosophy, but also in the further development of it in the future. Naturally, it is also an important theoretical problem in Marx's *Anthropology Notes* in his later years, but we cannot draw the conclusion that *Anthropology Notes* is a return to early humanism.

It is true that in Marx's early ideological development, the issue of human beings occupies a prominent and important position. Young Marx made a serious study of the nature of human beings, the relationship between man and nature, and the relationship between man and society. However, even when emphasizing the importance of human beings, young Marx's views on human beings are significantly different from the abstract humanism represented by Feuerbach. *Manuscripts of Economics and Philosophy of 1844* was regarded by Western scholars as a work that concentrately reflected the humanism thought of Marx, but in this work, the speculative logic from human nature and the scientific logic from economic facts were intertwined in this work. Although Marx had not consciously realized the differences between his thought and Feuerbach's humanism at that time, he had actually begun to study man and society from the perspective of social productive labor. In later *The Holy Family*, *The German Ideology*, and *Theses on Feuerbach*, Marx went on exploring human beings along this way of thinking, and came to the scientific conclusion that human nature was the sum of all social relations. So, it is against the historical fact to attribute young Marx to the humanism Marx.

If the *Manuscripts of Economics and Philosophy of 1844* has not completely escaped the influence of Feuerbach and has the trace of abstract humanism, and thus provides a justification for the Western scholars to fabricate "Humanist Marx", it is deliberate distortion to regard Marx's *Anthropology Notes* in his late years as the work of humanism. Because the study object of *Anthropology Notes* is not human beings, but society, especially prehistoric society and oriental society, and it is the perfection and deepening of the important principles such as the essence, structure and motive force of prehistoric society and the development way of human society of historical materialism. In *Manuscripts of Economics and Philosophy of 1844*, there is the history of regarding human society as the alienation and reversion of human nature, while in *Anthropology Notes*, Marx uses the development of material production to explain the development of social history, believing that the growth of social wealth will lead to the process of taking wealth as the only ultimate goal, namely the end of capitalism, because this course contains elements of self-destruction, on which a more advanced social system will be established, namely socialism and communism system.[294] Marx, in combination with the disintegration of primitive society, profoundly explained that the development of human personality was restricted by economic conditions, not the requirements of human nature and self-actualization. In *Anthropology Notes*, instead of talking about human nature in an abstract way, Mark connected human nature with class nature, and affirmed that in a class society, one's "personality itself was the personality of a class".[295]

Western scholars also admitted that Marx's thought in his later years embodied his "turning point"[296] in epistemology and methodology. Instead of objectively and fairly evaluating this "turning point", they simply attributed it to the transformation from philosophical anthropology to empirical anthropology, thus achieving the goal of dismembering Marx with humanitarianism.

---

[294]*Marx/Engels Collected Works*, Chinese Edition 1, Vol. 45, Page 398, Beijing, People's Publishing House, 1985.

[295]*Marx/Engels Collected Works*, Chinese Edition 1, Vol. 45, Page 647.

[296]See Lawrence Krader: *The Ethnological Notebooks of Karl Marx*, See *Research Materials on Marxism-Leninism*, 1985, Division 1, Page 198~199.

Another "argument" for Western scholars to humanize Marx in his later years is that in his later years, Marx was a romantic who was nostalgic for the past, instead of a proletarian revolutionary. Levine, a contemporary American scholar known for creating "opposition" between Marx and Engels, believed that in 1853, when Marx began to study the history of Oriental society and anthropology, he gradually lost interests in economics, and in the second half life, Marx's interest was completely concentrated on the collapse of the primitive society. And accordingly, Marx put an end to his criticism of capitalism and his study of the history of economics and economic development in Western Europe in the 19th century and became a nostalgic thinker who praised the primitive society and despised the modern society. [297] Donald Kelly, another American scholar who studied Marx's thoughts in his later years, also thought that Marx, from 1879 to 1883 till his death, had studied and developed his anthropological perspective, and turned from the problem of class struggle to that of the new anthropology itself. The most striking thing about Marx in his later years was that he seemed to be transcending historical materialism, which was confined to economics and class analysis. Kelly concluded that "Marx was his first revisionist."[298]

Is that true? Absolutely no. History tells us that revolution is Marx's unremitting pursuit throughout his life. Engels once said: "Marx was above all a revolutionary. In some way, Marx participated in the cause of overthrowing the capitalist society and the state system it built... In fact, this was his lifelong mission."[299] Marx once participated passionately in the European revolution. He spoke highly of the

---

[297]See Norman Levine: *Dialectical Materialism and the Russian Village Society*, See *Social Science Trends in Foreign Countries*, 1985, Division 7, Page 8.

[298]Donald Kelly: *Marxist Anthropology in His Late Years*, Published on *Journal of History of Ideas*, April-June, 1984.

[299]*Karl Marx and Frederick Engels: Selected Works*, Edition 1, Vol. 3, Page 575.

awakening of the Oriental countries in the 1950s and 1960s. He struck the death knell of capitalism with his pen as a hammer in *Das Capital*. Even in his later years, Marx remained concerned about the revolutionary cause of the proletariat. In 1881, two years before Marx's death, he wrote in a letter to his daughter, Jenny (Jenny Caroline "Jennychen" Marx Longuet), that: "They (See Marcel Longuet, Marx's grandson—Note of the quoter) are facing the most revolutionary period ever experienced by man."[300] One of the important motives of Marx's research in anthropology in his later years is to provide theoretical guidance for the proletariat revolution.

After the failure of the Paris Commune in 1871, world history entered a new era, and "the bourgeois revolution in the West has come to an end. The East was not mature enough to realize this revolution."[301] During the period of peaceful development, capitalism in Western Europe stepped up its predation and aggression against the Oriental countries. After the mature capitalist relations of production and the ancient non-capitalist relations of production of the East came into contact with each other, contradictions and confrontations took place, and the process of world history is accelerating. The outcome will not only determine the fate of these ancient nations themselves, but also determines whether they can "reverse to impact on Europe", which to a large extent, determines the fate of the European revolution. Marx objectively and concretely examined the history and current situation of these rather special social formations in the East, which was the theoretical preparation for the arrival of a new revolution. Even in his study of Morgan's ancient social theory, Marx was clearly aware of the practical significance of such a study. Marx believed that Morgan's work contributed to the transitory nature of capitalist history, and the understanding of the objective inevitability of

---

[300]*Marx/Engels Collected Works*, Chinese Edition 1, Vol. 35, Page 179.

[301]*Selected Works of Lenin*, Edition 2, Vol. 2, Page 438.

the whole human society leading to communism.

Seen from the experience and lessons of the failure of the Paris Commune Revolution, the question of the peasant allies was raised prominently. As early as the middle of the 19th century, Marx had clarified the importance of the alliance of workers and peasants based on the experience of the European countries in 1848, especially the French Revolution: If the proletariat established the alliance of workers and peasants, it would become a chorus of the revolution of the proletariat, otherwise it would inevitably become a cry of solitude. The revolutionary practice of the Paris Commune not only confirmed the correctness of Marx's thought, but also put forward the problem of the allied forces of the world proletariat at a deeper level. The fact that the revolution of the Paris commune was subjected to the joint repression by the French and Prussian bourgeoisie suggested that the proletariat cannot be considered only by one state but must be examined from the political pattern of the world.

Since the emergence of capitalism, because of the development of productive forces, the production and consumption of all countries have become cosmopolitan. Just as capitalism has subordinated the countryside to the cities, it has made the uncivilized and semi-civilized countries subordinate to the civilized countries, has made the peasant nation subordinate to the capitalist nation, and has made the ancient empire of the East subordinate to the capitalist powers of the West. By the second half of the 19th century, the question of relations between the developed capitalist countries of the West and the countries of the East had actually become a question of relations between the bourgeoisie and the peasants in the world. In this way, it was an important subject for Marx in his later years that how to solve the problem of the allied proletariat in the world.

In his later years, Marx not only summarized the experiences and lessons of the European proletarian revolution, but also paid great attention to the possibility of revolution in the East.

After 1870s, under the constant erosion of capitalism, various social contradictions have been intensified, and revolutionary crises will arise at any time. Under the general background of the development of world history, Marx focused on the possibility of a revolution in Russia. In September 1877, Marx wrote to Sorge: "This crisis is **a new turning point** in European history. I've studied the situations of Russia on the basis of unofficial and official Russian raw materials. Russia is already in front of the door of revolution, and all the factors necessary for that are ripe... This time, the revolution will begin in the east, which has always been a safe fortress for counter-revolution and a reserve army."[302] Marx was not an abstract humanist who was full of nostalgia in his later years. His enthusiasm for the proletarian revolution was not abated at all. The difference was that Marx looked to the East.

In his later years, Marx discussed the economic crisis in the capitalist world, and thought that the non-capitalist Russia would have the possibility of a revolution first. This is undoubtedly a new conclusion, which not only reveals the new trend of the development of world history, and meanwhile reflects the great change of Marx's thought. Marx used to focus his attention on the advanced capitalist countries, such as Britain and France, but now he has turned to the backward non-capitalist country—Russia. In the past, Marx believed that only the proletariat of the Western capitalist countries had acted together, can the victory of the socialist revolution be achieved, but now he believed that Russia and the East may break out the revolution first. In the past, Marx mainly studied the capitalist mode of production and its corresponding relations of production and exchange, but now, he added the study of the land ownership relationship in non-capitalist countries. Western scholars ignored these objective facts and arbitrarily denied Marx's attention to the proletarian revolution in his later years, with the aim of humanizing Marx.

---

[302]*Marx/Engels Collected Works*, Chinese Edition 1, Vol. 34, Page 275, Beijing, People's Publishing House, 1972.

Marx not only probed into the possibility of Russian and Oriental proletarian revolution, but also put forward the great subject of the times that how to combine Marxism with the actual situations in Russia and Oriental countries. Under the historical conditions at that time, the spread of Marxism in Russia and the Orient faced difficulties: in Russia and Oriental countries with the preservation of many traces of ancient society, especially commune land ownership and patriarchal system, some people did not understand the basic spirit of historical materialism, ignored the particularity of the historical conditions of the oriental society, treated the Marxist theory of social development mechanically, and compared the scientific communism with their subjective imagination. These errors can be divided into two categories: one is the Pan-Slavic and the populist utopian socialists in Russia, who believe that the village community is the growth point of socialism and the Russian peasants have a natural socialist instinct, conceiving that without the proletariat and without material conditions, the rural communes would be revived so that they could enter socialism and communism without capitalism. The other is bourgeois liberal thinkers, who ignore the historical condition differences between the East and the West, and regard the collapse of the Russian rural commune as a natural trend, as in Western Europe, believing that it is also a historical necessity for Russia to follow the capitalist path. On the face of it, there are differences of opinions between the two schools of thoughts, but in fact, they are apparently acquiescing while contrary-minded: Both of them regard Marx's theory of origin and development of Western capitalism as an abstract historical philosophy which can be applied to all historical times.

In March 1881, in his letter to Вера Ивановна Засулич, a Russian female revolutionist, Marx made a clear statement that his theory of the historical inevitability of capitalism was "clearly limited to the countries of Europe", that is to say, the judgment can only be made by combining the observation and analysis on the historical fate of the peoples who preserved all kinds of ancient social relations with local history and the present situations. This has solved the methodological problem of how to apply Marxism to Russia and the vast majority of backward countries and regions in the Orient. It can be seen from this that how could Marx's interests in his later years be completely focused on the collapse of the form of the primitive commune, and that how could it go beyond the theory of class analysis and class struggle and concentrate on the exploration of new anthropology.

In his later years, Marx did not give up his exploration of proletarian revolutionary theory or his study of economics. As far as the creation of *Das Capital* is concerned, after Marx turned to the study of anthropology in his later years, he did not ignore the creation of *Das Capital*. In September 1867, after the publication of volume 1 of *Das Capital*, Marx seized all available time to continue to study and write the following volumes and prepared to publish new editions. According to historical records, from the second half of November to December in 1879, "Marx wrote the second and third volumes of *Das Capital*, and studied the historical data of land relations."[303]; from October 1880 to March 1881, "Marx continued to write volumes II and III of *Das Capital*, and studied a large number of official documents (blue books) and literature on the economic development of the United States"[304]; and from October 30th 1882 to January 12th 1883, "Marx lived in Venter Noor, and worked on the preparation of the third German edition of volume I of Das Capital"[305]. It can be seen that Marx did not give up his criticism of capitalism or his study of economics until the last moment of his life. Even though Marx studied the works of American and European anthropologists, taking *Anthropology Notes* is not completely unrelated to *Das Capital*. Engels had ever made an explanation on this, saying that: "Marx studied everything by examining its historical origin and its premise, and therefore, to him, every single problem is natural to produce a series

---

[303] *Marx/Engels Collected Works*, Chinese Edition 1, Vol. 19, Page 677.

[304] *Marx/Engels Collected Works*, Chinese Edition 1, Vol. 19, Page 683.

[305] *Marx/Engels Collected Works*, Chinese Edition 1, Vol. 19, Page 694.

of new problems. He studied the history of primitive times, agronomy, land relations of Russia and America, geology, and so on, mainly to write the most perfect chapter on land rent in the third volume of *Das Capital*."[306]

It is impossible for Western scholars attempting to draw the conclusions of romanticism from Marx in his later years. Indeed, in *Anthropology Notes*, Marx emphasized the positive significance of the interpersonal relationship of primitive collectivism in history and anthropology, affirmed the courage, integrity and fortitude of primitive democracy and primitive man, mercilessly exposed the one-sidedness of alienation of human nature and repression from capitalist social relations, and noticed the destruction of capitalist civilization to the survival and development of backward nations. But it is not enough to prove that Marx yearned for the era of human desolation and hated the uproar of industrial society, for he neither fully affirmed the primitive society nor simply negated the capitalist society. He did not praise the ignorance and savagery of primitive society and the character of the primitives such as barbarity, crafty and fanaticism that followed the emergence of private property, but fully affirmed the progressive role of capitalist society in human history. In view of the crowning calamity of the backward nation by the capitalist "advanced civilization", Marx, on the one hand, gave full moral sympathy, and on the other hand, rested the hope for the future on their conscious and full use of all the positive achievements created by capitalism. How can Marx be regarded as a nostalgic thinker who praised the primitive society and despised of the modern society just according to Marx's affirmation of some of the advantages of the primitive man and primitive society in his later years in *Anthropology Notes*? Marx was not an advocate of "Doomsday theory", nor a romantic illusionist, but an optimist of history.

Marx is just Marx, the one as the creator of Marxism. The fictional "Third Marx" is

---

[306]*Marx/Engels Collected Works*, Chinese Edition 1, Vol. 22, Page 400.

consistent with his thoughts in his youth and adulthood, that is, to continuously deepen his understanding of the laws of society and history and to constantly enrich and develop historical materialism. Western scholars divided a complete Marx into three just for the purpose of distorting and tampering with Marxism.

2. Unconfused "Confusion in Old Age"

The trend of Marx's thought in his later years has been a historical mystery for a long time, which puzzles many researchers of Marx's thought. Marx biographer Mehring once described Marx's old age as follows: after 1873, with the reemergence of the proletarian revolutionary movement, Marxism began to spread throughout the world, and the political horizon suddenly opened up, but the twilight was increasingly approaching Marx and his family. "During this whole period, his life is just a chronic death"[307]. He even quoted Engels as saying on the day of Jenny's death: "Moore is dead, too"[308]. It is proved that Marx stopped his theoretical exploration in his later years because of health reasons and heavy emotional blows. This is Marx, "a historical old man who was enveloped in the twilight and suffering from disease", in his later years in Mehring's writing.

Soviet scholars discovered Marx's thought track in his later years for the first time, but did not pay enough attention to it. In 1921, Lenin sent Riazanov, president of the Marx and Engels Research Institute, to collect Marx's and Engels' manuscripts abroad. Among them, *Anthropology Notes* of Marx in his later years were collected. However, the Soviet scholars represented by Riazanov not only fail to fully realize the theoretical value of these "notes", but were also incomprehensible to Marx's turn to the study of anthropology in his later years, and regarded it as an

---

[307]Mehring: *Karl Marx: The Story of His Life*, Page 670, Beijing, People's Publishing House, 1972.

[308]Mehring: *Karl Marx: The Story of His Life*, Page 673.

"unforgivable pedantry"[309].

For the first time, Western scholars noticed the theoretical significance of Marx's study of anthropology in his later years, but simply incorporated it into the humanistic ideological system, and took it as the basis for the discovery of "the third Marx". Although it is not tenable for Western scholars to study the humanism tendency of Marx's thought in his later years, people cannot avoid such a "puzzling" question that: Why did Marx study anthropology, prehistoric society and oriental society in his sickly old age? It is difficult to answer the challenges posed by Western scholars and grasp the whole thought system of Marxism completely and accurately without solving this "historical mystery".

Some scholars believed that the reason why Marx studied the prehistoric society and the oriental society in his later years was to get rid of the "confusion in his old age", and the reason for the confusion was that his revolutionary prophecy had fallen through, and his expectation of revolution vanished like soap bubbles in real life. Because of his "confusion", Marx began to doubt his basic theory, and he wanted to re-examine historical materialism.

However, this so-called "confusion in his old age" was entirely a result of fiction and speculation. As mentioned above, Marx did not lose confidence in the proletarian revolution in his later years, but casted his eyes to the oriental according to the world situation at that time. In his later years, Marx never doubted historical materialism, nor his own point of view on the universal law of the development of world history, but tried to verify, enrich and develop it through the study of the prehistoric society and the oriental society. So what are the theoretical motives for Marx's study of the prehistoric society and the oriental society in his later years?

As we all know, it is Marx's great mission of his whole life to reveal the universal laws of the development of human society. In order to accomplish this important

---

[309]*Research Materials on Marxism-Leninism*, 1987, Division 1, Page 160.

mission, Marx firstly examined the most developed and complex social organization in the history of capitalist society, analyzed its social structure in a comprehensive and systematic way, and revealed the law of the emergence, development and extinction of capitalist society. On the basis of the general approach to the study of society derived from the study of capitalist societies, he examined all the underdeveloped social organizations of pre-capitalism. But before the middle of the 19th century, almost no one knows the prehistoric state of society and the state of social organization before the whole history of literature. The early bourgeoisie enlightenment thinkers, such as Grotius (Hugo Grotius), Hobbes (Thomas Hobbes), Rousseau and others, generally used the theory of contract to describe the initial state of human society, and believed that human society once had the natural state of having neither state nor private property based on the principles of natural law. Rousseau even called this time as the golden age, because there was no violence, no exploitation and no oppression, and everyone was equal. In fact, this is an illusion, and Marx's understanding of prehistoric society also had an illusion.

Marx's first relatively concentrated work on the early human society was *The German Ideology*, which was co-authored by him and Engels. In this work, Marx examined several major forms of ownership in history according to the different stages of the development of the division of labor, namely, tribal ownership, ancient commune ownership, state ownership, feudal or hierarchical ownership and modern capitalist ownership. Marx believed that tribal ownership, as the first kind of ownership form in the history of the human society, which is the original form of human society, was compatible with the underdeveloped stage of productive forces and division of labor. The primitive production activities, which are dominated by hunting, fishing and animal husbandry, and the division of labor which are only natural in the family, can only produce the primitive collective ownership and the social structure based on the family. However, in patriarchal families, the embryonic form of slavery has been existed hiddenly. The husband's domination of the labor force of his wife and children has formed the earliest essential aspect of this ownership, and meanwhile formed the basis for the emergence and development of other forms of ownership. In Marx's view, tribal ownership could be developed into both ancient slave ownership and medieval feudal ownership.[310] This kind of tribal ownership has a primary nature to other forms of ownership. The theory of succession of ownership forms is the embryonic form of Marx's theory of social formation. As the understanding of prehistoric society in this period is basically a blank, Marx has to use logical means to grasp the process of social development, so there must be limitations.

On the one hand, he tried to regard tribal ownership as a form of public ownership, because, in his view, real private ownership, whether in ancient or modern nations, appeared only with the emergence of portable property, whereas in tribal ownership, there was only real estate. And therefore, the tribal ownership is not a typical form of private ownership. However , on the other hand, Marx did not affirm that the tribal ownership was a form of public ownership, because there was private property—real estate in the ownership, and there was also hidden slavery with domination on the labor of others. So, the concept of tribal ownership did not fully coincide with the nature of the primitive public society. The situation of the patriarchal family cannot simply be regarded as the typical condition of the primitive society, but at most the product of the collapse of the primitive society.

The contradiction in Marx's understanding of tribal ownership obviously affected his scientific understanding of the process of social development. When Marx and Engels stated their basic views on social and historical development in *The Communist Manifesto*, they believe that "all social history so far is the history of class struggle"[311], which is undoubtedly not enough to reflect the true appearance

---

[310]See *Karl Marx and Frederick Engels: Selected Works*, Edition 1, Vol. 1, Page 68~69.

[311]*Karl Marx and Frederick Engels: Selected Works*, Edition 1, Vol. 1, Page 250.

of the history of human society. As for this, in 1888, Engels explained that: "in 1847, the prehistoric state of society and all the social organization before literature and history, is almost completely unknown."[312] In this case, even though the logic of the theory has grasped the basic clue that private ownership originates from the public ownership, it is impossible to make a breakthrough in the study of the initial human society.

In 1850s, people's lack of understanding of prehistoric society remained unchanged. This meant that it is possible for Marx to complete the task of comprehensively expounding all the historical processes and laws of human society from ancient to present only after a series of major discoveries in anthropology and archaeology were found. However, the urgency of Marx's study of social history did not allow him to interrupt his investigation of prehistoric society. It was in this historical background that Marx began to study the Asian production mode, which was another stage of Marx's study of the early human society.

It was in the *Preface to Critique of Political Economy* of 1859 that Marx formally proposed the Asian production mode, but before that, he had studied the basic characteristics of the Asian production mode. In (the manuscripts of 1877-1858 of) *Preface to Critique of Political Economy*, Marx discussed the characteristics and nature of three forms of ownership: the form of Asian ownership, the ancient form of ownership and the form of Germanic ownership under the title of "Various Forms Before Capitalist Production", Marx believed that in the ownership of Asia, "the individual is only the occupant, and there is no private ownership of land."[313] So, the primitive form of this kind of ownership itself was direct public ownership.

---

[312]*Karl Marx and Frederick Engels: Selected Works*, Edition 1, Vol. 1, Page 251, Note ①.

[313]*Marx/Engels Collected Works*, Chinese Edition 1, Vol. 46 (I), Page 484, Beijing, People's Publishing House, 1979.

In ancient ownership, "ownership was manifested in the dual form of state ownership in parallel with private ownership", and in Germanic ownership, "commune ownership was merely expressed as a supplement to individual ownership", and "individual ownership is the basis of commune ownership."[314] According to the degree of collapse of land public ownership, Marx established the logical sequence of succession and development from Asian ownership to ancient ownership and to Germanic ownership. This logical sequence coincides with the historical development of the form of ownership: private ownership has been formed on the basis of public ownership of land, and the further development of private ownership is in a state of complete separation from and coexistence of state ownership., thus forming the form of free individual land ownership, and collective property is only a supplement to it. It can be seen that the three forms of ownership analyzed by Marx actually corresponded to the three main forms of human social development, namely, primitive society, slavery society and feudal society. Marx believed that in these three social forms, slavery and serfdom were derived form rather than primary form, and primary form was Asian ownership. In the first volume of *Critique of Political Economy* officially published in 1859, he pointed out: "A careful study of the forms of commune ownership in Asia, especially in India, will prove that how to produce its various forms of disintegration from the different forms of primitive commune ownership. For example, the Roman and Germanic archetypes of private ownership can be extrapolated from the various forms of commune ownership in India."[315]

It is on the basis of the research on the manuscripts of *Critique of Political Economy* that Marx, in the preface to *Critique of Political Economy* wrote in 1859, made a

---

[314]*Marx/Engels Collected Works*, Chinese Edition 1, Vol. 46 (I), Page 484, Beijing, People's Publishing House, 1979.

[315]*Marx/Engels Collected Works*, Chinese Edition 1, Vol. 13, Page 22 Note ①, Beijing, People's Publishing House, 1962.

classical summary on the basic process and laws of the succession of various social forms, including the Asian production mode: "generally speaking, Asian, ancient, the feudal and modern capitalist mode of production can be seen as a few times of the evolution of social and economic forms."[316]

However, there is still such a contradiction in taking the Asian production mode as the primary form of human society that logically, the land public ownership factors in the Asian production mode constitute the basis of the primary form of human society, and private ownership society is gradually derived from this basis. But historically, not only did the Asian mode of production coexist with other private ownership societies, such as slave society and feudal society, but when the Asian production mode in Western society tended to disintegrate, the Asian production mode of the oriental society still maintained its own strong vitality. Moreover, in the Asian mode of production, although the land is owned by communes, not by individuals, on each isolated commune stands a higher owner, namely, the despotic monarch. "The state here is the highest landlord." [317] And therefore, the establishment of the status of the Asian production mode as the primary form of human society only logically solves the problem of the development of the private ownership society from the public ownership, but does not solve the problem of the development of the Asian social form itself from the historical point of view. That is whether this mode of production, as a "primary form", must go through slave society, feudal society, and finally to capitalist society as the Western society does. If the Asian production mode can be directly transferred to the capitalist society after coexisting with the Western social development sequence for a long time, does this mean that the law of the succession of social forms is not of universal significance in the Oriental society? In short, when Marx placed the Asian

---

[316]*Karl Marx and Frederick Engels: Selected Works*, Edition 1, Vol. 2, Page 83.

[317]*Marx/Engels Collected Works*, Chinese Edition 1, Vol. 25, Page 891.

production mode in the development process of the successive changes of each human society forms for study, there was an inherent contradiction between logic and history, which was the contradiction between the Asian production mode as the "primary form" of human society logically and as a social form coexisted with other social forms and developed independently historically.

The possibility of resolving contradictions can only be realized after the conditions are in place to solve them. This means that it is possible for Marx to overcome the one-sided understanding of the "original form" of human society resulting from the lack of historical data, and to complete the historic mission of comprehensively expounding the historical process and general laws of human society from ancient to present only after a series of major discoveries in prehistoric society were made by anthropology, archaeology, and other disciplines. It logically requires Marx to move towards anthropology in his later years.

Since 1860s, anthropology, archaeology and other subjects that directly take prehistoric society as the object of study have made great progress. By the first half of the 19th century, in the Western European literature, there had been a great deal of materials on the Central American, North and South American Indians, the aboriginal peoples of Oceania Islands and Australian coast, as well as many peoples in Africa and Asia. Ways of life, such as slash-and-burn farming method and drilling wood to make fire, which were previously found only in historical documents, still exist in some of the relatively backward ethnic groups. The physique, appearance, and peculiar social structure, language form, marriage and family, religious ceremony, artistic style, and even the way of thinking of these peoples have attracted many European scholars, and therefore, a series of questions about human race and human culture are put forward.

According to Engels in the book *The Origin of the Family, Private Property and the State*, before 1860s, it was impossible to talk about family history at all. "Historical science is still completely under the influence of the Five Books of Moses in this respect."[318] This situation changed only after the publication of *Mother Right (Das Mutterrecht)* by the Swiss jurist Bachofen (Johann Jakob Bachofen) in 1861. His study of ancient marriage and family systems and matrilineal clans has provided some valuable materials and perspectives for the understanding of the nature and basic characteristics of the prehistoric society. In 1865, in his book *Primitive Marriage*, the British jurist McLennan (John Ferguson McLennan) directly inherited Bachofen's view that the matriarchy hereditary system was the original form of organization of human society. In 1860s, anthropology developed to a certain extent, however, the study of prehistoric society has not provided Marx with materials of decisive significance.

By 1870s, anthropology had made considerable strides, and people's understanding of prehistoric state had deepened greatly. There were also plenty of books on this respect. For example, *The Origin of Civilization and the Primitive Condition of Man* (1870) by Lubbock, *Primitive Culture Volume 1: Researches Into the Development of Mythology, Philosophy, Religion, Art, and Custom* (1871) by Tylor (Edward Burnett Tylor), *Lectures Delivered by Maine for the Inns of Court were the Groundwork of Ancient Law* by Maine, *Ancient Society* by Morgan, *The System of Commune Land Ownership and the Cause, Process and Result of Its Disintegration* (Общинное землевладение etc. Mosk.1879) by Kovalevsky, and T*he Aryan Village in India and Ceylon* by Phear, and so on. Some of these books directly examine the social structure, marriage and family of ancient peoples to reveal the early social overview of mankind; some reflect some of the basic characteristics of primitive society by examining primitive culture; and some infer the initial state of the long-gone human society by examining the social conditions of the backward nations. They not only deeply dissected the internal structure of prehistoric society, explored the mysteries of internal primitive social organizations, but also revealed

---

[318]*Karl Marx and Frederick Engels: Selected Works*, Edition 1, Vol. 4, Page 5.

the process of prehistoric social evolution and its general law. These important findings are of great significance for Marx to establish scientific prehistoric social theory and perfect historical materialism.

From a large number of abstracts, commentaries, supplements and elaborations on the works of anthropology in Europe and the United States in Marx's *Anthropology Notes* in his later years, we can see that Marx's study of anthropology not only further confirmed the universality of the basic principles of historical materialism, but also enriched and developed historical materialism in many ways.

As mentioned above, Marx regarded the patriarchal family as the earliest social organization in human history in *The German Ideology*, and considered that the social structure was only limited to the expansion of this kind of patriarchal family. However, in *Anthropology Notes*, Marx denied the previous view on the basis of the patriarchal family discovered by Morgan. He wrote that all previous great scholars, including Sir Henry Maine, considered Hebrew and Roman (patriarchal families) to be the oldest forms of family, and that these forms of family produced the earliest organized society. In fact, this is only the high stage of barbarism, far from ancient times.[319] This clearly shows that Marx had clearly recognized that patriarchy family was only a family form that existed at the end of primitive society , before it had a more original form of family .

Anthropology Notes also revised the argument that "all the history so far is the history of class struggle" proposed in *The Communist Manifesto*. He said: "**Fourier** (Jean-Baptiste Joseph Fourier) believed that the **monogamous marriage system** and **the private ownership of land** are the symbol of the **civilization era**. The modern family in the bud, not only contains senatus (slavery), but also contains **serfdom**... It contains all the confrontations that later developed extensively in

---

[319]See *Marx/Engels Collected Works*, Chinese Edition 1, Vol. 45, Page 377 and Page 587.

society and in its country in microcosm."[320] Marx has used the term "modern" here to restrict class confrontation or class struggle, which had been widely developed in society and its countries, and regarded class struggle as a later development rather than existed ever before. In this way, he corrected his over-generous time limit on class struggle in 1840s.

In the *Preface to Critique of Political Economy*, Marx used the "Asian production mode" to describe the primitive mode of production of human society. Morgan's rediscovery of prehistoric society had a great impact on Marx's traditional concept of "Asian production mode", which made it possible for him to fundamentally overcome the inherent contradictions contained in the concept, namely, the antinomy between the land public ownership and autocratic state. In Marx's view, Morgan's outstanding contribution was a complete reappearance of a true picture of primitive human society: there was no class, no private ownership, and no state in primitive clan organizations. In this way, the long-unknown "primary form" in the general process of human social development has been discovered. This "primordial form" not only remained in "Asia" for a long time, but was also the initial form of the clan that could be seen among the civilized peoples of ancient Greece and Rome, and it is the earliest universal stages in the development of human society, and therefore, it is inappropriate to recrown "Asia" before the primordial form of human society. Marx gave up the concept of "Asian production mode" in his later years, which showed that he realized the limitations of using this concept to express prehistoric society. There is no doubt that this is a positive result after a great theoretical deepening.

From this point of view, in his later years, Marx turned to the study of the prehistoric society and the oriental society, not because he doubted the basic principles of historical materialism, nor did he retreat from the historical

---

[320]*Marx/Engels Collected Works*, Chinese Edition 1, Vol. 45, Page 366.

materialism he created, but rather enriched and developed historical materialism, which was in line with the logic of the development of his whole ideological system.

3. Is Marx an Anthropologist?

In the eyes of some Western scholars, Marx is a typical anthropologist. The North American dialectical anthropologist school, represented by Stanny Diamond and others, believed that whether from the works of the young Marx or from that of Marx in his later years, a tradition of anthropological criticism of capitalist societies can be found. In his youth, Marx criticized the denial and alienation of human nature by capitalist relations of production from the angle of philosophical anthropology. In his later years, from the materials of empirical anthropology, he criticized the destruction of oriental culture by capitalist civilization. They also regarded the basic tradition of Marxism as a kind of historical dialectical anthropology with revolutionary conscience and foresight, and believed that there would be no Marxist tradition without anthropology.

The purpose of emphasizing the so-called "anthropological tradition" of Marxism and describing Marx as a typical anthropologist is to denounce and attack historical materialism. Either being ignorance of historical materialism or deliberately distorted, some Western scholars always put the study of people and historical materialism against each other, and believed that historical materialism ignores people, and did not study people. They not only accused Engels of turning Marxist philosophy from a dynamic theory into a dead social determinism system, but also accused "Old Marx" of abandoning "a path that might have led to a new humanitarianism. Following the narrow path of economic concepts of property and exploitation led to the dogma that prevails today"[321]. In later years, the publication of the *Anthropology Notes* delighted them, and they found that Marx, in his later

---

[321]D. Bell: *About the Change of Alienation*, Quoted from *Philosophical Discussion on the Theory of Man*, Page 176, Beijing, People's Publishing House, 1982.

years, had returned to the "broad avenue" he had taken in his early years. Donald Kelly thought that the most striking thing about Marx in his later years was that he seemed to be transcending historical materialism, which was limited to economics and class analysis. But is it the fact as they say that Marx in his later years is an "anthropologist" who is moving away from historical materialism?

Anthropology, as an independent discipline, was formed and developed in Western Europe in the middle of the 19th century. It focuses on the characteristics of a certain aspect of human beings, and is the knowledge of a certain aspect of human beings. *Anthropology Notes* in Marx's later years is a study of man and society, especially the prehistoric society and the oriental society, from historical materialism, further putting forward the oriental social theory on the basis of perfecting the theory of prehistoric society.

In Marx's Anthropology Notes in his later years, there were a large number of excerpts and comments about consanguinity. The emphasis on consanguinity is an absolutely important aspect of adhering to historical materialism. Engels once pointed out in *Die Mark*: "There are two spontaneous facts that almost dominate everything or all the nation's ancient history: division according to ethnic kinship and land ownership"[322] Later, he carried out Marx's last words and gave a scientific expression of this in highly classical language. These are the two theories of production, which hold that in a certain historical period and in certain areas, the social system is restricted by two kinds of production. One is the production of material materials and the social relations it produces, and the other is the production or breeding of human beings themselves and their kinship. It can be said that, if we don't grasp these two kinds of production and two kinds of basic social relations which are both materiality, namely, social relations of production and kinship, we can't really understand the social history of the ancient nations in

---

[322]*Marx/Engels Collected Works*, Chinese Edition 1, Vol. 19, Page 353.

the world, especially the ancient oriental nations.

The two kinds of production theories are the thought that Marx and Engels have always adhered to since the time of founding historical materialism. There are revelations of different degrees on the theory from *Critique of Hegel's Philosophy of Right* and *The German Ideology* to *The Communist Manifesto* and *Preface to Critique of Political Economy*, and from the *Manuscripts of Economics from 1857 to 1858* to *Das Capital*. As Marx devoted his life to the study of capitalist society, guided and summed up the actual struggle of the proletariat, he did not have time to make a centralized and systematic exposition. In addition, it should be noted that Marx had always believed that understanding the capitalist economy had provided the key to understanding the ancient economy, just as human anatomy provided the key to the monkey's anatomy. Moreover, he adopted this kind of method in his comparative study, and had already made an important summary of the important problems of various pre-capitalist social and economic forms, including the emergence and development of private ownership and the state. However, the development of historiography at that time had not provided sufficient information for the study of the primitive social formation based on kinship, and therefore, there was no condition to expound all kinds of pre-capitalist social forms in a systematic way, and to give full play to historical materialism. But now the situation is different. Not only does Morgan's writings provide sufficient historical basis for the two kinds of production theories of historical materialism, but what is particularly important is the development of world history that makes the historical fate of the ancient oriental society become a major issue of the times. These ancient societies are not simply equivalent to the ancient Greek and Roman society or feudal society, neither simply the "monkey body" in the Western sense. It is now necessary for Marx to personally and systematically dissect these rather special forms of society in the East, and to further elaborate his historical materialism. From Engels' testimony, we can see that Marx had planned to write a systematic treatise on the two theories of production based on his study on the ancient social history in his later years. However, his early death prevented Marx from realizing this grand plan.

The Origin of the Family, Private Property and the State written by Engels in the second year after Marx's death, is only "slightly compensated" for Marx's unfinished ambition, because the scale of Marx's *Anthropology Notes* in his later years is much more magnificent than Engels' *The Origin of the Family, Private Property and the State,* and the scope of space and time is much wider. In addition to the ancient peoples of Western Europe, it also covered a wide area of Asia, Africa and Latin America including Peru, Mexico to India and Algeria. At the same time, not only the study of the state of the most primitive society, but also the study of the realities of these ancient clans and their future are included; not only the study of clan relations and kinship, but also the study of land commune ownership are included; and not only did Morgan's scientific explanation of the clan mystery in ancient Greek and Roman society be excerpted in detail, but also criticized the opinion of historian Groat and others that the common kinship was the basis of the clan's own fictional concept. Marx pointed out that this common kinship was a "very important thing"[323] to the members of the clan of ancient Greece and Rome, and as the basis of the clan relationship, "it was not **conceptual**, but **material**, and **carnal in German**"[324]. This clearly shows the nature of the clan: The clan is the social organization based on the kinship created by the production of the human itself, and the kinship is the material social relations in reality. This fundamental character of the clan, even in the age of social class division, still plays its role. This is not only the scientific answer of Marxism to the ancient Greek and Roman social clan, but also the general meaning that, as long as the clan or clan relationship exists, we must attach importance to the study of kinship. Otherwise, we could not

---

[323]*Marx/Engels Collected Works*, Chinese Edition 1, Vol. 45, Page 503.

[324]*Marx/Engels Collected Works*, Chinese Edition 1, Vol. 45, Page 503.

understand the ancient society. And therefore, even after the emergence of the private ownership and class, the functions of the clan were dying out day by day, and the kinship was manifested in the patriarchal relationship, which still played a strong normative role in the society and embraced economic and class relations. This is reflected in the patriarchal family, an important link in family history.

Marx attached great importance to this link. He pointed out that this patriarchal family "includes not only servkus (helotism), but also **serfdom**, because from the very beginning, it was related to the **servitude** of farming in the field. It **epitomized** all the confrontations that developed extensively later in society and in its country."[325] That is to say, in all fields of social life and national life in this historical period, there is a strong projection of this patriarchal relationship. This situation is particularly evident and lasting in the history of the Oriental countries. In the notes written by Kovalevsky, Marx examined the brand created by the development of kinship in the evolution of commune land ownership, affirmed the results of Kovalevsky's research. In India, for example, the clan commune, the extended family commune and the form of public land with different direct consanguinity have been preserved, even in the last stage of the commune system-the rural commune, there is still the brand of kinship in terms of the land relationship.

It is the theory of prehistoric society that is closely related to the two theories of production. Marx made a long and deep study of human prehistoric society. As early as in *The German Ideology*, Marx pointed out that the first social form of the development of human society was public ownership rather than private ownership. From 1850s to early 1870s, he studied the rural communes remained in the East and the West, "deduced" the archetypes of ancient communes or ancient public societies from these concrete communes from different regions with different forms, and wrote *Various Forms Before Capitalist Production*. However, due to the

---

[325]*Marx/Engels Collected Works*, Chinese Edition 1, Vol. 45, Page 366.

historical conditions at that time, Marx had not yet formed a scientific prehistoric social theory. In *Anthropology Notes* in his later years, based on a large number of historical data and cultural anthropology research results, Marx pointed out the method of staging the prehistoric society, and revealed the essence and development process of primitive public ownership by taking the development of productivity and changes in the form of marriage and family as a clue.

In his book *Ancient Society*, based on the production of material materials, Morgan divided the prehistoric society into the era of savagery and the era of barbarism, and divided each era into three stages including lower, intermediate, and advanced staged with each stage marked by a certain number of inventions and technologies. As a result of the progress in the production of material materials, technology and inventions belong to the productive forces. According to the condition of productive forces, we can divide the different stages of the primitive society's development, and we can generally describe "the development picture of mankind's reaching the beginning of the civilization era through the era of savagery and the era of barbarism"[326]. So Marx used Morgan's staging method in *Anthropology Notes*, and described the level of productivity development at each stage in a very clear language. But Marx didn't copy Morgan's staging method completely. For example, Morgan believed that the symbol of the transition from the era of savagery to the era of barbarism was pottery, while Marx classified some tribes that knew nothing about pottery but had invented primitive agriculture as the lower stage of development in the barbaric era.

As an objective basis for the staging of primitive society, in addition to the clues to the development of productive forces, attention should also be paid to the track of the change of the relations of production. The basis of the relations of production in primitive society is the integration of the whole producer and the means of

---

[326] *Karl Marx and Frederick Engels: Selected Works*, Edition 1, Vol. 4, Page 22~23.

production under the connection of kinship. As for this, Marx also made a dynamic description in *Anthropology Notes*. In the primitive society entering the matrilineal clan period, the whole producer connected by kinship directly combined with the increasing "tools of production created by civilization", through the collective labor of the clan, the material goods on which people depended for survival were produced. At this time, in addition to their qualifications as a collective member, a share of a social product of an individual or a small collective should be added to the factor of their own participation in the labor that creates the product. In this way, the public ownership has changed from the single structure of the primitive group of kinship to the multi-level structure of the individual, clan and tribe. As a result of the appearance of metal tools, the first great division of labor took place in society. Nomadic tribes were separated from other tribes. The multi-level public ownership in primitive society entered the stage of disintegration, and the public ownership gradually decreased and transformed to private ownership.

In the process of the disintegration of the public ownership in primitive society, private ownership also gradually occurred at various levels within the clan. In *Anthropology Notes*, Marx excerpted a large number of materials recorded in the works of Kovalevsky and expounded the question. In his opinion, from the historical point of view, whether in ancient or in modern nations, real private ownership occurred only with the emergence of the individualization of movable property. In what order do various forms of movable property become private property? Firstly, it was the personal property limited to those for personal use and personal work; secondly, it was the family property, which was not created and used by individuals, but created and used jointly by people who were not closely related to each other; and thirdly, it was communal property including material goods created and used on a broad basis. Marx not only described the process of privatization of movable property from individual to family and to commune, but also described the process of privatization of real estate—land. The process of privatization of real estate—land was much more complicated than the privatization of movable property, but generally speaking, the process of land privatization also went through all the process from the initial tribal public, to the clan public, the family commune public, and then to the individual family private, and finally completed the qualitative transformation from public to private.

In *Anthropology Notes*, Marx not only elaborated two kinds of production theories and examined the prehistoric society, but also explored the nature and development path of the oriental society, and formed the "oriental social theory".

The so-called oriental social theory is relative to the Western social theory. The Western social theory is mainly based on Britain, France and Germany, and it is Marx's comprehensive system theory on the historical development, current situation and future transition to communism of Europe, especially Western Europe. Whereas, the oriental social theory is mainly based on the oriental world, which accounts for the vast majority of the population and has a wide geographical area, especially in India, Russia and China, and is the theory about the historical development, the current situation and future transition to communism of the oriental society.

As early as the beginning of the establishment of Marxism, the social problems in the oriental society aroused the attention of Marx. Hegel's exposition on the prevalence of autocratic system in the oriental World in *Philosophy of History* once impressed Marx deeply. But Marx did not understand the characteristics of the oriental society at this time, and he covered the oriental world under the unified thought of "world history".

In 1850s, Marx began to study the characteristics of the oriental society. On July 22nd 1853, in the article of *The Future Results of British Rule in India*, Marx clearly put forward the concepts of "Asian society" and "Asian society" for the first time, and distinguished it from "Western society".[327] Marx believed that, compared with

---

[327]See *Karl Marx and Frederick Engels: Selected Works*, Edition 1, Vol. 2, Page 7.

the "Western society", "Asian society" had the following characteristics.

First, there is no private ownership of land, which is a key to understanding oriental society. On June 2nd 1853, in the letter to Engels, according to the materials in *Travels in the Mogul Empire* by François Bernier, Marx pointed out that "Bernier was quite right to see that the basis for all phenomena in the East (he was referring to Turkey, Persia and Hindustan) was **the absence of private ownership of land**, which was even a true key to understanding the Kingdom of the East."[328] In the reply dated June 6th of Engels to Marx, Engels agreed with this kind of view and said: "There is no private ownership of land, and it is surely a key to understanding the whole East and is the basis of all the oriental political and religious history.[329] Engels attributed the reason for the absence of private ownership of land to the geographical environment of these countries. He said: "Why did the peoples of the East fail to achieve private ownership of land, or even feudal land ownership? I think this is mainly due to the nature of the climate and the soil, especially the Great Desert, which passes from the Sahara through Arabia, Persia, India and Tatar to the highest part of the Asian plateau. Here, the first condition of agriculture is artificial irrigation, which is a matter for the village community, the province or the central government."[330] In June 10th of the same year, Marx wrote *The British Rule in India*, which took advantage of Engels' idea, but his views were not exactly the same. Except Engels' idea that the characteristics of the geographical environment was the reason why there was no private ownership of land in the East, Marx also added another important reason, that is, the low level of productivity. He pointed out: "Saving water and sharing water are the basic requirements, which in the West,

---

[328]*Marx/Engels Collected Works*, Chinese Edition 1, Vol. 28, Page 256, Beijing, People's Publishing House, 1973.

[329]*Marx/Engels Collected Works*, Chinese Edition 1, Vol. 28, Page 260.

[330]*Marx/Engels Collected Works*, Chinese Edition 1, Vol. 28, Page 260~263.

such as in Flanders and Italy, have brought private entrepreneurs into a voluntary union; but in the East, because of the low level of civilization and the large size of the land, there is no voluntary union, so there is an urgent need for a centralized government to intervene."[331] Marx regarded "the degree of civilization", that is, the different development level of productive forces, as the main reason for the difference of land ownership between the East and the West, which not only put forward the theory of oriental social particularity, but also planted the seeds of negating the theory of oriental social particularity.

Second, in the basic economic organizations of society, the oriental society is dominated by rural communes. Marx pointed out: "since ancient times, a special social system, the so-called **village community system**, has emerged in India. This system makes every such small unit an independent organization, leading a closed life."[332] The reason why this closed life can be maintained for a long time is that in rural communes, the scope of production is limited to self-sufficiency, and agriculture and handicraft are combined. As for this kind of rural commune, Marx thought it was an important obstacle to the development of oriental society. Because even when the rural commune gradually disintegrated under the erosion of capitalism, the clan patriarchal relationship and kinship, which was its companion creature, was still very strong, and its long isolation still constrained the creativity of the society with neither an intention to hope for social progress nor action to promote it. On the contrary, at the beginning of the Western Middle Ages, the Malk commune system quickly collapsed under the impact of the land partition system, and replaced it with the manor system of the territory. Although the manor system also has such characteristics as self-sufficient and closed to the outside world, this social and economic organization has been in a state of instability

---

[331]*Karl Marx and Frederick Engels: Selected Works*, Edition 1, Vol. 2, Page 64.

[332]*Karl Marx and Frederick Engels: Selected Works*, Edition 1, Vol. 2, Page 66.

because of the frequent changes in land relations. And therefore, the Western manor system has not constituted a major obstacle to the development of Western capitalism.

Third, in terms of social political relations, on the basis of the state ownership of land and the rural communes, the oriental society has generally formed an autocratic government with a high degree of centralization by the central authorities. Because the rural commune is self-sufficient and closed, the society is broken down into many identical and unrelated atomic organizations. The isolation between communes forces the commune to transfer its power to govern the public affairs of the whole society to an organ of authority—the state with power over the communes,   just as Marx said: "Like all the peoples of the East countries, the Indian people also hand over the main condition on which their agriculture and commerce are based, that is, large-scale public works, to the government."[333] In this way, all governments in Asia cannot but carry out an economic function, that is, to set up public projects, and the public affairs of society can only be interfered by the central government.

Marx believed that Asian society had stagnated for a long time and had no internal motive for development, and that only the invasion of Western capitalism could shake its foundation, and brings about a real revolution in Asia. The reason why Western capitalism was able to promote the transformation of the social structure of the East and to make the East walk from its stagnant history was that Western capitalism represented a more advanced mode of production with advanced productive forces and advanced science and technology, so that it can avoid the conquest of the civilized nation by the barbaric nation that appeared in history, but it cannot escape the result of assimilation by the civilized nation.

Marx believed that, from the point of view of pure personal feelings, the

---

[333]*Karl Marx and Frederick Engels: Selected Works*, Edition 1, Vol. 2, Page 66.

disintegration of the social structure of the East and its inclusion in the historical system of the world was a disaster for the oriental nation, because "it would be sad to see with their own eyes that the peaceful social organizations of these numerous industrious patriarchal systems have collapsed, disintegrated, and been cast into a sea of misery, and that their members have lost both their ancient forms of civilization and their ancestral means of livelihood."[334] However, "from a historical point of view," the social system on which the oriental civilization is based can no longer manifest the spirit of historical initiative. It has always been the solid foundation of the oriental autocratic system and runs counter to the development of world history. In this sense, no matter how capitalism is completely driven by extremely despicable interests and commits incalculable crimes against all nations in the process of opening up world history, it has, after all, served as an involuntary tool of history, and opened the way for the universal communication of all nationalities in the world.

It is from the concept of "world history" that Marx thought that the impact of Western capitalism on the traditional social structure in the East and the destruction of the rural commune organizations was "the largest and the only **social revolution** in Asia.[335] The most direct result of this "social revolution" was to push the oriental society into the course of world history, to force it to accept the civilized fruits of Western capitalism and to participate in national exchanges throughout the world, and to have to embark on the road opened up by Western capitalism.

However, since the second half of 1870s, new changes have taken place in oriental and Western societies. Western capitalist economies have entered a long and stable stage of development. However, the particularity of the oriental society has not

---

[334]*Karl Marx and Frederick Engels: Selected Works*, Edition 1, Vol. 2, Page 67.

[335]*Karl Marx and Frederick Engels: Selected Works*, Edition 1, Vol. 2, Page 67.

been eliminated because capitalism has opened up a vast world market, especially the village community system in the east still maintains a strong vitality. This makes Marx feel that the formation of "world history" does not entirely depend on the development of capitalism in the world, so Marx in his later years has once again got a sense of urgency to study the social problems of the East.

When Marx studied oriental social problems in his later years, an important breakthrough in theory was the revision of his conclusion in 1850s that the oriental society must follow the capitalist path. When excerpted *The System of Commune Land Ownership and the Cause, Process and Result of Its Disintegration (Общинное землевладение etc. Mosk.1879)* by Kovalevsky, he gave a high appraisal to the book. This is because the book extensively deals with one of the core issues of oriental society: commune land ownership. But Marx did not agree that Kovalevsky's those ideas that mechanically applying the Western model to the oriental society. He criticized his theory of Western centralism and opposed taking the development road of the Western society as the only yardstick to measure the development road of the oriental society.

Consistent with the idea of opposing Western centrism, Marx, in his *Anthropology Notes* in his later years, mercilessly exposed the colonial aggression of capitalist countries in the oriental society. If Marx called the British aggression against India and China a "social revolution" in the beginning of 1850s, Marx changed this view in his later years. In his excerpt from Kovalevsky's work, he wrote: "Both British Indian officials and the international jurist based on them such as **Sir Henry Maine** attributed the decline in the ownership of the Punjabi commune only to **economic progress**... In fact, the British themselves are the **main** (active) **culprits** responsible for the decline."[336] Marx believed that the destruction of the oriental commune system by Western capitalism would soon result in a war against all in the oriental

---

[336]*Marx/Engels Collected Works*, Chinese Edition 1, Vol. 45, Page 300.

society. This war will undoubtedly bring Oriental society into a very long and painful process, "not to propel the local people to move forward, but to make them retreat."[337] Is this the future destiny of the oriental society? This question has been puzzling Marx in his later years.

Since 1877, Marx has begun to explore the possibility of Oriental society surpassing capitalism. In his letter to the editorial office of the *Chronicle of the Motherland* in November, Marx elaborated his ideas in this aspect for the first time. In this letter, Marx mainly refuted a view imposed on him by Russian populist theorist Николай Константинович Михайловский. In an article, he arbitrarily believed that Marx, in *Das Capital*, turned a historical overview of the origin of capitalism in Western Europe completely into a historical philosophical theory on the general path of development, thus requesting all nations, regardless of their historical environment, to follow this path. Marx pointed out in his letter: "If he does so, he will give me too much honor and at the same time he will inflict too much insult on me."[338] Marx therefore explained that the general theory of historical philosophy was not a master key to grasp the completely different results produced in different historical environments. On the contrary, "the greatest advantage of this historical philosophical theory is that it is transcendental."[339] On the basis of this principle, the Western development model cannot be mechanically set in the oriental society. But for the development of the oriental society, Marx answered very carefully and cautiously, saying: "I have come to the conclusion that if Russia continues to walk on the way it began in 1861, it will lose the best opportunity that history can offer to the nation, but will suffer from all the extremely tragic consequences of the

---

[337]*Marx/Engels Collected Works*, Chinese Edition 1, Vol. 19, Page 448.

[338]*Marx/Engels Collected Works*, Chinese Edition 1, Vol. 19, Page 130.

[339]*Marx/Engels Collected Works*, Chinese Edition 1, Vol. 19, Page 131.

capitalist system."[340] Here, Marx suggested that the oriental society could go beyond the basic idea of the capitalist historical stage.

The possibility of the Oriental society surpassing the development of capitalism and the conditions for its realization was brought up again and again in the last few years of Marx's life. In the letters and the drafts of the letters dated February to March 1881 written to Вера Ивановна Засулич, a Russian female revolutionist, Marx concentrated on this issue. It happened that this letter and the drafts of the letter were written by Marx after a thorough study of and detailed excerpts from the works of Kovalevsky and Phear. And therefore, it can be said that Marx's letter to Вера Ивановна Засулич is actually the direct embodiment, application and summary of the theoretical achievements of *Anthropology Notes*.

Of course, it must be pointed out that the Russian rural commune, put forward by Marx in his later years, could go directly to socialism without "the Caudine Forks of the capitalist system", which has a strict difference between the theory of populists in Russia in the 1960s and 1970s. The rise of populists as a trend of thought was determined by the specific historical background of Russia at that time. After the reform of serfdom in Russia in 1861, capitalism was fully developed, and the survival and development of the ancient Russian agricultural village community were seriously threatened. The populists, representing the interests of some rich peasants, of course hated capitalism and believed that Russia had a special situation, which was not suitable for the development of capitalism, and the rural commune was the symbol of "beauty" and "sacredness", which was the hope of Russia. So, the populists proposed to go back to "ancient" and "folk". Obviously this is an illusion contrary to the law of social progress. However, Marx's vision did not shirk from the fact that capitalism had developed in Russia with the essence to consider how Russia can take a better form to accept and take advantage of all the

---

[340]*Marx/Engels Collected Works*, Chinese Edition 1, Vol. 19, Page 129.

positive achievements made by capitalism. Obviously, one is realistic to face the future, and the other is "going back to ancient times" in fantasy. Hence the view of Western scholars that "populist theory constitutes the fourth source of Marx's thought"[341], and that "late Marx's thought is full of populist sentiment"[342] is untenable.

In order to further understand the true meaning and theoretical value of Marx's assumption, it is necessary to analyze the historical background and main basis of this assumption. Marx came to this conclusion mainly from the analysis of the specific historical conditions in Russia at that time, which can be summarized in the following aspects:

(1) The vitality of the primitive commune is much stronger than that of the capitalist society. There is no "historical environment" in Russia which can completely destroy the structure of the commune, because it is not the hunting object of the foreign conquerors, as in the case of the East India, but an independent sovereign state. Russia, and therefore, is the only European country to preserve the "agricultural commune" throughout the country.

(2) The public ownership of land forms the natural foundation of collective production and collective occupation.

(3) The historical tradition and national culture of Russia show that peasants are accustomed to the relationship of labor combination, which facilitates its transition from a small land economy to a collective economy. Moreover, the Russian peasants have to some extent carried out collective management on unallocated

---

[341]Teodor Shanin: *Late Marx and the Russian Road: Marx and the Peripheries of Capitalism*, Preface, New York "Monthly Review" Journal, 1983.

[342]See Marian Sawer: *Marxism and the Question of the Asiatic Mode of Production*, Page 63~67, Hague, 1977.

grasslands, in drainage works and other undertakings of common interest.

(4) The special historical condition of the coexistence of the Russian commune and the capitalism of Western Europe, which widely exists in the whole country, proves that Russia is extremely disadvantageous and unfeasible to take the Western European capitalist road again; it is impossible for Russia to build up a huge industrial system that has been conceived for centuries in Western Europe, not to mention a whole set of exchange institutions including banks, joint-stock companies, etc. From a purely economic point of view, Russia can only get rid of the desperate state of its agriculture through the development of its own agricultural commune, and it is futile to use the British capitalist tenancy to get rid of this desperate situation.

(5) The coexistence of the Russian commune and the capitalism of Western Europe also has a unique advantage that the big capitalist industry that coexists with it provides it with all the conditions for collective labor.

(6) The future of Russian society depends on the revolution. Only the Russian revolution can create the historical conditions for the normal development of the Russian commune, thus making the rural commune a factor of Russian rejuvenation.

It was only on the basis of analyzing these social and historical conditions in Russia that Marx put forward:" Russia can use all the positive achievements of the capitalist system in the communes without passing through the Caudine Forks of the capitalist system."[343]

In his later years, Marx expounded the basic idea of the development of oriental society, which was an important amendment to the theory of social development formed in 1850s. He broke through the conclusion that the oriental society must

---

[343]*Marx/Engels Collected Works*, Chinese Edition 1, Vol. 19, Page 435~436.

take the capitalist road, and preliminarily discussed the possibility and reality of the Oriental society passing through "the Caudine Forks of the capitalist system". Although Marx did not completely solve the problem of the development road of the oriental society in his later years, however, his idea contained something of universal theoretical significance and methodological significance. It shows the basic spirit of Marxist historical philosophy: the dialectical unity of the universal inevitability of the law of historical development and the dynamic movement selection of human historical activities. History is not a special personality that uses man as a tool to achieve its own ends. History is nothing more than the activities of people who pursue their own goals. In the face of historical laws, people do not have the freedom to "transcend" or "choose", but have the freedom to recognize and use the rules to actively choose their own specific ways of activities. When history is at the crossroads of various possible development possibilities, the concrete realization of historical inevitability depends entirely on the choice of the subject. Although this choice cannot transcend the natural process of the development of social formation, it can reduce the shock and pain of the process.

Although Marx only conceived the idea of transcending the capitalist system from the special object of Russia, a backward oriental country, with no clear opinion on the future fate of other peoples in the more backward East that already in the "Caudine Forks of capitalist system", we can also extract his general views on the development of socialism throughout the Eastern world from his "special" view of the Russian revolution.

In his later years , Marx had gradually formed such a prophetic view that the socialist revolution had **"the nature of the world"**.[344] Marx also clearly saw that, with the exception of Russia, almost all the oriental countries had become colonies and semi-colonies, and the traditional public ownership had been destroyed to

---

[344]*Marx/Engels Collected Works*, Chinese Edition 1, Vol. 45, Page 712.

varying degrees. With the rapid development of world history, they all lost the good opportunity of active selection of history. The commune could no longer be the historical starting point for them to realize a new type of public ownership society; the invasion of the colonialists caused strife and division within the nation, thus undermining their powerful solidarity against foreign oppression. History has doomed these peoples to be in such disaster and misery for a long time to come. Marx once paid great attention to the survival and liberation of these nationalities at that time. He foresaw the possibility of realizing socialism in the oriental society from the analysis of the Russian problem and revealed the necessary prerequisite for realizing this system.

From this we can see that the focus of Marx's *Anthropology Notes* in his later years is not the empirical argumentation and concrete development of the theory of human nature, nor does cultural anthropology form the core of Marx's thoughts in his later years. Surely, we also acknowledge that Marx's later years was the beginning of the great development of anthropology. He did participate in the thinking, research and construction of this new discipline, and expressed many important views on many basic theoretical issues (such as the development of classes, countries and social groups in anthropology) of anthropology, which has important enlightenment to the development of contemporary anthropology. However, Marx is not a professional anthropologist after all. It is still a fictitious contemporary "theoretical myth" to insist that Marx found a "Marx of anthropologists" in his later years, and that Marx had a systematic "theory of anthropology".

4. Misunderstanding of "Anthropological Marxism"

In 1920s, Italy Marxists proposed the relationship between Marxism and anthropology. In 1960s, various forms of Marxist anthropology school and ideological trend have appeared in Western academic circles. T. Botmore, a famous contemporary British expert in Marxist studies, summed up this trend into two opposing factions or tendencies: structural anthropology in Europe and America and dialectical anthropology in North America.[345]

Dialectical anthropology holds that Marxism is still very young, and can even be said to be in its cradle, and thus has great prospects for development. This school regards Marxism as a tool for criticism, and advocates that it must be distinguished from ideological Marxism. This school also regards Marx as a representative figure of dialectical anthropology and believes that Marx denies the existence of all historical laws. Stanley Diamond, the representative of this school, said: "Marxist anthropology is real. Marxism tradition can be seen as a kind of anthropology with revolutionary conscience, thoughtful and dialectical anthropology. He added: "The purpose Marx pursued all his life was to concretize the image of the possibility of humanity he had explained as a young philosopher, and he began to have only one vision, which ended by the *Note on Social and Cultural Anthropology (Ethnology)* that he left.[346]

From the viewpoint of dialectical anthropology, we can see that in addition to repeating the old tune of "Marx in his later years is the return of humanism to the philosophy of young Marx", this school also draws the "new" conclusion that Marx, as a dialectical anthropologist, denies the existence of universal laws of social development, which is also a misinterpretation of Marx.

As mentioned above, it is Marx's great mission throughout his life to understand and grasp the universal law of the development of human society, and a major theoretical subject that must be solved in historical materialism. As the founder of historical materialism, Marx made an indefatigable exploration of this and revealed the general law of the evolution of human society from the lower level to the higher level.

---

[345]See T. Botmore: *A Dictionary of Marxist Thought*, Page 23~25.

[346] Stanley Diamond: *The Marxism Tradition as A Dialectical Anthropology*, Published on *Dialectical Anthropology*, Amsterdam, 1975 First Issue.

In 1840s, Marx described the development of the whole history of human society as five stages of evolution, namely, tribal ownership, ancient commune ownership and state ownership, feudal or hierarchical ownership, capitalist ownership and future communist ownership according to his study of European history. But at this time Marx did not regard these social forms as insurmountable from the point of view of world history. From 1850s, Marx began to study Asian society, on the basis of the comparison of Eurasian society, replaced the concept of "tribal ownership" by "Asian production mode", and regarded the Asian, ancient, feudal and modern bourgeois modes of production as several eras of the evolution of social and economic forms. Here, Marx had clearly brought the theory of the succession of social forms into the scope of "world history," demonstrating that the development of world history has its own inherent laws, and that all nations and countries, no matter how different they are, must follow the common law of the development of world history. However, due to the lack of raw materials, Marx can only grasp the original form of human society by studying the old Asiatic mode of production in the eastern society which coexists with capitalism. He said: "If you look closely at the forms of commune ownership in Asia, especially in India, you can see how the various forms of dissolution that emerged from the different forms of ownership of the primitive commune, for example, the archetypes of Roman and Germanic private ownership can be extrapolated from various forms of commune ownership in India." [347] Based on this, some Western scholars believed that Marx affirmed the various possibilities of pre-capitalist economic form, so Marx advocated the multi-line theory of social development. [348] But if we carefully analyze Marx's exposition, it is not difficult to find that Marx's division of original ownership cannot be the basis of "multi - line theory".

---

[347]*Marx/Engels Collected Works*, Chinese Edition 1, Vol. 13, Page 22 Note ①.

[348]See Umberto Melotti: *Marx and the Third World*, Page 4, Beijing, The Commercial Press, 1981.

From the static point of view, Marx juxtaposed the three forms of ownership, that is, they were all the transition from the primitive form to the derived form. But from the dynamic point of view, we can see that the "derived form" produced by the three forms of ownership is not parallel in itself, but is successive replacing each other in turns of time. Asian ownership, as the strongest and long-stagnant form of ownership, did not directly produce "derivative form", so Marx regarded it as the first stage of the evolution of human history. However, in history, ancient ownership derived slave society (ancient Rome), while Germanic ownership through the conquest, directly developed into a feudal society based on serfdom, so Marx regarded them as the second and third stages of historical evolution. Since 1860s, Marx had further perfected the theory of primitive society on the basis of a large number of previous research achievements. At this time, Marx regarded the Asian commune, the ancient commune and the Germanic commune as the final stage of the primitive society after the disintegration of patriarchal nation, which was the transition form from public ownership to private ownership and from class free society to class society. Hence, the first stage of human society is not the Asian production mode, but the whole primitive society including the above forms. Thus, Marx had scientifically revealed the law of the development of human society from the lower level to the higher level.

Another major argument that Western scholars believe Marx denies the existence of universal laws of human social development is that Marx put forward the idea of passing through "the Caudine Forks of the capitalist system" in his later years. Ordol Qinning, a professor at the University of Manchester, England, pointed out that Marx had recognized that there were many development paths in the pre-capitalist society as early as in *Outline of Critique of Political Economy in 1857-1858*, and the *Anthropology Notes* in his later years shown the diversity of the social development paths in a world dominated by capitalism. In his view, since Russia can enter socialism directly without passing through "the Caudine Forks of the capitalist system", how can the evolution of the five social forms in turn become the universal law of the development of human society? Two distinct problems have been confused here: one is whether there are universal laws in the development of human society and the other is the question of whether there are particularities in the development path of various nationalities and countries. The envision of passing through "the Caudine Forks of the capitalist system" put forward by Marx in his later years is the revelation of the particularity of the Oriental society emerged in the development of the road, it does not deny the universal law of social development, but takes it as the premise. Although the development path of each country and nation is different, the direction of their development is consistent with the social evolution direction.

In his later years, when Marx conceived that the development of Russian society might pass through "the Caudine Forks of the capitalist system", he clearly stated that this was based on the development of world history to the capitalist stage as a prerequisite. Marx pointed out, if Russia existed independently from the world, and if it can only achieve the economic achievements of Western Europe from primitive society to capitalist society on its own, then, the Russian commune was doomed to perish with the development of Russian society. However, since Russia is at the same time as capitalism, it only needs to absorb all the "positive results" of the capitalist mode of production and develop and transform the ancient form of its rural commune, and it is possible to realize the "leapfrogging" the social development path.[349] Engels later gave further play to Marx's idea, saying that only when the capitalist economy flourished in his hometown, making backward nations see how capitalism serves the whole society by treating modern industrial productive forces as social assets can backward countries embark on this path of shortening the development process. This is to say that it is the history of the world that has evolved to the capitalist age provides the conditions for the "leapfrogging"

---

[349]See *Marx/Engels Collected Works*, Chinese Edition 1, Vol. 19, Page 437 and Page 444.

of the backward countries, which shows that the development path of each country and nation is restricted by the universal law of the development of human society.

Dialectical anthropology attempts to draw a conclusion from Marx's thoughts in his later years that Marx denies the existence of universal laws of social development, while structuralist anthropology tries to find the basis of "pluralistic determinism" in Marx's thoughts in his later years. Maurice Gaudrier, the representative of structuralist anthropology, believes that in Marx's "anthropology works" and ancient social works, his structuralism viewpoint and method can be "found". Gaudrier believes that in Marx's view, the function of kinship is not only a kind of production relationship, but also a foundation and superstructure. Taylor believes that in the kinship, a variety of determinants can be found. In Althusser's words, it is called pluralistic determinism. All in all, in their opinion, Marx's study of anthropology in his later years reflected his "negation" of his original economic determinism, and Marxism became a pluralistic determinism.

However, if we read Marx's *Anthropology Notes* carefully, we can see that Marx talked about the relationship between the economic base and the superstructure in *Anthropology Notes*, but he did not equate the two, nor had the meaning of superstructure determinism. On the contrary, he stressed that superstructure generally lagged behind the development of economic foundation. In *Ancient Society*, Morgan argues that the system of kinship is passive, that it records the progress that has taken place in the family over a long period of time, and only when the family has fundamentally changed can it change radically. Marx commented on it that: "The same goes for **political, religious, legal and general philosophical systems**." [350] Secondly, Marx believed that, the country as a superstructure, compared with the economic basis, was by no means primary. He wrote in *Lectures Delivered by Maine for the Inns of Court were the Groundwork of*

---

[350]*Marx/Engels Collected Works*, Chinese Edition 1, Vol. 45, Page 354.

Ancient Law by Maine: "The unfortunate **Maine himself does not know at all**: where there is a **state** (after the primitive commune), that is, the **politically** organized society, the state is by no means **primary**, but only **seems** so."[351] He also criticized Maine's fundamental mistake of "treating **political superiority,** whatever its specific form or the sum of its various factors, as something that is socially based and based on itself". He made it clear that the state, moral and other superstructure factors, "ultimately all based on **economic conditions**"[352].

Marx, in *Anthropology Notes*, did talk about the decisive role of kinship in prehistoric society, but this must not be the basis of "pluralistic determinism". Marx believed that kinship played a decisive role in prehistoric society not in the sense of social origin, but in a special phenomenon in prehistoric society of mankind. When mankind had just separated from the animal kingdom, whether in terms of the relationship between man and nature, or in terms of the relationship between men and men, it was natural kinship that dominated. Moreover, the less development of labor, the more limited the number of labor products and the wealth of society, the more the social system will be dominated by kinship. How can Marx's explanation of a historical phenomenon in a specific range can be raised to the height of social ontology, and the conclusion of "multiple determinism" be concluded?

In addition, Marx never regarded kinship as the basis and superstructure. He clearly pointed out that the nature of kinship "is not **conceptual**, but **material**."[353] Western scholars are always used to imposing their ideas on Marx and then announcing the discovery of "new" Marx. This unwise technique can only prove that they do not really understand Marx's writings.

In conclusion, Marx was not in the "lonely corner" or "thought desert", nor the

---

[351]*Marx/Engels Collected Works*, Chinese Edition 1, Vol. 45, Page 645.

[352]*Marx/Engels Collected Works*, Chinese Edition 1, Vol. 45, Page 647.

[353]*Marx/Engels Collected Works*, Chinese Edition 1, Vol. 45, Page 503.

"return" to the early humanism, but the constantly developed rich theoretical treasure. If the thought of young Marx reveals the forming process of Marxist theoretical structure and the essence and value of Marxism as the essence of the spirit of the times in the sense of genesis, then the thought of Marx in the later years reflects the development and enrichment of his mature theory form, and reflects the practical value of Marxism in the contemporary era. Just as we cannot understand the inevitability of Marxism without understanding young Marx, we cannot truly understand the development of Marxism without understanding Marx in his later years. Just as we cannot understand the young Marx, if we cannot understand Marx in his later years, we cannot understand Marxism in a complete and accurate way.

CHAPTER 8   THE TREND OF "MARXISM RELIGION"

In various theories of dismemberment of Marx today, the trend of religion is increasing day by day. In the West, some people brazenly regard Marx as a "religious prophet" and Marxism as a "new religion". It has become a kind of fashion to talk about the so-called "prophet Marx and his religion" and converged into a reactionary trend of thought which cannot be ignored in the field of Marxist research.

1. The Breeding and Spreading of "Marxism Religion" Thought

The trend of religious thought is breeding and spreading from the problems of the relationship between Marxism and religion. Its general characteristic is to blur the boundary of the two, confuse the difference between the two, and regard them as something close, similar or identical. The representatives confuse Marxism with some religious system, such as Christianity, or simply refer to Marxism as "the religion of industrial century" or "atheistic religion".

This trend of thought came into being in the 1930s. Some Western scholars made a fuss about *Manuscripts of Economics and Philosophy of 1844*, the early work of Marx which had just been published, dressed up Marx as a moralist and a religious thinker, and distorted Marxism as a religion of ethics and humanitarianism. These ideas won great applause in the Western ideological world, and became a fashionable point of view. It was after the Second Word War when it spread widely in Europe and the United States as a trend of thought. Since 1950s, representative figures of this trend of thought in the United Kingdom, the United States and Latin American countries had begun to publish numerous advocacy articles. Donald McRae, the British scholar, wrote in the *Cambridge Journal* that Marxism was a religion, and "its God is a personified history". In Latin America, religious eschatology of historical materialism is widely popular.

M. Cashas, one of the greatest representatives of Argentine bourgeois philosophy tried to find the religious hierarchy which can gave Marxism the "messianic nature" in the Marxism of human and freedom.

In the 1960s, the trend of thought of "Marxism religion" prevailed, and many articles and works of "comparative" Marxism and Christian doctrine appeared, drawing a farfetched analogy of Marxism with Christianity. There were a number of such articles compiled in *Marxism and Christianity*, chiefly edited by H. Aposecker in New York in 1966. Giulio Gilardi published a book of the same name in 1968. In the book, "Soviet defectors" and "a Chinese who no longer believes in Marxism" are used to prove that Marxism is a "materialistic religion". Connected with this kind of theoretical atmosphere, Christians and Marxists began a certain degree of dialogue and contact in social and political life. In 1964, the 21th General Assembly of the United Church of Canada considered that there were good reasons for Christians to contact with Marxists. In the same year, Hall, an American Marxist, initiated a dialogue between Marxists and believers.

In the 1970s and 1980s, the trend of thought of "Marxism religion" became more and more widespread. Lohrman, an American Christian missionary, called for "integration" of Marxism and religion, and reminded people that "early Marxism" and "early Christianity" had "a lot in common". Radical theologian Ding Dean put forward the idea of "post-theism", calling for the establishment of a new theology "based on the combination of Marxism and the original revolutionary nature of the *Bible*". Robert Wieson, a professor of political science at the University of California in the United States, systematically discussed the viewpoint that Marxism was a new religion in the books *Why is Marxism* and *Marxism as a Religion*.

In recent years, this anti-Marxist trend of thought spread to China, causing great ideological confusion. It is an important realistic task for Marxists to analyze and criticize its fallacy, expose and eliminate its harm.

2. Marx as a "Prophet"

It is the common purport of many Western scholars to take delight in talking about "the prophet Marx". It is not surprising, because seeing Marx as a prophet is a basic argumentation and an important part of his "Marxist New Religion". To regard Marx as a religious prophet is nothing more than to describe Marxism as a prophet's religion.

It should be noted that here the prophet is nothing but a religious prophet. Superficially, it seems completely reasonable to interpret the prophet as a "predictor", that is people who have made some forecasts and predictions about historical development and social phenomena, but in fact, according to the Western cultural tradition, the so-called "prophet" refers to the one who makes a major religious prophecy in a religious setting with a religious identity. Generally speaking, a prophet is a prophet of religion or a person like a prophet of religion.

And therefore, it is most natural to understand the prophet as a religious prophet in the eyes of the West. It is in this sense that those in the West who describe Marx as a prophet use the word "prophet". Here, Marx was painstakingly portrayed as a prophet of religion. American pragmatist philosopher Sydney Hook said in his *Marx and Marxists-Vague Heritage* that Marxism was "a new religion", "this religion declared that history is God, and Karl Marx is the main prophet of history." Parsons (Howard L. Parsons), an American scholar, said in the article *The Prophetic Mission Of Karl Marx*[354]: "Marx was a prophet. He denounced the sins and corruption of the time, whipped the rich and the enemy, and called on the people to listen to him, to join his ranks, and to build sublime and wonderful system through the uprising. Only he could see clearly that the system was shimmering on the horizon." Binkley also said: "Regard Marx as a philosopher, a prophet or the founder of a new religion,

---

[354]Parsons: *The Prophetic Mission Of Karl Marx*, See Aposecker: *Marxism and Christianity*, Page 146~158, New York, 1966.

so that we can understand the importance of Marx a little more clearly."[355]

Because the "prophet" mentioned by the Western scholars has a specific meaning, so they are not interested in the specific content of Marx's prophecy. To them, what is important is not the specific content of Marx's prophecy, but Marx's religious identity as a prophet. When they described Marx as a prophet, they imposed on Marx what he firmly rejected from the beginning. They set Marx in a fixed historical role, portraying Marx as a predictor in the frame of a religious prophet. Although they often talked about many of the predictions Marx had made, and spent a great deal of time arguing that these predictions were inaccurate, between Marx's specific predictions and the prophet's image, the latter always came first to them

Binkley described the so-called prophet image of Marx in detail. Unlike Fromm who only said that Marx had inherited "the Western thought tradition of each period from the prophet through Christianity, the Renaissance to the Enlightenment", he found this kind of tradition from Marx's family, which is the influence of the enlightenment thought in the 18th century on Marx's father, and found the family origins of Marx's "zeal in prophecy". He not only saw "almost the metaphorical expression of prophet" in the alienation of labor thought of young Marx, but also recalled the image of Amos, a Hebrew prophet in the 8[t]h century BC, in his recollection of Marx.[356]

Comparing Marx with Amos, Binkley found two common points: first, Marx's prophecy on the demise of capitalism and Amos's prophecy on the death of the

---

[355]Binkley: *Conflict of Ideals: Changing Values in Western Society*, Page 96.

[356]Amos, the Jewish prophet in the *Old Testament*, was active in the 8th century BC. He announced many prophecies to the Jews, especially the perishing of the Jewish state Israel and the Jewish state. Although he was only the third of the 12 little prophets in the *Old Testament*, he was undoubtedly one of the most famous religious prophets in Jewish history.

State of Israel are both moral predictions, which are all based on moral reasons. There is no doubt that Amos's prophecies have moral implications, and all the calamities he prophesied were the results of the Jews acting unjustly and angering God. His horrendous prophecy of the destruction of the State of Israel was a severe condemnation of the loss of justice and the general depravity of the Jews of that time. The reason for this destructive prophecy is entirely moral. Binkley looked at Marx the same way and quoted the saying of Karl Popper (Sir Karl Raimund Popper) that: "there is no doubt that the secret of his religious influence lies in its moral appeal. His critique of the capitalist system came into effect mainly with a moral critique." Secondly, Binkley believed that Marx, like Amos, not only prophesied but also resorted to action. He wrote that: " Marx is not an idle dreamer, looking forward to a " new world " like a miracle , but more like the prophet Amos in the *Old Testament* , telling people what they must do in order to truly get free." Because of the two fabricated "common grounds", Marx became a religious prophet like Amos.

But Binkley's analogy is not only far-fetched, but absurd. There is no doubt that Marx predicted the ultimate demise of capitalism, but it was not based solely on moral reasons, as Amos did. Although Marx also made a moral denunciation of the evils of capitalism, at the beginning of his sentence of death on the capitalist system, he crossed the narrow scope of moral indignation and was based on the correct understanding of the objective law of capitalism's operation. Although Marx predicted the inevitable victory of communism, he was not like the humanists who always stretched the truth and the utopian who liked to shout that were eager and content with the prophecy of the future ideal society. The utopian socialists not only predicted the future ideal society, but also described the ideal picture of the future in a prophetic manner. If socialism and communism have their own "prophets" and "seers", then this is not Marx, but the utopian socialists and utopian communists. In the view of Marxism, the so-called "prophets" and "seers" of socialism or communism are only sarcastic words. Marx and Engels laughed more than once at Weitling, the utopian communist who considered himself as the "prophet" of communism and the "savior" of the working class. Engels, in the *History of the Communist Alliance*, mentioned Weitling, "the prophet who was driven from one country to another, with a ready prescription in his pocket to make a paradise on earth, feeling like everyone's trying to steal his prescription."[357] As early as 1846, Marx had criticized Weitling's Salvationism and the wild manner of "prophet" at a meeting of the Communist Communications Commission in Brussels.

In the viewpoints of Marx and Engels, the workers' movement needed and had its "prophets" and "seers" only in its infantile early years. If it relied solely on these prophets to lead the way and draw inspiration and strength from their prophecies, the socialism can only always be in its own utopian period, for the socialist "prophet" itself is an unconscious and immature socialist, who lack of scientific recognition of socialism movement. If socialism wants to change from utopia to science, it must always bid farewell to its own "prophet".

The difference between Marx and utopian socialists is the difference between thinkers and prophets, and is also the difference between scientists and moralists. Marx is not a man who predicted and acted only on moral indignation and ideal zeal (and so did the utopian socialists), but is a person who, through empirical examination and scientific research, changes the theory of socialism from a utopia to science, or rather, a person who gives the scientific foundation and basis for the prophecy of socialism (which distinguishes Marx from the pioneer of utopianism). And therefore, strictly speaking, Marx did not "predict" the demise of capitalism and the victory of communism, but "proved" it with science.

The difference between a scientist (thinker) and a prophet (moralist) is obvious. As the English scholar A. Kennet believes, the prophet is superficial, sensitive and passionate, while the thinker is profound, objective and dispassionate. The

---

[357]*Karl Marx and Frederick Engels: Selected Works*, Edition 1, Vol. 4, Page 194.

prophet's task is to "express the immature beliefs of his audience impressively", so as to preach and exhort the public. He does not need systematic and profound ideas and theories.[358] Spinoza has realized this three hundred years ago. He said in the preface to *Theological Politics* that the prophets were authority only in moral matters. Their theories cannot convince us. What is important for the socialist movement is not to hope to inspire the enthusiasm of the working class by the words of prophets, but to point out their path with the theoretical argument of scientific socialism. When criticizing the meaning of the Salvationism of Weitling and expounding the importance of arming the socialist movement with science, Marx pointed out that if there were no strict scientific thoughts and correct theories to call on the workers, it would be an empty and hypocritical missionary, with an impassioned prophet on the one hand, and fools who listened to him with open mouth on the other hand, which would only lead to the destruction of the socialist movement.[359]

The reason why Western scholars are keen to "restore" Marx's "just status" as a prophet is to replace the Marx as a scientist with the Marx as a prophet, to replace the Marx as a thinker with the Marx as a moralist, and to eliminate the scientific nature of Marxist theory and thus to replace the socialist reality with the socialist "prophecy". If Marxism is just a moral prediction of socialism, rather than a scientific guide, such Marxism is harmless to capitalism and can be accepted by the bourgeoisie.

3. Absurd Analogy: So-Called Common Ground between Marxism and Religion

It is only a prelude to "comparative study" of Western scholars to dress up Marx as a religious prophet, far from the whole content of his "Marxist New Religion". In

---

[358]See A. Kennet: *Carlyle*, Page 109 and Page 158, Beijing, China Social Sciences Press, 1987.

[359]See *Human Prometheus*, Page 45, Beijing, People's Publishing House, 1983.

fact, the portrayal and evaluation of historical figures are not their real interests. They are not content to compare Marx with the religious prophets. What they are keen to do is to make a "comparative study" of Marxism and the Christian system, and to find out "what they have in common" in order to point the spearhead at the Marxist scientific system. As for this, Binkley said unabashedly: "It is obvious to readers that Marx's ideas are much similar to Hebrew-Christianity."[360]

All kinds of Marxist critics have appeared to write books to turn Marxism into a religion. It is asserted in *The Complete Man*, by the French theologian Yagu Marisan when referring to the extant communism that this is a religion, and the most arbitrary, assuming that it must be appointed to replace all other religions; and that it is an atheistic religion with dialectical materialism as its doctrine, and communism as a system of life as its ethical and social expression. French "new philosophies", Levy and Gruksman, both vilified Marxism, attacking Marxism as "the opium of the people", and saying that there are two major churches in the world today: The Christian Church and the Marxist Church. The British philosopher Bertrand Russell said: "I think the world's major religions such as Buddhism, Hinduism, Christianity, Islam, and communist beliefs are all false and harmful."[361]

They racked their brains to find what Marxism and religion had in common. Albert Camus, the French "absurd philosophy", compared the teachings of communism to Christianity in his *Rebellion*, and found the so-called three "similarities": Firstly, "the two doctrines share a world outlook"; secondly, both of them are creative fatalism; and thirdly, both of them demand a new kind of obedience and order in the name of history. American R. Tucker has further discovered four things in common: Firstly, both of them have an all-encompassing unified worldview; secondly, the fall and

---

[360]See Binkley: *Conflict of Ideals: Changing Values in Western Society*, Page 104.

[361]Bertrand Russell: *Why I Am Not a Christian*, Page 8, Beijing, The Commercial Press, 1982.

atonement of man are proposed in the same philosophy of history; thirdly, Christianity thinks that man must be reborn if he wants to be saved, while Marx realized that a new type of regenerator must stand up and pursue the realization of ideal; and fourthly, both of them require the unity of thought and action.[362] Abandoning their incomprehensible phrases and summarizing their new findings, the "similarities" of the so-called Marxist and Christian doctrines are broadly expressed in three aspects: the commonality of the world view, the historical view and social function.

It is astonishing to talk about the commonality of Marxism and the doctrine of Christianity in terms of the world view, and it would be more ridiculous to say that the two "share the same world view". Because the essential difference between the two is the difference between the world views. Moreover, this kind of difference is absolutely clear that one is theism, while the other is atheism; and one is idealism, while the other is materialism.

Except empty words and crazy talks in dreams, what else can there be to find common ground in the worldview between Marxism and Christian doctrine? For example, as Tucker says, both of them are unified and inclusive as world views. This is nothing in common! The nature of the worldview is to provide mankind with as complete and unified a view of the world as possible. Any worldview can be said in a sense to be all-encompassing in nature. Despite the systematization of the theories, the degree of completeness and foothold of the expression of each worldview are not the same, as a world view, it provides the greatest possible integrity for both its environmental conditions and specific believers at that time, which can show nothing to explain the commonality of Marxism and Christian doctrines in the world view. Camus went further than Tucker, saying that the two shared a world view. But his next example was, "in the view of the Christianity and

---

[362]See Binkley: *Conflict of Ideals: Changing Values in Western Society*, Page 104.

Marxism, that nature must be dominated". This is a strange and vague argument. Because Marxism of transformation of nature is based on the recognition of the objective existence of nature itself and the priority of man and his consciousness, while the Christian doctrine of dominating nature is that all things are created by God for human beings. As for Russell's claim that Marx's "universal optimism" is closer to religious theism, the absurdity is even greater than that of Tucker and Camus. He said: "Marx claims to be an atheist, but maintains a cosmological optimism that can only be grounded in theism."[363] This is obviously the imposition of religious teleology on Marx. Is it true that, just as Christians believe that the hidden God has prepared a good home for them, so Marx believes that there is a similar purpose in the universe in favor of the proletariat? In fact, Marx did not concentrate on the sky above his head, as Russell said, and did not talk abstractly about the optimistic universe or look for an optimistic purpose in the dark, nor did he claim to have discovered it, instead, he always helped the working class to find ways to realize its own interests in real life.

What Western scholars talk about most and most vigorously is the so-called common ground between Marxism and Christian doctrines on history. Tucker thinks their "philosophy of history" is the same. What Marxism calls the suffering and liberation of the proletariat is the fall and salvation of the people in Christianity. The French philosopher A. Benoit considered the historical theory of Marxism to be "a secular form of Christian historical theory".[364] Because in his view, the communist picture of Marxism is the same as the apocalyptic schema of Christianity.

Eschatology is the theory of religion about the end of the world. Christian

---

[363] Russell: *A History of Western Philosophy* Vol. II, Page 344, Beijing, The Commercial Press, 1976.

[364] A. Benoit: *Nominalism Foundation of an Attitude to Life*, See *New Rightists*, Page 137, Paris, 1979.

eschatology holds that human beings will come to the end of the world, that everyone will be judged on the end of the world, or go to heaven or hell, and that each will have its own place. However, before the end of the world, Christ came to the world as the king for a thousand years. This is the millennium that Christians are waiting for—the end of the world. Western scholars either equate the future of communism with the Christian kingdom of the millennium, or the heaven after judgment. Tucker straightly declared that "historical materialism is a form of eschatology". Western Marxist philosopher Ernst Bloch also used religious eschatology to explain Marxism, called communism as "utopia", and believed that its value lied in that it cannot be realized and can only bring "hope". The Polish philosopher Kolakowski also said that Marxism was a "secular eschatology", "believing that heaven is waiting for us in front of us". They all tried to compare communism to a "millennium kingdom" or heaven to vilify and belittle "communism".

Western scholars not only equate communism with religious eschatology, but also confuse the proof of the inevitability of the realization of communism of Marxist historical view with the Christian idea of the inevitable coming of the end of the world, and confuse the optimism about the future of the communists with Christians' expectation of the end of the world. They point the finger at Marx's idea of the inevitability of the law of history. Henri de Man, in his *Socialist Psychology*, called the historical laws of Marx as a new god, and called it as "a harsh and cruel God, who has a clear and peculiar inherent kinship with the Lord in the *Old Testament* and the Calvinist gods of the doomed pioneers of capitalist culture" [365] ,"One believes in determinism, which means that one turns to supernatural forces in order to arouse fear among enemies and confidence in his

---

[365]See *Selected Materials of Old Revisionism Philosophy*, Division 1, Vol. 6, Page 112, Shanghai, Shanghai People's Publishing House, 1965.

own ranks."[366] In commenting on American Maxwell Eastman's *Marx, Lenin, and Revolutionary Science*, Stracher of Britain enthusiastically said that Marx's philosophy "is a bible of a new religion, which 'reveals' to us that the world is rapidly and definitively transforming itself into a socialist utopia in a mysterious and insoluble way, without any effort of our own."[367] Karl Popper condemned Marxism as a "wild" belief, because the historical prophecy of communism requires people to "help achieve what is inevitable!"

Although under the guise of "comparative study," it is in fact a completely absurd analogy to equate the Marxist view of history with the Christian eschatology, because its method is unscientific. It either appeals to abstract analogies of external characteristics, or appeals to the so-called common psychological foundation and emotional elements, regardless of the content of thought itself. They pull two absolutely incomparable and farfetched theories together to draw abstract analogies only on the basis of outward specious similarities, and draw conclusions that suit their needs. They even play lexical tricks. For example, in order to show that Marxism is the same as Jewish-Christian in its "way of understanding" of history, Russell even compiled the following formulas for comparative studies in his academic book—*History of Western Philosophy*:

Yahweh (Jehovah) = Dialectical Materialism

The Savior = Marx

The Voters = The Proletariat

The Church = The Communist Party

Jesus's Second Coming = Revolution

---

[366]*Selected Materials of Old Revisionism Philosophy*, Division 1, Vol. 6, Page 111.

[367]*Selected Materials of Old Revisionism Philosophy*, Division 1, Vol. 6, Page 62.

Hell = Punishment for Capitalists

Christ as the King for a Millennium = The Communist Union[368]

Any man of normal mind will laugh at such absurd analogies. Apart from playing with words, he did not put forward any common points in the content of objective ideas as evidence. In fact, as long as the specific ideological contents of Marxist and Christian views of history were concerned, his lies would be exposed at once.

To find support for its abstract analogy, Russell appealed to the common grounds in "emotional content" and "psychological basis" between Marxism and the Christian doctrine. He looked at his own "series of formulas" and said with satisfaction: "The left words mean the sense of the right words. It is this emotional content familiar to Christian or Jewish people that makes Marx's eschatology worthy of faith."[369] Here, the concept and vocabulary is not the reflection and generalization of objective content, but the emotional substitute of words that do not have the meaning. What is the objective comparison and just conclusion?

Western scholars also try to erase the opposition between Marxism and religion by comparing the social roles of Marxism and religion. Kolakowski said that Marxism is "a doctrine of blind faith", and "its efficacy is only a religious nature". They believe that both Marxism and religion can attract the oppressed and guide them to fight. Russell believed that, like early Islam, communists were "inspired by the belief that a god called 'materialism' is fighting with them and, in due course, helping them win."[370] It seemed to them that since the Marxists had faith in the struggle for communism, it was as if they were religious. Marxism, of course, had also become a

---

[368]Russell: *A History of Western Philosophy*, Vol. I, Page 447~448.

[369] Russell: *A History of Western Philosophy*, Vol. I, Page 447~448.

[370] *Translation Collection of Modern Western Historical Philosophy*, Page 126, Shanghai, Shanghai Translation Publishing House, 1984.

religion. This absurd view, if not out of extreme ignorance of Marxism, is malicious and disingenuous with an ulterior motive. The struggle over this issue in the field of ideology for more than half a century fully proves this.

4. Two Kinds of Beliefs: The Opposition between Marxism and Religion

Through the thought tendency of Western scholars to convert Marxism into religion, it is not difficult for people to see that they share a latent premise that belief is religion, and they are completely identical. In the eyes of some Western scholars, science and belief are two independent relations, while Marxism is a kind of belief rather than science, and belief is nothing more than religious belief, so Marxism is also a kind of religion and is a new religion at most. They do not argue that Christianity is a scientific system, but demonstrate that Marxism is a belief system to mix Marxism with Christian doctrines. For example, Koenig, the Cardinal of Austria, namely, the head of the secretariat responsible for dialogue with non-believers in Vatican, said that atheism of Marxism was based not on science but on faith, because modern scientific experimental materials and empirical methods cannot refute God as the supreme being and cannot become the scientific basis of atheism of Marxism, so he concluded that Marxism was an atheistic religion.[371]

It is appropriate for Western scholars to do so, for since there is no other kind of belief than religion, so long as Marxism is proved to be a belief, it will be done. Thus, to do so, they tried to highlight the inspiration of Marxism to its followers, and even to exaggerate and "praise" the efficacy of Marxism beliefs at the expense of words. However, they did not notice that there was a huge loophole in their thinking process, and the key was not whether Marxism was a belief, but what kind of belief it was, was it scientific belief or religious belief?

---

[371]See A. Mesritenko: *Contemporary Foreign Marxism-Leninism Philosophy*, Vol. II, Page 584, Beijing, Social Sciences Academic Press, 1986.

Indeed, there are some superficial similarities between Marxism as a belief and religious belief, such as both of them arise from human practice, reflecting (correctly or inversely) certain social realities, and showing a kind of subject mentality including cognition, emotion, will and so on. But here the common ground is secondary, and the distinction is primary and fundamental. Moreover, it is these commonalities that form the basis of the distinction between the two. This distinction is not a special distinction between specific beliefs (such as between two religions), but the essential differences between the two kinds of beliefs, which are mainly the differences between the objects of belief.

Marxists believe in scientific propositions that can be proved, while religious believers believe in unscientific propositions that cannot be verified. Taking the object of belief as a proposition on epistemology for investigation, we can see that Marxism and religion are two fundamentally different beliefs.

Religious belief will be put aside by scientific proof as correct, directly using and exaggerating conclusions unproven or impossible to prove, making it something that is original and beyond epistemology, and giving it absolute faith. Religious belief makes a common gap between scientific knowledge and belief, believing that only a belief in something that cannot be scientifically tested is a true belief. The religious people believe that this belief has its own rational yardstick, and it is not related to scientific knowledge. Although it often tried to attach scientific conclusions in the prosperous times of science, it will not measure itself by science. Many Westerners hold the view that a proposition, if proven, is knowledge and irrelevant to faith; if it is proved wrong, it is false and irrelevant to faith. Belief in the pending proposition is faith only when the proposition has not been tested or tested but has neither been proved nor falsified. In fact, this kind of view is unilateral that it looks at belief from the perspective of religion, and does not include scientific belief in their definition of belief, so, many Western scholars cannot see the fundamental differences between Marxism and religious belief.

The belief in Marxism is the belief in the true understanding of the truth proved by science, the internalization of scientific knowledge into belief, and the use of it to guide action. Here, scientific knowledge and belief are no longer fundamentally opposed to each other, but united as the two interrelated and transitional links of practice itself in the practice activities. This kind of unity preserves the difference between the two, which is the difference between the two links with no meanings of the difference between the two independent entities. Just as the Soviet philosopher Copperning put it: "Marxist epistemology holds that scientific knowledge does not coexist with any belief, but only coexist with the belief based on scientific evidence and scientific proof to guide people to the actual realization of scientific ideas."[372]

In terms of the object of belief, the great communist ideal that Marxism believes in and pursues is the greatest goal of human practice, while the religion believes in and pursues a supernatural being—God, which has completely lost the character of human practical goal, so it appears to be far from, or even irrelevant to the practical goal of human transformation of the world. The object of religious belief has gone through a process of separation from the goal of human practice, and greatly lost the fundamental nature of the object of belief. So when the reasonableness of the communist ideal is easily understood in the object of human activity, the religious God cannot be understood by practical goals and become an inscrutable mystery. And therefore, theologians have racked their brains to discuss the existence of God and how it exists, but it remains elusive.

The lofty goal of communism is not only the sustenance of man's ideals and aspirations, but also the realistic goal that can be achieved through practical activities, and therefore, the goal of communism is the unity of material and spiritual values, and the spiritual value depends on and serves the material value.

---

[372] Kopnin: *Introduction to Marxist Epistemology*, Page 272, Beijing, Realistic Publishing House, 1982.

However, the religious God, due to the loss of the objective characteristic, becomes a pure spiritual value embodiment, that is, spiritual sustenance. Originally, people concentrate their attention, energy and enthusiasm on the goal of their own activities in order to achieve it. In the trust and realistic pursuit of their own goals, people naturally feel spiritually happy and full, get encouraged, inspired, and comforted, but this is a positive consolation combined with the encouragement of actual action, and the consolation is not the primary. But in religion, man assigns his spirit to God only for psychological consolation. This consolation flows into cajole and paralysis because there is no actual content. Man becomes the object of idleness from the subject who sets up and pursues the goal voluntarily, and kneels down before God, the omnipotent subject, looking forward to grace.

The belief mentality is composed of cognition, emotion and will. The unique subjective factor of "belief" lies in the center of the belief mentality, and in the interaction with the cognitive, emotional and will activities of the belief subject. Marxist scientific belief and religious belief are fundamentally different and opposite in the emergence of belief. Religion's belief in God is formed mostly by the participation of feelings and emotions, do not believe because of recognition, nor disappear as a result of recognition. Scientific discoveries often do not shake the illusory beliefs of religious believers. Religion often sweeps aside the consequences of scientific discoveries or suppresses and nullifies scientific discoveries within its reach; on the contrary, emotional change and the need for action often make the religion believers change their beliefs. In scientific belief, that is, Marxism, the situation is quite the opposite. Belief was born and disappeared as an attitude of understanding subject to epistemological standards of truth and falsehood. Knowledge must conform to its object, while the belief must accord with the understanding of the object that reflects it correctly, and the credibility should be in accord with the truthfulness. Although the factors of emotion can hinder or promote the generation and disappearance of the belief, the belief here is mainly based on the level of understanding of the objective object.

The interaction between belief and cognition, emotion and will also has the other side, that is, the influence of belief on cognition, emotion and will. In scientific belief and religious belief, the nature and characteristics of this influence are different. In religion, belief is caused by blind feelings and will, which in turn exacerbates blindness of feelings and will. All kinds of religious feelings and religious acts are subject to the belief in God. What doctrine is or what God requests, what people's feelings or will are. Absolute belief in doctrine hinders people's true understanding of objective things. But the scientific belief of Marxism is just the opposite. Because belief appears with knowledge and is consistent with knowledge, belief in scientific faith in turn promotes people to carry out scientific understanding and exploration activities. The more developed the cognition, the more accord with the request of scientific belief, and the belief in scientific truth makes emotion and will based on reason and knowledge, and avoids the random and blind display of emotion and will.

The examination of the belief mentality should not be confined to its own internal factors, but also examine the externalization or embodiment of these factors in its connection with the object of belief. In this way, the three factors including internal cognition, emotion and will of the belief mentality will be externalized into three kinds of relationships between the subject and object of belief, that is, the three ways in which the subject of belief grasps the object of belief, namely, theoretical confirmation, emotional experience and behavioral pursuit.

Just as both Marxism and religion have three factors including cognition, emotion and will in their belief mentality, there are also three ways including theoretical confirmation, emotional experience and behavior pursuit in the belief subject's grasp of the belief object. But the importance and function of each way are different in these two beliefs, which are determined by the different objects of belief.

In religion, since the proposition it believes in cannot be scientifically proven, there is no truthfulness in the recognition of theoretical confirmation on the belief object—God. Most believers do not believe in God through theoretical proof, and many people do not have such expectations of reason. Compared with the theoretical confirmation, emotional experience plays a more important role in religion, and it is the foundation of all religious beliefs and attitudes. Moreover, the external behavior of religious belief existed to achieve inner experience, so it does not have the significance of changing the world. It is because of the special status of emotion experience in religion, it is easy for us to understand why the mentality of religion easily become a blind passion—religious fanaticism.

Scientific theoretical confirmation is the basis of Marxist scientific belief, which determines the scientific nature of this belief. Of course, in Marxist scientific belief, emotional experience also exists, but it is based on theoretical confirmation, to the limit of theoretical truth, and serves the pursuit of the lofty goal of communism. The pursuit of this kind of behavior is the end-result of Marxist scientific belief. It is not for the purpose of emotional experience, but directly for the practical activities of changing the world. Only this kind of belief truly accords with the positive essence of human faith. Religion, as an old form of belief, is nothing more than a perverted manifestation of human nature in an upside-down historical era.

The founder of Marxism has always made a strict distinction between his theory, religious belief and theological theory. As we all know, Marx began to expound his theory in the criticism of religion and the capitalist society on which it depended. Marx thought that religion was the opium of the people, and " the criticism of religion is the premise of all other criticism". Engels continued to reveal the illusion of religion and scientifically revealed the nature and origin of religion: "All religions are reflected in the imagination of the external forces that govern the daily life of people in people's minds. In this reflection, human power takes the form of superhuman power.[373] From its inception, Marxism broke away from all religious

---

[373]*Karl Marx and Frederick Engels: Selected Works*, Edition 1, Vol. 3, Page 354.

beliefs and resolutely opposed attempts to establish a so-called new religion in the future. Engels made a theoretical settlement of many famous figures who advocated the creation of a new religion after the decline of Christianity, such as hero worship of Thomas Carlyle, Goethe's labor worship, and Feuerbach's so-called religion of love. He wrote: "it is said that a new religion, namely, the pantheistic hero worship and the labor worship, should be created. At least we should wait for such a religion to emerge in the future. But it is simply impossible..."[374] In his later years, Engels also criticized Feuerbach's fascination with religion and his attempt to replace the old one with a "new and true religion."

The emergence of Marxism turned communism from utopia to science. One of the important signs of this change is that the combination of Marxism and the workers' movement makes it completely free from the influence of religious belief in its guiding ideology. Before Marxism came into being, utopian communist theorists, in order to attract the masses of workers, and because of their ideological limitations, once openly publicized the similarities and consistency between communism and Christianity, hoping to find the spiritual strength from Christianity and the rationality of the labor movement from the similarity with the early Christian movement. This is inevitable before the birth of Marxism and its combination with the labor movement, because the working class is just beginning to awaken, and is undoubtedly characterized by the spontaneous movement of the oppressed in history and the struggle against religion. But the emergence of Marxism means that the working class has its own scientific beliefs; that the working class has changed from an independent class to a self-class; and that communism has changed from a utopian to a scientific one. Since then, Marxist theory has merged with the communist movement, and any attempt to mix Marxism or scientific communism with religion is wrong and incompatible with the interests of the working class.

---

[374]*Marx/Engels Collected Works*, Chinese Edition 1, Vol. 1, Page 649.

The founders and classical writers of Marxism not only tried to remove the influence of religious beliefs on the communist movement, but also opposed attempts to turn communism into a certain religion. For example, Marx and Engels severely criticized Clegg, who preached communism as a sentimental religion of love in the United States. So it is with Lenin's criticism of Bodanov and Bazarov. When Gorky invited Lenin to Hippley (Bogdanov, Bazarov, etc. was also there at that time), Lenin resolutely refused and said, "I can't, nor do I want to talk to those who advocate a combination of scientific socialism and religion." [375] Lenin always opposites science and religion, and points out that "to exclude the law of science is in fact only the law of smuggling religion".

Just like making the myth of "Two Marx" and making the myth of "the opposition between Marx and Engels", it will inevitably reveal the false essence in the face of scientific truth and revolutionary reality, and will be spurned by the proletariat and the masses of the people who want to overthrow capitalism and engage in socialist revolution and construction to attempt to make Marxism religious. The fact that Marxism is a science and that Marx is a revolutionist and a scientist will certainly be widely accepted by more and more people all over the world and be used to guide their revolutionary practice with the development of history.

---

[375]Krupskaya (Nadezhda Konstantinovna Krupskaya): *Memories of Lenin*, Page 161, Beijing, People's Publishing House, 1960.

CHAPTER 9   MARXISM GOING FORWARD IN PRACTICE

Our time has provided unprecedented conditions and opportunities for the creative development of Marxism. The questions raised by reality call for Marx. Gramsci once said something very insightful that Marx was the founder of the spirit of a historical era, which would probably last for centuries, until the political society was destroyed and the adjusted society was established. Only then would his worldview be transcended.

Marxism must be both persisted and developed. Practice is the most powerful, which will not only punish the dismemberment of Marxism, but will also break the deadlock that dogmatizes Marxism. In such a period of great change, the so-called "crisis" may appear. In fact, this so-called theoretical crisis is precisely the period in which Marxism has rapidly advanced itself in the face of challenges. The closed state of the crisis is the real crisis.

1. Reflection on Historical Experience: Dialectical Unity of Persistence and Development

Stalin and Mao Tse-tung are leaders of the international communist movement. Their death was mourned by the people, but it also brought a new turn to the end of the personality cult and the promotion of the Marxism. The contradictory combination of pain and expectation, and mourning and new marching horn shows that Stalin and Mao Tse-tung are great historical figures with some tragic color.

On March 5th 1953, Stalin died. A few years later, in February 1956, at the 20th Congress of the Soviet Communist Party, Khrushchev (Nikita Sergeyevich Khrushchev) finally displayed a banner against the personality cult. Then, on June 30th, he published the *Resolution of the Central Committee of the Soviet Communist Party on Overcoming the Personality Cult and Its Consequences*. Khrushchev's handling of Stalin's problem obviously has shortcomings in ways and methods, but it should be admitted that opposing Stalin's personality cult is requirements of the reality.

On September 9th 1976, Mao Tse-tung passed away. This was the death of the leader of the world's largest socialist country and the largest proletarian party after Stalin. Two years later, the Third Plenary Session of the 11th CPC Central Committee was held in December 1978, which highly appreciated the ongoing discussion on "Practice is the only criterion for testing truth", and put forward the problems of a historical and scientific understanding of Mao Tse-tung's great achievements and a completed and accurate mastering of the scientific system of Mao Tse-tung's thought. In fact, it is the beginning of an implicit and proportionate criticism of Mao Tse-tung's personality cult in a Chinese way.

During their lifetime, Stalin and Mao Tse-tung could overcome the mistakes in their own leadership within a certain period of time and to a certain extent. For example, Stalin's criticism of victory in the period of total collectivization of Soviet agriculture; Mao Tse-tung's criticism of the unhealthy atmosphere in the equalitarianism and communism in "Great Leap Forward" and "People's Commune", and the self-examination at the National People's Congress (NPC) with 7,000 attendees in January 1962 illustrated this point. But the destruction of the principle of collective leadership and democratic centralism has blocked the possibility that they can completely correct their own mistakes. Their mistakes were corrected only after their death by opposing the cult of personality, which are the new problems of Marxism in the development of socialist countries after the proletariat seized power.

Among them, there are many lessons to be learned.

Not long after Stalin's death, *The Communist Party is the Leading Power of the Soviet People*, an article published on *Pravda* on June 10th 1953, and *The People Are the Creators of History*, an article of the Editorial Office of the magazine *The Communist Party* published in August of the same year, began to raise the question of opposing the cult of personality. Articles in this field were published one after another, gradually loosening the spell of dogmatism of people for a long time, which led to the public opposition to the cult of personality at the 20th Congress of the Communist Party of the Soviet Union in February 1956.

In China, after the death of Mao Tse-tung, the question of personality cult was not immediately raised. On the contrary, for a period of time, the principle of "two whatevers" was emphasized. The theoretical bringing order out of chaos mainly focuses on reversing the theory reversed by "the Gang of four", without touching on how to fully understand and comprehensively understand Mao Tse-tung's thoughts. Despite the fundamental changes that have taken place in politics, the basic question of how to treat Marxism and Mao Tse-tung's thought is still wandering on the old ideological track.

However, practice is the strongest. The economic and political contradictions accumulated since 1957, especially during the "Cultural Revolution" period have slowed the development of productive forces and science and technology, thus putting the most acute question in front of the people: Whether "to follow the established policy" and follow the original routine, or to build socialism with Chinese characteristics in accordance with the actual situation in China? In order to follow the latter path, we must correctly treat Marxism, especially by breaking through the principle of "two whatevers". To achieve this, we must find a higher authority than Marxism and Mao Tse-tung's personal authority, which is the principle of practice. The discussion on "practice is the only criterion for testing truth", which was launched in the first half of 1978 in China, has made this most common and fundamental principle of Marxism special the special and wonderful function of politics and theory, and the key to the locking of people's minds.

In Stalin's time, the special status of the Communist Party of the Soviet Union made the influence of Stalin's theory and practice beyond the scope of the Soviet Union. The Stalin issue became an international issue. Breaking down the personality cult of Stalin had varying degrees of influence both on the socialist state and on the Communist Party, which was not in power. However, due to the complex international situation, the personality cult against Stalin, which began at the 20 Congress of the Communist Party of the Soviet Union, has turned into an international debate, and has formed a complex situation of contradictions of various natures. The voice of opposing dogmatism, opposing personality cult and creatively developing Marxism is intertwined with the call for non-Stalin to dismember Marxism in the name of opposing dogmatism.

History seems to be repeating itself. In 1976, especially in 1978, China began to criticize the cult of personality and the struggle against dogmatism that solidified Marxism. But the situation is different. The world has been evolving for 20 years. In particular, we learned and summarized Khrushchev's lessons in dealing with Stalin problem, and made a historical and scientific evaluation of Mao Tse-tung. In China, since the discussion of "practice is the only criterion for testing truth", especially since the Third Plenary Session of the Eleventh Central Committee began on 1978, it has not been a non-Mao movement against Mao Tse-tung, but a movement to truly uphold and develop Marxism-Leninism, Mao Tse-tung thought, seeking truth from facts and emancipating the mind.

This is a decade of ideological liberation and a decade of creatively advancing Marxism. Through the discussion that "practice is the only criterion for testing truth," people have come to realize that what Marxism provides is not a ready-made answer, but the fundamental theory and method of understanding and transforming the world. To achieve the great achievement of socialist construction, the Chinese Marxists must combine the universal truth of Marxism with China's reality, creatively push forward Marxism and build socialism with Chinese characteristics. If everything starts from the original, and if the ideology is rigid, the vitality of Marxism will be destroyed, and the socialist society will again fall into stagnation. This understanding is costly, which condenses more than 70 years of international experience since the October Revolution, and the experience of 30 years of socialist construction in China.

In the past ten years, in various fields of social theory, there has been an exploratory and creative use of Marxism, which has extended to many theoretical fields with "practice is the only criterion for testing truth" as the breakthrough point. No matter in terms of the questions discussed, or the depth and breadth of its discussion, it is beyond the reach of the "Cultural Revolution" and its predecessors. In particular, the ideological liberation movement has promoted the reform of the economic and political systems, and the deepening and development of the reforms have turned to the guidance and demonstration of theory. This interaction of mutual influence and circular advance is very favorable for the creative development of Marxism.

But there are always two sides to everything. It is absolutely right to oppose the "two whatevers", to advocate seeking truth from facts and emancipating the mind, to break the rigid state of thought and to carry forward the spirit of daring to explore. But some people attempt to turn it into a non-Maoist movement that totally negates Mao Tse-tung's thought. They preach "school of thought", "pluralism" and "outdated theory", which oppose adherence to Marxism and the development of Marxism. They regard adherence as dogmatism and development as the complete negation of the fundamental principle of Marxism, which in fact is the denial of the reality of Marxism in the name of development.

Persistence and development should be dialectical unity. Only by adhering to Marxism, that is, moving forward along the road opened up by Marxism under the guidance of Marxism, can it be possible to develop Marxism creatively. Similarly, only by creatively developing Marxism and constantly combining new realities, summing up new experiences and solving new problems can Marxism be thoroughly adhered to. Without the persistence of development, it must be dogmatism.

As a matter of fact, true persistence will certainly involve development, because at different times and places, under different conditions, and in the face of different problems, it is necessary to face the reality creatively to always adhere to Marxism. This cannot be done by adhering to "book worship" and carrying out the principle of "whatever". On the contrary, a theory truly worthy of creative development must include insistence, that is, the use of the stances, views and methods of Marxism-Leninism, and the confirmation of its basic principles. There was not, is not and will not be a so-called creative Marxism, which deviates from the basic principles of Marxism.

Personality cult is not a sincere belief in Marxism, but a superstition. If we say that religious superstition is "personification of God", that is to say, the god in the fantasy turns into a real existence; the personality cult is the deification of man-man becomes an absolutely correct and almighty God, which is a false image. This false image, although can arouse some enthusiasm and expectation for a certain period of time, in the long run, stifles the minds of people and stifles the initiative and creativity of the people. As a result, not only will it not lead to the crisis of Marxism, on the contrary, it is a good medicine for breaking the stagnation, overcoming the crisis and reinjecting vitality into the solidified Marxism to oppose personality cult.

We should oppose the personality cult and persist Marxism-Leninism and Mao

Tse-tung thought, which is an important conclusion drawn from the reflection of historical experience.

2. Marxism and Contemporary Capitalism

From the point of view of the history of Marxist development, Marxism has entered a period of self-reflection by opposing the personality cult, and through the study of contemporary capitalism, it has reproved itself and developed itself.

This period, viewed from the outside, seems to be the so-called crisis period. In fact, it is precisely the period in which Marxism has the most creative possibility and necessity for its development. After the Second World War, especially in recent decades, the changes of capitalism have raised many new questions, which require scientific answer. Questions-answers to the questions-development is the law of Marxism development.

The analysis of capitalist social formation is the most important part of Marxist theory. It can be absolute to say that not only *Das Capital*, but also the vast majority of the works of Marx and Engels, are directly or indirectly closely related to the study of capitalist society. It is an important point of Marxist theory to reveal the development laws of capitalist society and to elaborate the great historical mission of the proletariat. And therefore, without the theory of capitalism, there would be no Marxism.

Some of the more serious Western scholars acknowledge that the basic principles of Marxism's capitalist theory are not out of date. For example, the American scholar Heilbroner said in Chapter 4 of *Marxism: For and Against*: "I am much more certain of Marx's analysis of what capitalism is, whatever its problems in explaining what capitalism will become. This social analysis of capitalism, which starts with simple commodities, is, I think, one of the most noteworthy and thought-provoking minds we've ever seen... As long as capitalism exists, I don't believe we can ever declare any mistake in his analysis of the intrinsic nature of capitalism."[376]

But many scholars, based on the changes in capitalism, simply deny the scientificity and rationality of Marxism's analysis of capitalism. Wright Mills believed that "all kinds of theories of Marxism were branded as Victorian capitalism". "Classical Marxism is no longer able to accurately explain the reality of advanced capitalism, but rather a kind of political empty talk using the 'desired tone'."[377] Toffler (Alvin Toffler) believes that Marxism is the product of the second wave, namely, the product of the industrial revolution. Today, It is like still using a magnifying glass in the era of electron microscopy to use Marxism to diagnose the internal structure of a high-tech society. Habermas, the most famous representative of the Frankfurt School of thought, also believed that modern capitalism was late capitalism, that it had eliminated the contradiction of liberal capitalism, and that Marxism was no longer applicable. In a word, some scholars believe that the labor theory of value of Marxism has been replaced by the knowledge theory of value, that the theory of surplus value has been replaced by the theory that profit is the reward of organization management production, or even the theory of risk reward, that state intervention has completely eliminated anarchy and crisis, that the new middle class has replaced the opposition between the proletariat and the bourgeoisie, that the integration of the proletariat with the capitalist system and the theory of the proletariat's historical mission have become obsolete; and that the future of capitalist society is not socialism, but information society, post-industrial society, etc. In a word, Marxism is no longer applicable to contemporary capitalist society.

In fact, Marxism has never denied the changes in the capitalist society itself. It was

[376]Heilbroner: *Marxism: For and Against*, Page 62.

[377]Mills: *The Marxist*, Page 135.

Marx and Engels themselves who regarded the capitalist society as a living organism, and emphasized its variability. As early as 1848, in *The Communist Manifesto*, they has pointed out: "It is where the bourgeoisie era differs from all past eras in the constant changes in production, the continuous turbulence in all social relations, and the perpetual instability and change."[378] Marx and Engels, who lived in the 19th century, could not go through the changes behind them, but they could not conclude that the Marxism law analysis of capitalist society as a social form is out of date.

In the capitalist theory of Marxism, what has the greatest vitality is not the exposition on the tragic situation of the proletariat or the prophecies of the revolutionary prospects of individual countries, but the analysis of the basic contradictions of the capitalist society as an independent social formation, namely, the contradiction between socialization of production and private possession of production means.

In the contemporary capitalist society, this contradiction has not disappeared. Even in the most developed capitalist society, some changes have taken place in the specific forms of ownership, but the shareholding system has not changed the fundamental nature of capitalist private ownership. A small amount of scattered shares is not worth mentioning on the nature of the enterprise, and the real possession of the means of production is not a small amount of stock holders, but a few big capitalists. In capitalist society, the essence of the joint stock system is not the disappearance of private ownership, but its deformation, which is a way to fund of the large monopoly group. However, the whole capitalist production is becoming more and more socialized because of the development of productive forces and the revolution in science and technology. The large monopoly groups in developed

---

[378]*Karl Marx and Frederick Engels: Selected Works*, Edition 1, Vol. 1, Page 54.

capitalist countries are not only likely to highly concentrate and reasonably divide production, exchange and circulation at home, but also to implement some kind of division of labor and cooperation worldwide through multinational corporations, so as to develop the socialization of production to the maximum the extent of capitalist society.

The secret of Marx's theory of the capitalist mode of production is the theory of production of surplus value, which reveals the exploitative and exploitative relations between the bourgeoisie and the proletariat under the capitalist system. Despite the development of the contemporary scientific and technological revolution makes the working conditions, economic income and living conditions of the proletariat different from those of the early capitalist period, it does not fundamentally change the nature of the relations between the proletariat and the bourgeoisie. The proletariat is still the wage laborer and still depends on selling the labor force for a living. The level of wages is a matter of labor price, which does not change the nature of employment, and the proletariat is still the creator of the surplus value. Although the development of science and technology and the automation of production constantly turn the workers from direct labors into supervision and management of the production process and the working hours are relatively reduced, the surplus value is not the product of machines, but the product of labor (including mental work directly invested in human production). It is only that, compared with the early days of capitalism, the production of surplus value is more and more dependent on intellectual expenditure, and the production of relative surplus value replaces the production of absolute surplus value to some extent.

The contemporary technological revolution has not led to the disappearance of the proletariat in capitalist society, but to the expansion of their ranks. It has changed the structure of the working class, not the absolute number. Although the numbers of the traditional industrial sectors, such as steel, coal, shipbuilding, and textile industry decreased, the new industry, especially the tertiary industry is developing rapidly. The ratio of blue-collar workers to white-collar workers has changed. The number of workers in the traditional sense, that is, simple manual workers, is decreasing, and the ranks of the intellectual proletariat are constantly expanding. From the point of view of an enterprise, the demand for workers is reduced by high technology and automation. However, the development of productive forces can lead to the emergence of a new social division of labor and new production departments, and from the perspective of the whole society, it increases the demand for workers. This argument is entirely correct that it is the expansion of the workforce with the development of capitalism.

There is an intermediate class in contemporary capitalist society, but there is no intermediate class, namely, the trend of the dissolution of the proletariat and the bourgeoisie in the middle class. Marxism's argument that capitalist society is increasingly divided into two classes, the proletariat and the bourgeoisie, does not exclude the intermediate class. The existence of the intermediate class in contemporary capitalist society is not because of the small production stability and vitality, but because of the functional need of the social structure. The developed capitalist needs a large number of teachers, doctors and engineers, and needs a large number of managers and management personnel. But the intermediate class is also unstable with the trend of polarization existed among them, so the development of capitalist society makes the intermediate class constantly divided and condensed.

Marxism's argument about the inevitable transition of capitalism to socialism has not been invalidated. Although after the Second World War, especially in the past 20 years, Western developed countries have not yet formed a revolutionary situation with economic development and stable situation, it cannot be concluded that the capitalist society is eternal; or that the prospect of capitalist society development is not a socialist society, but a society such as information society, post-industrial society and technology electronic society. In fact, the later so-called "society" is the change in the technological form of the productive forces within the capitalist society, not the fundamental change in social relations.

In contemporary times, capitalist relations of production still have some possibility of accommodating the development of productive forces. It is difficult to predict how long the life span of capitalist society is now. The key question is whether we can regard the formation of capitalist society as the eternal and final form? No. It took a few hundred years for capitalist society to replace feudal society, and there is still a feudal, semi-feudal system in some parts of the world today, but no one would think thereof that feudal society is eternal. It is a great change in the history of mankind for socialism to replace capitalism. From the transformation of the world, it takes a long time for two social systems to coexist from the victory of socialism in one country to the dominant position in the world. It's been only over 70 years since the October Revolution, how can it be argued that the capitalist system is permanent? The working class, especially the awakened working class, will not be reassured for a long time by the improvement of life in the position of being employed and exploited, especially the ills of the capitalist society, which has aroused the strong discontent and protest of the workers. The development of productive forces and science and technology in the developed capitalist countries in the West does not foreshadow the convergence of socialism and capitalism. Instead, it is necessary and possible for the whole society to share the main means of production and turn the production results into the common wealth of mankind. The more developed capitalism is, the closer it is to the socialist society rather than the farther away it is from the socialist society.

However, the Marxist theory on capitalism must be developed, and the characteristics of modern capitalist society should be carefully studied from the actual situation, and a new and correct understanding should be drawn from it.

Generally speaking, the classical writers of Marxism overestimated the maturity of the capitalist system at the time. Whether it was in 1840s when Marx and Engels founded Marxism or the early days of capitalism, the contradictions exposed at that time was the contradiction in the early stage of capitalist industrialization. After the Second World War, especially in recent decades, the development of productive forces and the rise of scientific and technological revolution in major capitalist countries show that the capitalist system can also accommodate the continued development of productive forces. The capitalist system plays an important role in easing social and class contradictions and promoting the development of productive forces by adjusting property and distribution relations, in particular by strengthening government intervention in the economy and macro-control.

In recent decades, great changes have really taken place in contemporary capitalism. We must discuss the new features of capitalist society in economic, political and ideological aspects, the changes in the industrial structure, employment structure, the structure and living conditions of the working class of the capitalist societies, the policies carried out by bourgeois countries, and the ways, conditions and characteristics of capitalism to socialism. However, this kind of discussion must be based on the analysis of the basic contradiction and essence of the capitalist social formation by Marxism. Without this fundamental foothold, the so-called recognition of capitalist society will consciously and unconsciously deviate from Marxism.

3. Two Trends of Socialist Reform: Marxism and Anti-Marxism

The history of theory and practice of scientific socialism has gone through three stages: the first stage is socialism from utopian to scientific, which is the period of Marx and Engels; the second stage is socialism from ideal to reality, which is the period of the establishment of the socialist system began with the October Revolution; and the third stage is the transition of socialism from the "one country" model to the search for a road suitable for the construction of its own country, which is the current period of economic and political restructuring in socialist countries. These three periods were not absolutely successive, but intersecting. The socialism from utopia to science did not end when Engels died in 1895. It should be said that the process of socialism changing from an ideal to a reality continued to include the verification, supplement and development of Marx and Engels' theory of scientific socialism, while the reform of socialist countries should be the self-improvement of socialist system, which is to continue to turn socialism from ideal into reality.

In accordance with the development phase mentioned above, we have seen three kinds of ideas about the socialist system. One is the scientific socialism founded by Marx and Engels, which is a kind of idealistic social system, and a theoretical grasp of the essential characteristics of the socialist system; one is the reality of the socialist system that has appeared on the earth since the October Revolution; and the third one is the overall objective of the reform, which is the socialist system established through the reform of economic and political systems, and can also be called as socialism with its own characteristics. The dismemberment of Marxism often takes place in the course of two transformations.

The first time transition is from theoretical socialism to realistic socialism.

Marx and Engels' theory on socialism is to examine communism as a social form opposed to capitalism. Starting from the full development of large industries, socialized mass production and the commodity economy under capitalist conditions, and from the analysis of the inherent contradictions in the capitalist mode of production, they expounded the trend and law that capitalism was bound to be replaced by higher social forms, divided the lower and higher stages of the development of communist society, and pointed out the basic characteristics of ownership, distribution, class relation and superstructure from the angle principle of distinguishing the two stages. Marx and Engels gave up the characteristics of the nation and grasped the law of the change of social form. This analysis is scientific, and theoretically and logically rigorous and consistent.

However, the socialist system established successively since the October Revolution in Russia occurred in countries where the productive forces were relatively backward, capitalism was underdeveloped or very underdeveloped. Hence, they were obviously not exactly the same as the socialist society conceived by Marx and Engels on the basis of the highly developed capitalism. On this basis, some people attacked Marx and Engels' theory of scientific socialism as utopian socialism and a new utopia, which is completely wrong. Marx and Engels devoted their whole lives to opposing all kinds of utopian socialism, from opposing "real socialism" to opposing Dühring's utopian socialism. Marx and Engels opposed dogmatic predictions of the future, opposed a detailed description of the characteristics and construction of socialism and to the restraint of people's hands and feet. In 1880, in his book *The Impact Of Population Growth On Social Progress*, Kautsky described how a communist society would regulate and control the production of people, and Engels responded in a letter to Kautsky: "Anyway, the people of communist society themselves will decide whether or not to take certain measures to this, when and by what kind of means, and take what kind of measures. I don't think I have a mission to suggest and advise them in this aspect."[379] Marx and Engels have always believed that the problem of how to build socialism should be solved by people's practice.

The leap of socialism from theory to reality is the great proof of Marxism's scientific nature.

The second transition from the mode of one country to the road of socialist

---

[379]*Marx/Engels Collected Works*, Chinese Edition 1, Vol. 35, Page 145~146.

construction suitable for its own characteristics is another leap.

In the decades after the October Revolution, during the Stalin period, the Soviet Union gradually established a planned economic system based on a single public ownership, highly centralized and managed by executive order. Other successor socialist countries have adopted the Soviet model to some extent, and this system has its historical function for a certain period of time. In the course of decades, the Soviet Union turned a backward tsarist Russia into a superpower capable of competing with the United States, surpassing Britain and France, and traveled through the centuries of developed capitalist countries in the West in a relatively short time. But, with the development of productive forces and the rise of science and technology revolution, this kind of excessively centralized and rigid system has exposed its various disadvantages day by day, so it is necessary to carry out the reform of economic and political system.

After decades of socialist construction, the socialist countries that have seized political power advocated reform again. Does it mean that Marxism is no longer effective? That socialism is not working? No. Some argue that the failure of the socialist attempt will be the legacy of the 20th century, and that some Western politicians are clamoring that communism has collapsed, which is only unrealistic somniloquism.

The socialist reform does not prove that Marxism ineffectiveness, but proves its truth. The most profound root of socialist reform is the contradictions between the development of productive forces as well as the rise of science and technology revolution and the original system, which requires changing some drawbacks of the original economic system and political system in order to meet the needs of the productive forces, and promoting its development. That is to say, the root of socialist reform lies in the basic contradictions of socialist society.

The socialist reform has also proved that it is impossible to achieve the level envisaged by Marx and Engels in the short term in carrying out socialist construction in economically backward countries. However, from the perspective of long-term goals and the height of the development of social formation, the coexistence of various forms of ownership, the coexistence of various distribution systems, the production and exchange of goods mediated by money, and even the capitalist private economy, all kinds of non-labor and even exploitation of people, is, after all, a certain stage in the course of human history, rather than the end of the history. Reform is to find a way to truly build socialism in its own country. In this sense, socialist reform is not getting farther and farther from the ideals of Marx and Engels, but getting closer and closer.

We acknowledge that in the two transitions of socialist theory and practice, new questions were raised beyond Marx's and Engels' view at the time. For example, in the first transition, the most acute question is how to carry out socialist construction in backward countries; in the second transition, there were questions such as the stage of socialist development, how to carry out socialist macroeconomic regulation and control, how to combine planned economy with market regulation, how to make use of the commodity and monetary relations, how to correctly implement the principle of distribution according to work, how to carry out the construction of material civilization and spiritual civilization, and how to carry forward socialist democracy and perfect socialist legal system. The solution of these problems will inevitably promote the development of Marxism.

As a result, there will inevitably be two different types of reform: one is to adhere to Marxism as the guide and to regard reform as the self-improvement of the socialist system; and the other is to oppose Marxism and advocate social democracy, to advocate privatization in the economy, democratization in the system and pluralism in theory, which is in fact a retrogression in the name of reform. And therefore, we should adhere to the socialist orientation of reform and Marxism, which is something that any socialist country should never waver.

4 To be a True Marxist

Who is the true Marxist? This is an old problem and a new one.

In late 19th century and early 20th century, Lenin raised this question when he opposed the revisionism represented by Bernstein.

In the second half of 1950s, the question was raised in the controversy of the international communist movement.

At present, the problem is more acute and more complex worldwide.

On the one hand, according to the principle that Marxism must be combined with the reality of each country, Marxists in each country should find a road to socialism according to the characteristics of their own country, especially after gaining political power, and should establish socialism according to the characteristics of their own country. Since people understand and use Marxism according to the actual conditions and cultural traditions of their own country, there must be differences.

On the other hand, there are many interpretations of Marxism in the world. Starting with Lukács' *History and Class Consciousness* in 1920s, after the Second World War, especially in the past 20 or 30 years, all kinds of Marxism have sprung up.

It is the objective reality of the present age with a variety of understandings of Marxism. Some philosophers believe that there are at least 15 kinds of Marxism; some believe that there are five barriers to Marxism: Eastern Europe, Western Europe, Yugoslavia, the Soviet Union and China; some believe that there are three major schools: Marxism in the Soviet Union, Marxism in China, Marxism in Europe and the Communist Party of Europe, and so on. Their basic views are different or even opposite to each other. Who is the real Marxist?

We oppose the pluralism of truth. Marxism is monistic in terms of its truthiness and scientificity, and the monism of truth lies in its objectivity.

However, the application of the universal truth of Marxism can be concrete and diverse. Not only will there be differences in the process of combining Marxism with the situations of various countries, but also in the theoretical research of Marxism. Because of the different scopes of research problems and the different perspectives of observing problems, Marxism will be understood, enriched and developed from different aspects. This can collect not only the experience of socialist revolution and socialist construction in various countries, but also the practical experience and summary of different countries ad nationalities into Marxism, and can promote the development of Marxism through the mutual supplement of various viewpoints. Of course, the creative development of Marxism is an extremely complicated process, which requires us to always adhere to the principle that "practice is the only criterion for testing truth", to distinguish between truth and fallacy, between right and wrong, and to deeply study and critically examine various schools of thought known as Marxism. In the contemporary era, we must especially oppose the theory of "Marxist obsolescence", and oppose the distortion of Marxism by Freudianism, existentialism, structuralism or any other doctrines.

To insist on Marxism is not to dogmatize Marxism, and dogmatists are not Marxists. Engels once admonished: "Don't copy the words of Marx and me, but should think like Marx according to your own situations, and only in this sense can the word 'Marxist' have a reason to exist."[380] When Lenin refuted dogmatism in *On the Revolution of Russia*, there was a reference to "'Marxism' like Marx"[381]. Marx is opposed to dogmatizing his theory. To be a Marxist like Marx, we must always insist on combining the universal truth of Marxism with the actual conditions of the revolution. Only in this way can we go on along the road opened up by Marx and Engels forever.

---

[380]See *A Lamp of Wisdom*, Page 91, Beijing, People's Publishing House, 1983.

[381]*The Collected Works of Lenin*, Chinese Edition 2, Vol. 43, Page 371, Beijing, People's Publishing House, 1987.

CONCLUSIONS   THE FUTURE BELONGS TO MARXISM

There is no monolithic dynasty in the world, and no immutable ideological system. In the history of mankind, many ideological systems have gone from prosperity to decline after a long or short period. The prosperity of all kinds of schools of thought and a hundred schools of thought in ancient Greece and Rome and in the Spring and Autumn Period and Warring States Period of China has become a historical vestige.

The length of the existence of an ideological system depends, first and foremost, on the extent to which it meets the needs of society. Social needs are the basis upon which an ideological system can emerge and survive. The broader and stronger the social basis for such needs, the longer the system that meets the needs of this society exists. Secondly, it depends on the nature of the system of thought, including its truthfulness, transmissibility and adaptability. It is hard for an inscrutable, obscure and closed ideological system to last.

Relatively speaking, Marxism is a relatively young ideological system, which is in the ascendant with a period of only a century and a half since its birth.

Marxism has great social needs. From the first victory of socialism in a country to the fact that socialism has become a dominant social formation in the world, this is a very long historical stage. The historical mission undertaken by Marxism is just beginning, and is far from over. So far, mankind has not found any theory or doctrine that can replace Marxism. Whether it is Freudianism, existentialism, structuralism, logical positivism, or whatever else, in terms of the partial scope or in its own field of study, there may well be some merits, but generally speaking, they cannot explain history and reality scientifically and cannot be the guiding principles for the liberation of mankind.

After the birth of Marxism, especially since the Second World War, many schools of thought appeared in the West, but they did not live long enough, like the lantern of a horse, but only Marxism remained its great attraction. In today's world, the rise of Marxism is itself a proof of the strong vitality of Marxism.

Marxism is extremely adaptable. From its emergence, it began in several of the more developed capitalist countries in Western Europe, but in terms of its spread, it quickly spread worldwide beyond Western Europe, North America, Asia, Africa and Latin America. It can take root in countries and regions with different cultural traditions, different races and nationalities, and different languages, because it can be combined with the actual conditions of each country, can be nationalized and can be adapted to the needs of different situations.

Marxism is practical and mass in nature. In history, many ideological systems have a limited range of activities, which are often spread in the narrow circle of a small number of intellectual classes. But Marxism has gone out of the study room and out of the scope of pure intellectuals, and combined with the activities of millions of people. If it is said that some ideological systems tend to decline with the death of its founders because of their narrow range of activities, the broad mass base of Marxism made it not interrupted by the death of its creators. During the lifetime of Marx and Engels, a number of Marxists emerged in the first and second international periods. After the death of Marx and Engels, with the extensive establishment of the revolutionary political party of the working class and the victory of the socialist revolution in some countries, a number of Marxists appeared in all countries. On the basis of the wide spread of Marxism, Marxists have emerged in large numbers and successively from generation to generation.

The vitality of Marxism also lies in its creativeness. Historical experience has proved that no ideological system that regards itself as the ultimate truth can exist for a longer period of time. Marxism has always opposed the ultimate truth, believing that it is contradictory to the basic law of dialectical thinking. An absolutely perfect understanding is just as absurd as an absolutely perfect social system.

As the founders of Marxism, Marx and Engels spent their whole lives summing up new experiences and exploring new problems, and never stopped creative researches. The outstanding achievements of the successors of Marx and Engels lie not only in adhering to Marxism, but also in developing Marxism under the new conditions and continuing to push it forward.

We should make a proper distinction between Marxism and Marx and Engels. Marxism, of course, cannot be separated from Marx and Engels. It was founded by them, but it cannot be equated to them. Marx and Engels are the subjects who founded this theory, while Marxism is an objective ideological system. The life of Marx and Engels is limited, and they died in 19th century; whereas Marxism, as an ideological system, develops according to its own logic and laws, and its life cycle is quite long. And therefore, our evaluation yardstick of Marx and Engels should be different from the requirements on Marxism.

Our assessment of Marx and Engels should be historical, because they are historical figures. We cannot demand them by ignoring the background of their times. We can't deny them because they don't see the science and technology revolution, the atomic bombs, computers, and genetic engineering after they have passed away. The great feat of Marx and Engels lies in the fact that they accomplished tasks that their contemporaries could not do, and created a new doctrine for mankind-Marxism, which is an ideological system more scientific and critical than any of the ideological systems of their predecessors.

Our evaluation of Marxism should be realistic, that is, to what extent contemporary Marxism promotes Marxism, whether they use Marxism to solve or attempt to solve the new problems facing contemporary capitalism and contemporary socialism and to sum up the new achievements of the scientific and technological revolution. The essence of Marxism is always contemporary, but not historical. And therefore, Marxism has its reasons and bases for long-term existence.

There is no doubt that the relationship between the successors of a school of thought or an ideological system and its founders is complex. The spread of Marxism in various countries and its integration with the specific conditions and cultural traditions of each country will certainly change the content and form of Marxism. But different from other ideological systems, it is not reflected in changing its content to meet the new social conditions and the needs of particular classes, but in advancing along the path of truth opened up by the founders of Marxism. It is not far from the truth, but constantly adds new particles for the understanding of truth.

Will mankind have only one ideological system—Marxism in the future? In our time, arguing about this distant future can only divert attention of the people from the struggle of contemporary ideology, and ignore the great responsibility that how we should creatively develop Marxism in combination with the contemporary issues. It is extremely unwise to push aside the current reality with abstract and cumbersome arguments.

In fact, as long as we deeply examine the history of human thought, it is not difficult to answer this question. In the history of human thought, all kinds of ideological systems evolve, but the knowledge acquired under these ideological systems does not disappear. Like a mountain of earth, the layers of knowledge constitute the whole of human knowledge.

Similarly, in Marxism system, we should see the difference between Marxism as the theoretical form of the proletariat and as human knowledge and scientific truth. Marxism, as the theoretical form of the proletariat, contains a specific class relationship and class content, which will disappear when its historical mission is completed, but as a scientific truth, it will be incorporated into the sea of human knowledge. Even if there will be a doctrine or ideological system a few years later, as long as it is scientific, it will inevitably build on the scientific achievements that Marx has made and include it as the most important source and content. In this sense, Marxism is permanent.

Some people are talking about the so-called crisis of Marxism. We recognize that the development road of Marxism is tortuous. Marxism has changed from the theory of a few advanced elements in 1840s to that of the working class as a whole and the guiding ideology of each socialist country, and has been moving forward along a rising routine in more than 100 years. However, since the middle of 1950s, it has seemed to have retreated along a downward path. Some of the former socialist countries have abandoned Marxism; in some capitalist countries, Marxism has separated itself from the workers, gradually returned to the classroom and the study room, and became a pure academic study. In fact, this is not a crisis of Marxism, but a crisis caused by deviation from Marxism. This kind of crisis is bound to promote the exploration and thinking of the real Marxism of contemporary times, and further develop Marxism creatively.

The power of truth is invincible!

The future belongs to Marxism!

POSTSCRIPT OF THE ORIGINAL EDITION

This book is the product of my collaboration with several of my students. I put forward the structure and context of the book. After discussion, the chapters and sections are confirmed and wrote separately. The details of each chapter are written as follows:

Chen Xianda: Introduction, Chapter 1, Chapter 9 and the Conclusions;

Hao Lixin: Chapter 2 and Chapter 3;

Liu Huaiyu: Chapter 4;

Huang Xing: Chapter 5;

Zhang Kangzhi: Chapter 6;

Liu Mingru: Chapter 7; and

Liu Jianjun: Chapter 8.

Finally, I confirmed the final edition, and Zhang Kangzhi and Hao Lixin assisted me to confirm the final edition of this work.

The writing and publication of this book has been enthusiastically supported and helped by Shanghai People's Publishing House. In particular, Gao Zhiren, the executive editor, and Song Huizeng took great efforts, which are highly appreciated!

Chen Xianda

In the end of March 1990

www.ingramcontent.com/pod-product-compliance
Lightning Source LLC
Chambersburg PA
CBHW021120270326
41929CB00009B/975